IMAGES
of America

In The Somerset Hills

The Landed Gentry

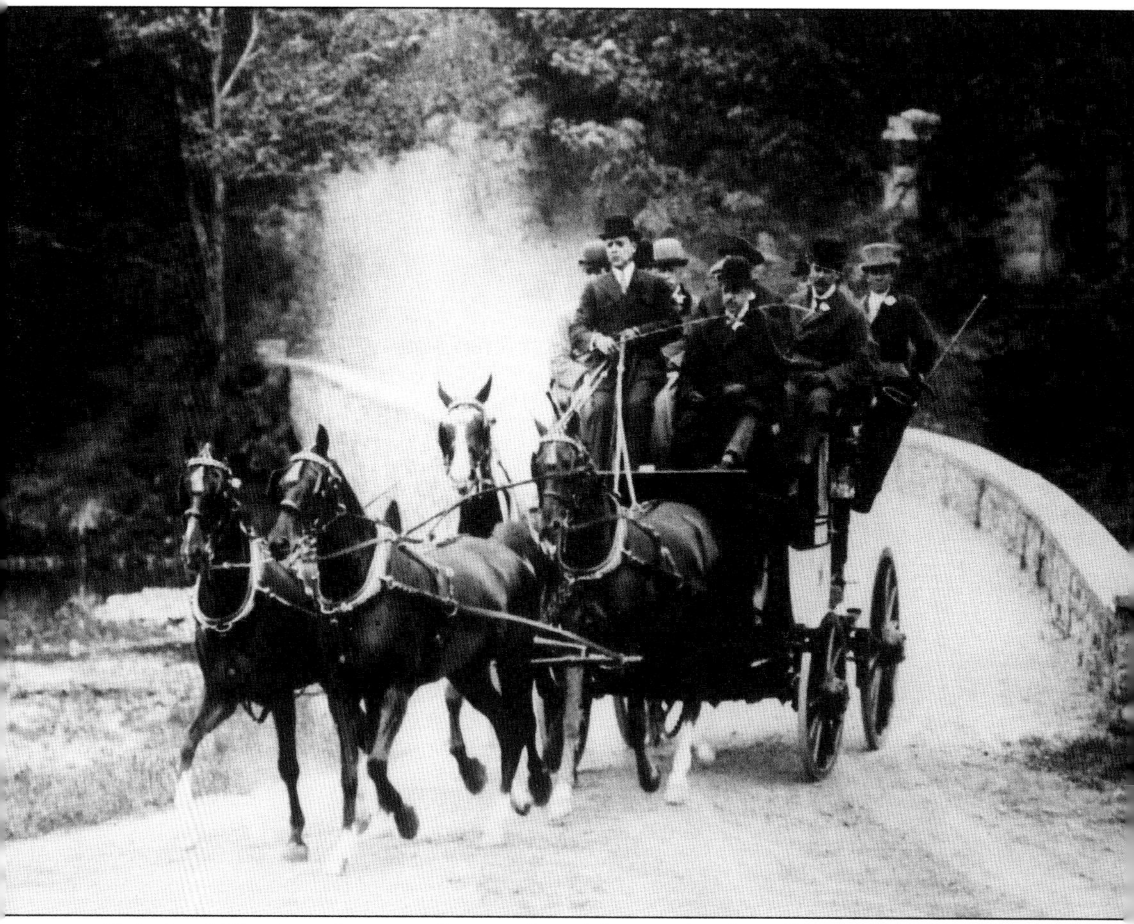

C. Ledyard Blair is at the reins of his coach-and-four, with a few of his friends. They are leaving Blairsden by the back gate, and crossing his private bridge over the North Branch of the Raritan River, just below the Ravine Lake dam, about 1913. (Anthony Villa.)

IMAGES
of America

IN THE SOMERSET HILLS
THE LANDED GENTRY

William A. Schleicher and Susan J. Winter

ARCADIA
PUBLISHING

ISBN 978-0-7385-6422-7

Published by Arcadia Publishing
Charleston, South Carolina

Printed in the United States of America

Library of Congress Catalog Card Number: 2008938092

For all general information contact Arcadia Publishing at:
Telephone 843-853-2070
Fax 843-853-0044
E-mail sales@arcadiapublishing.com
For customer service and orders:
Toll-Free 1-888-313-2665

Visit us on the Internet at www.arcadiapublishing.com

Contents

Acknowledgements

To the many people who shared their treasured photographs and stories with us, we extend our heartfelt thanks: The Behr family, Mike Deak, Dean Durling, Hugh Fenwick, Oliver D. Filley Jr., Kip and Steve Forbes, James S. Jones, Lorraine Hunt Kopacz, Kenneth B. Schley Jr., Dorothy Stratford, William Turnbull, Jack Turpin, Anthony and Peter Villa, and John von Stade.

We would also like to thank the following organizations for giving us access to their archives: the *Bernardsville News*, the Bernardsville Public Library Local History Room, the Branchburg Historical Society, Chatfield's, the Clarence Dillon Memorial Library, Duke University William R. Perkins Library, the Gill St. Bernard School, the Masters of the Essex Fox Hounds, The New York Historical Society, the Peapack Gladstone Library, the Ronald Reagan Presidential Library, Rutgers University Alexander Library Special Collection, the Somerset County Historical Society, the Somerset County Library, *The Somerset Messenger Gazette*, the U.S. Equestrian Team, and the White House.

Finally, we would like to thank our spouses, Dorothy and Norm, for tolerating our eccentric ways, permitting the distractions, and abiding the mess.

Please note that the names in parentheses at the end of captions indicates the source of the photograph, not the source of the information.

"Good reader, blame not the wrytter,
for that that is myssing in this booke is not his faulte.
What he hath founde—as nere as possybell he could—he hath set down."

—from an English parish register, 1582.

Introduction

In the decades following the Civil War there arose a class of industrialists and financiers who amassed great fortunes in building the infrastructure of our expanding nation. Much of this wealth and power was concentrated in New York City, where it was hemmed in by two rivers, and surrounded by squalid conditions. The rich began to look to the English Victorian aristocracy for a desirable lifestyle to model. Their wealth enabled them to live as well as or better than any of the great nobility of Europe, and they felt more akin to others of similar position, be they American or European, than to those of ordinary means.

The English aristocracy set the example of having a city home and a country estate. The wealthy New Yorkers sought to establish for themselves a country seat. These estates would have to have acreage on a grand scale. It was thought that they should be located in beautiful countryside, but not too far from New York. The location should have privacy, but also should provide opportunities for association with others of similar social and economic position. There should be enough land to produce the meat and vegetables to provide food for the country estate and the city house as well. These were some of the standards established for the landed gentry.

In the early 1870s, two men who were to become the key motivators in luring wealthy New Yorkers to the Somerset Hills discovered the area quite by accident. George B. Post's wife suffered from rheumatism, and one day, while visiting his cousin and family doctor's farm on the Bernardsville mountain, Mr. Post wondered if the climate would be advantageous to his wife. He bought the 104-acre Ballentine farm.

George Seney, president of the Metropolitan Bank of New York, had been a regular guest at Frank Oliver's boarding house on the Mendham Road for a number of years. In 1871 he bought the place from Oliver and named it Highland House. In 1872 he built the Somerset Inn on the site and began to invite wealthy New Yorkers to come out and enjoy the fresh country air. Those who stayed at the inn often went on to establish summer estates in the area, many of which were designed by the renowned architect George B. Post.

The area was soon carved up into estates. Farmers were offered cash for their land, and in some cases, they were permitted to stay on and farm the place for the new owner. From Jockey Hollow to Burnt Mills, and from Gladstone to Far Hills, the estates were contiguous. The area had quickly become exclusive and impenetrable. Within these boundaries resided men of such enormous wealth and power that they virtually ran this country. John Dryden founded the Prudential Insurance Company and was elected to the United States Senate in 1901. The Stevens family owned Hoboken, refined the steamboat, established the first railroad, won the America's Cup, and founded the Stevens Institute of Technology. Charles Pfizer was the son of the founder of the great pharmaceutical and chemical company. The Roeblings had built the Brooklyn Bridge, and invented the cable that made suspension bridges possible. The list of movers and shakers who found a country home here could go on for pages.

To build the great estates, skilled stone masons, wood carvers, and men of all trades were brought in from Europe. Farmers, gardeners, grooms, and coachmen were needed. In the house there were butlers, cooks, and upstairs and downstairs maids. Many of the estates employed thirty to forty full-time servants. The house staff lived in the house. The grooms and coachmen lived over the stables. The farmers and gardeners often lived in the homes of those from whom the land had been purchased, and the skilled craftsmen lived in town.

At first the wealthy land holders had to take a carriage to Morristown to catch a train into New York. It was the custom at that time for the wives and children to live in the estates full-time during the summer, and for the husbands to commute on weekends. Later, after the train came to Bernardsville and Grant Schley had it extended to Gladstone, it became possible for the men to commute on a daily basis. The five o'clock train became known as the "Millionaire's Special." Coachmen were expected to be at the station at precisely five o'clock to pick up their masters, and there were races to see whose coach would get up the mountain first.

As early as 1894, a group of men formed an association to establish a country club. J. Herbert Ballantine, George B. Post, Robert L. Stevens, and Edward T.H. Talmadge each pledged $8,000 to buy the land. The Smith farm, located in a small valley through which the North Branch of the Raritan River flows, was purchased for about $80 an acre. A dam was started in 1898 and was completed the following year, creating what we now call Ravine Lake. A clubhouse was built there, and a nine-hole golf course was established on top of the hill overlooking the lake. This was the beginning of the Somerset Hills Country Club, which continued there until 1917, when it was relocated to its present site.

By the 1880s it was becoming too built up around Montclair, New Jersey, for fox hunting, so the Essex Country Club sold its hounds, hunters (horses), and equipment to Charles Pfizer, who brought them to Bernardsville, and then Gladstone. From 1890 to 1913, the Essex Hunt was Charles Pfizer's personal property, and those who hunted foxes with him were his guests. Many were prominent men from estates in the area. Some were business associates, who took the train from New York for a weekend's hunting. Others were gentlemen from hunt clubs in other states, or abroad, who liked to experience the hunt in different areas, and with different breeds of hounds and horses. Finally, there were a few from Squadron A of the 7th New York National Guard cavalry unit who, tired of riding horses in a practice rink, looked to fox hunting as an opportunity to get some real riding experience. Mr. Pfizer was a generous host, and for those lacking their own mounts, he maintained a stable of some thirty fine hunters.

Over the years the area has retained its appeal. The Essex Fox Hounds still run three times a week. The Somerset (Ravine) Lake and Game Club still provides a swimming and boating facility to its members, and the Somerset Hills Country Club is as spectacular (and as exclusive) as ever. New clubs have been added to answer the demand, and several gentlemen have private polo grounds on their estates. The Far Hills Race Meeting continues to draw record crowds, and the U.S. Equestrian Team sponsors a number of equestrian events each year. Many descendants of the original mountain colony still live here, and new gentlemen of substance continue to aspire to the ownership of an estate in the Somerset Hills. Malcolm Forbes brought his family to the area in 1947, and Jackie Kennedy found a country place here after the death of the president. More recently, His Royal Highness, King Hassan II of Morocco, has purchased the beautiful Kate Macy Ladd Estate in Peapack.

One

The Great Estates

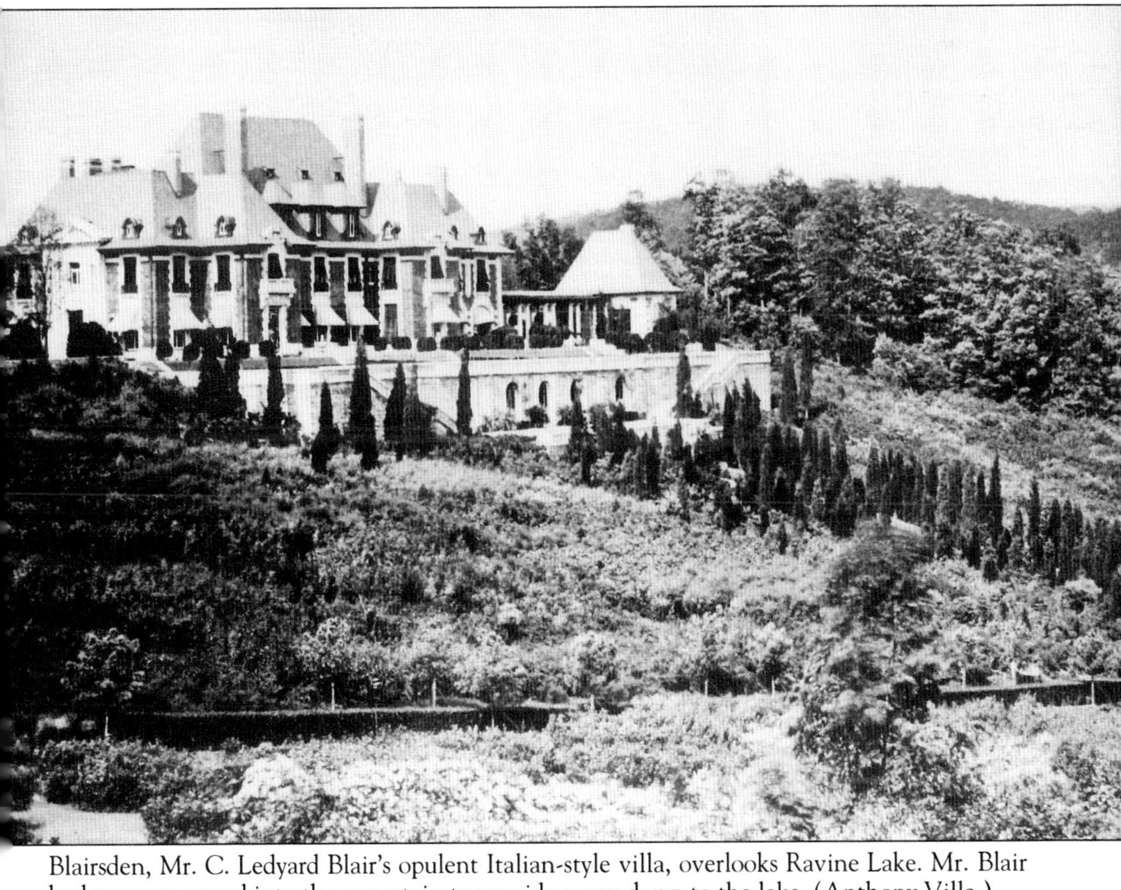

Blairsden, Mr. C. Ledyard Blair's opulent Italian-style villa, overlooks Ravine Lake. Mr. Blair had terraces carved into the mountain to provide a way down to the lake. (Anthony Villa.)

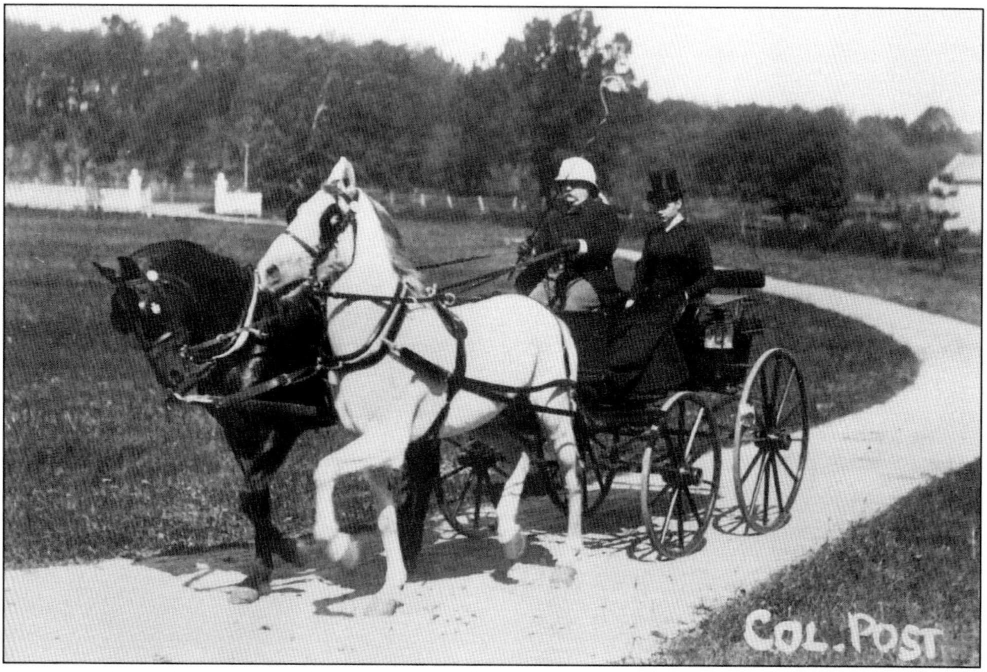

Renowned architect George B. Post is seen here in a phaeton on the grounds of his estate, Claremont, about 1895. Post had served under General Burnside at the battle of Fredericksburg during the Civil War, and rose to the rank of colonel in the New York National Guard by 1868. He was a tall man with a white walrus mustache that was stained slightly yellow by the cigars he smoked. (Chatfield's.)

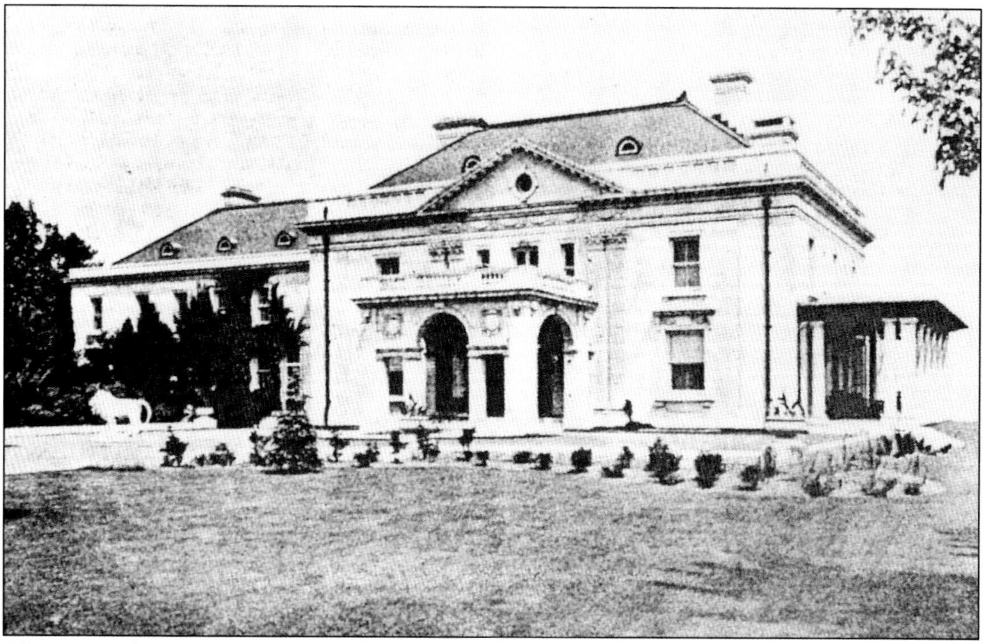

Claremont, the Bernardsville estate of George B. Post, was built in 1907, and is named after the country home of his grandfather, Joel Post, which overlooks the Hudson River in New York State. As a boy, George loved to go there. (The *Bernardsville News*.)

George B. Post is credited more than anybody with selling wealthy New Yorkers on the idea of establishing country estates on the Bernardsville mountain. Many of them he designed himself. He is also known as the creator of the skyscraper. Among the buildings he designed are the New York Times Building in 1889, the St. Paul Building (tallest in New York at the time) in 1897–99, and the New York Stock Exchange. (Turpin Real Estate.)

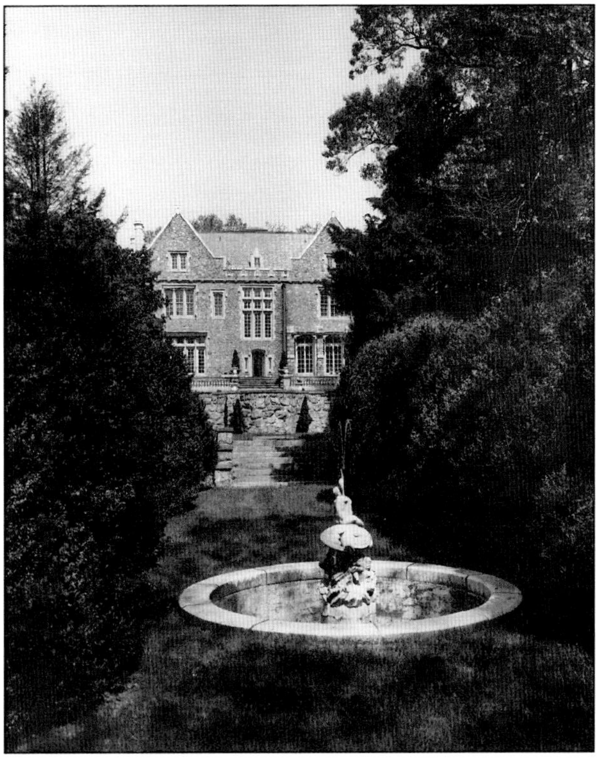

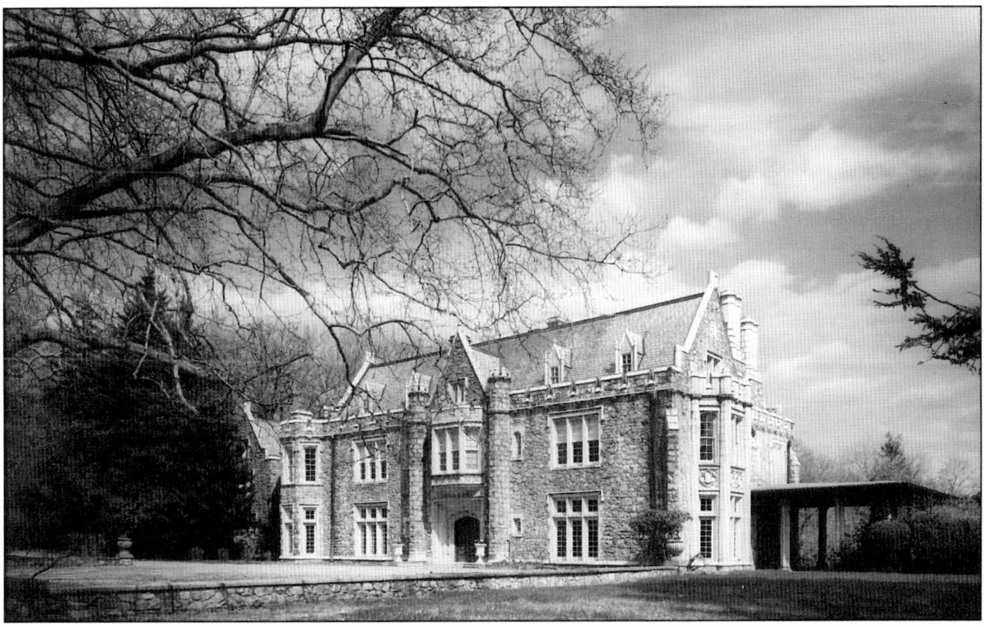

Kenilwood was designed by George B. Post as a wedding gift for his daughter, Harriet, upon her marriage to Thornton Wilson. The house was built in 1896–97. Later Harriet married Sumner Welles, secretary of state under President Franklin D. Roosevelt. This is one of the two most important examples of Gothic Revival architecture in America. The estate remained in the Post family until it was sold in 1988 to Mike Tyson. (Turpin Real Estate.)

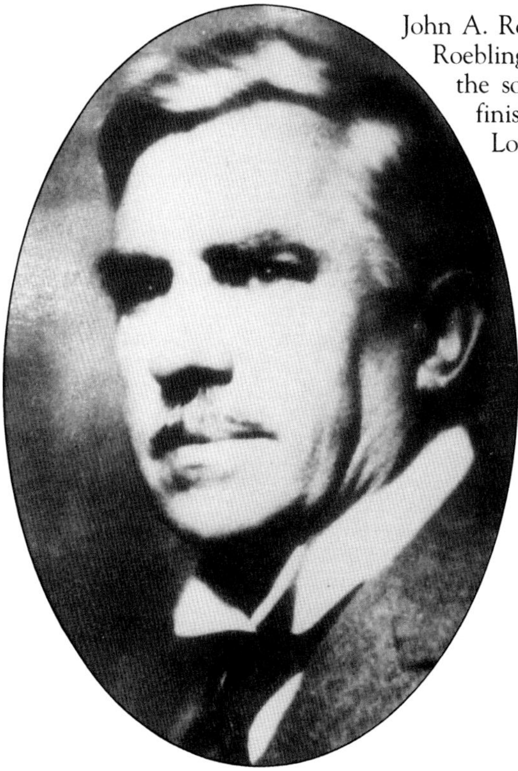

John A. Roebling was the grandson of John Augustus Roebling who planned the Brooklyn Bridge, and the son of Washington Augustus Roebling, who finished that bridge. (Bernardsville Public Library Local History Collection.)

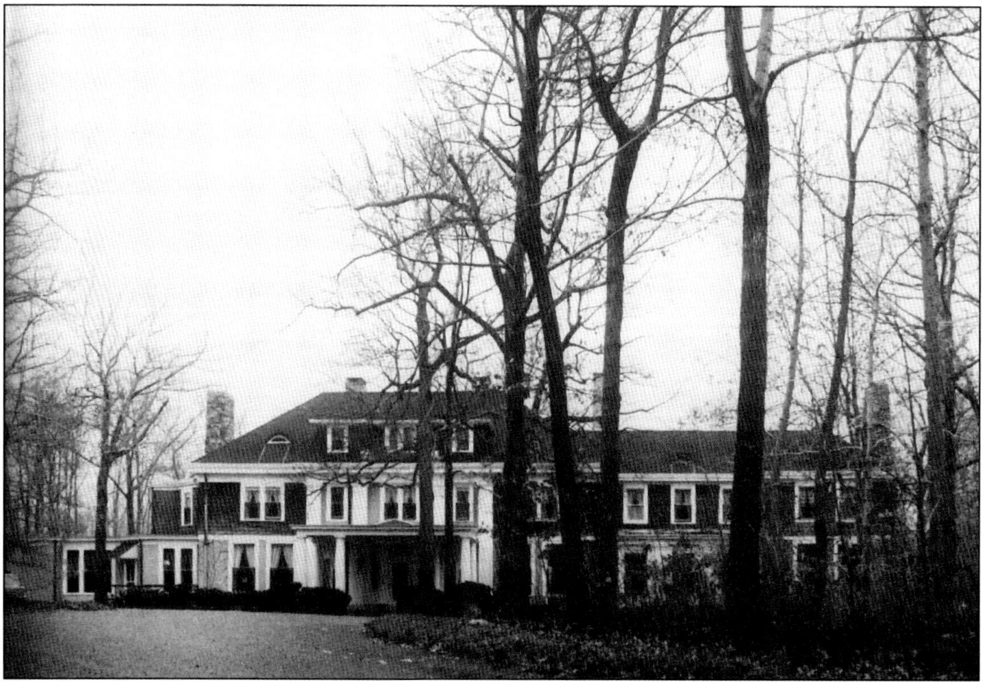

Mr. Roebling bought Boulderwood in 1908. During the depression, he was one of many wealthy estate holders who provided work for the local people who needed it. (Bernardsville Public Library Local History Collection.)

Henry Janeway Hardenbergh was born in 1847 to one of Somerset County's oldest families. He became an architect in New York City and a master of a new building form—the skyscraper. He designed the Waldorf Astoria and the Plaza hotels, but his most famous creation was the Dakota apartment house. (Somerset County Library.)

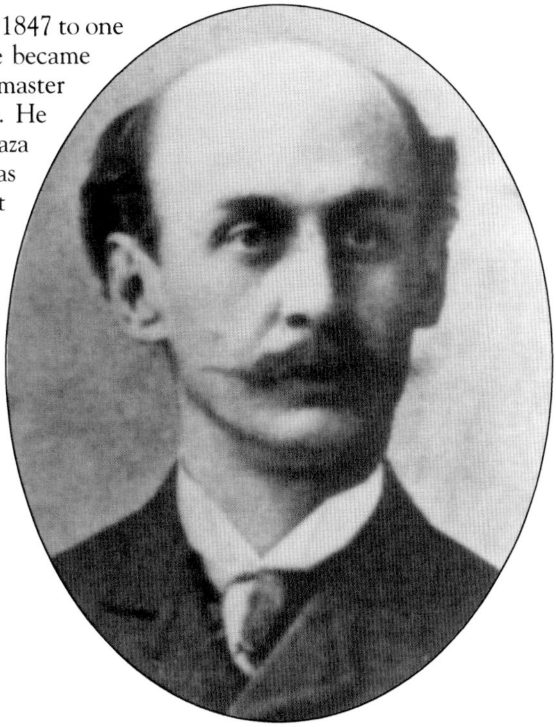

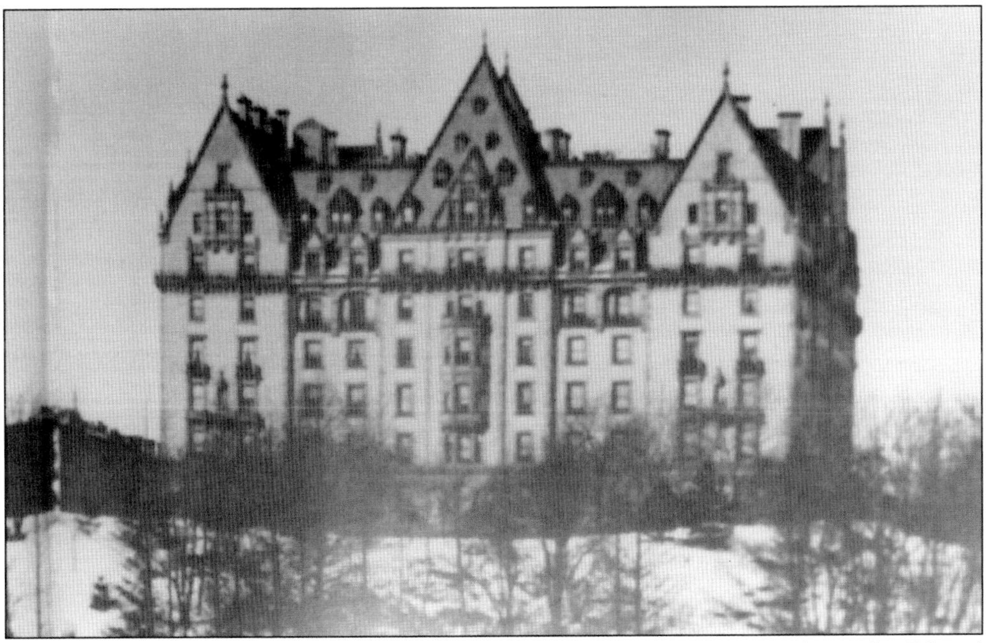

Henry J. Hardenbergh was commissioned to design the Dakota apartment house by Edward Clark, president of the Singer Sewing Machine Company. It was built so far west of the fashionable part of the city of the day, that critics said it might as well have been built in the Dakota Territory, so that is what he named it. He covered it with western and Indian symbols. Begun in 1880, it was sold out before it was completed. Famous residents have included Boris Karloff, Lauren Bacall, and John Lennon and Yoko Ono. (The New York Historical Society.)

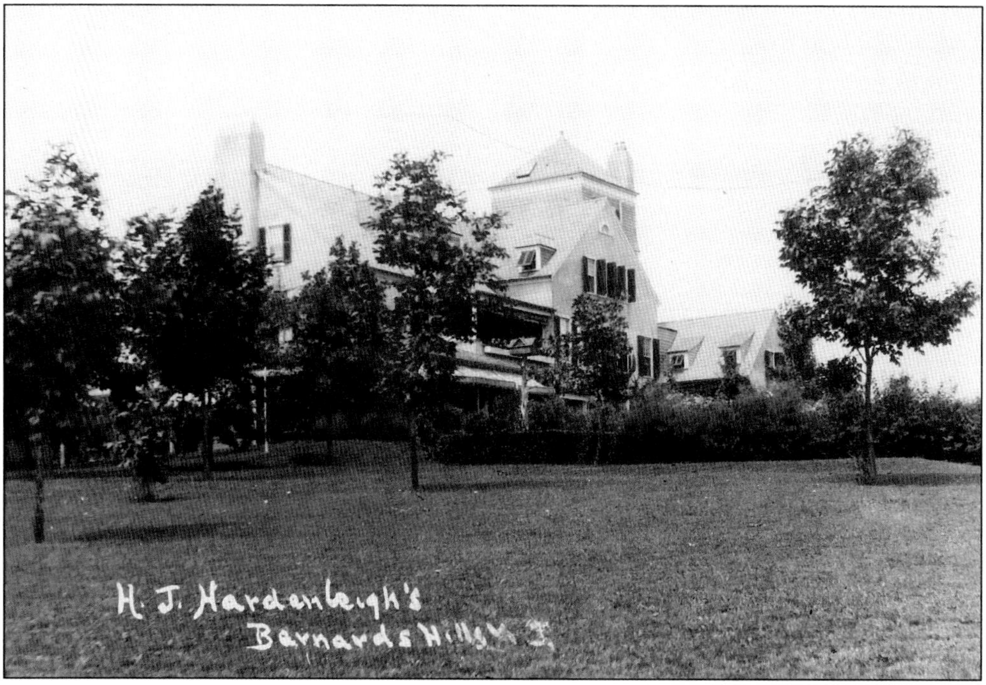

Renemede was the estate of Henry Janeway Hardenbergh in Bernardsville. The house was built in the 1880s, and had to be rebuilt after a fire about 1906. Mr. Hardenbergh died on March 13, 1918. (Bernardsville Public Library Local History Collection.)

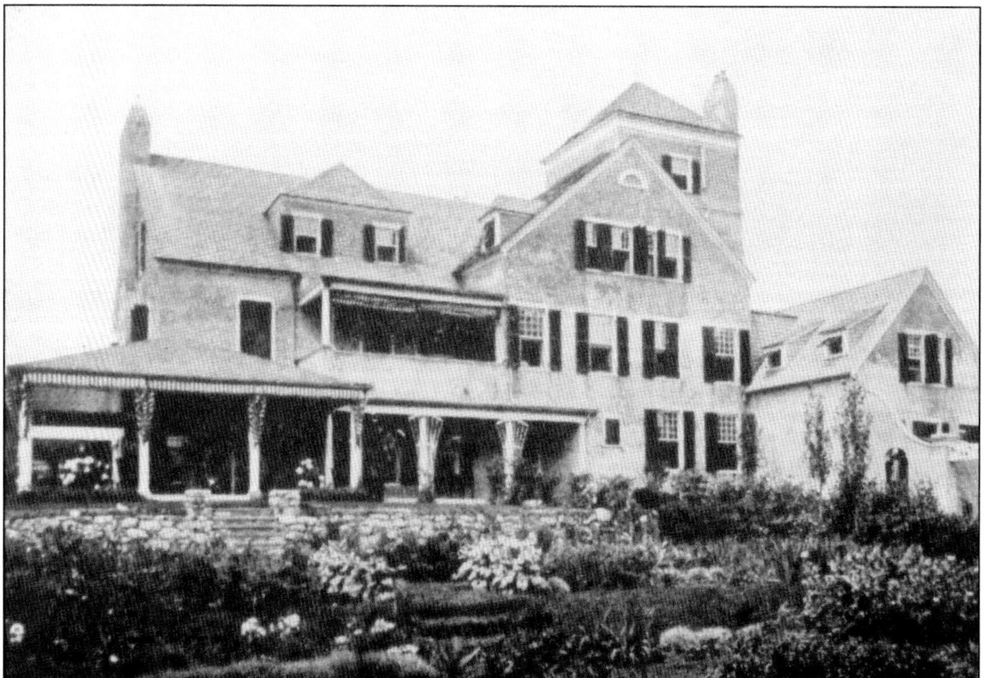

Another view of Renemede, the Bernardsville estate of Henry Janeway Hardenbergh, was taken about 1905. (Bernardsville Public Library Local History Collection.)

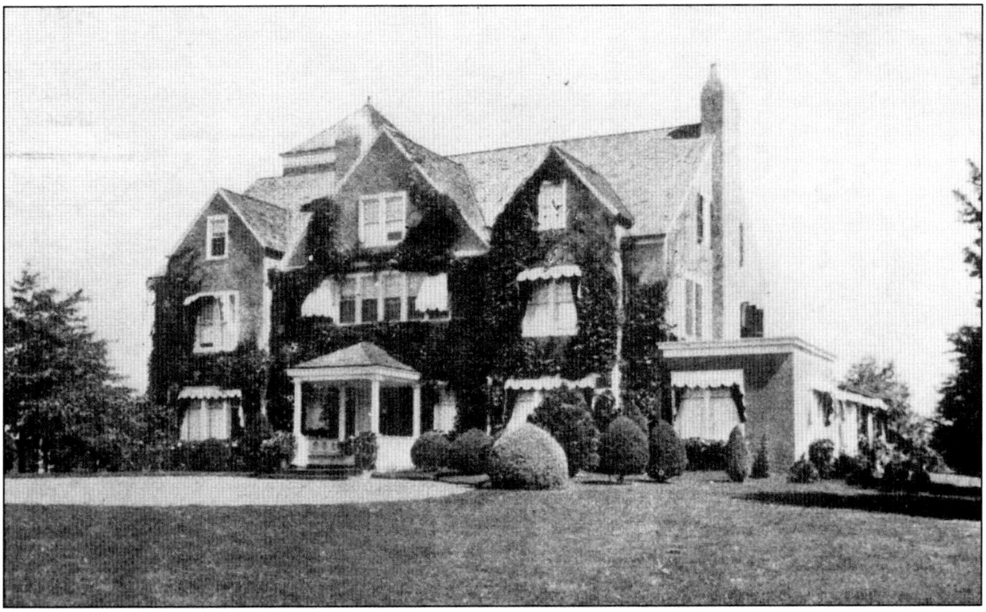

Renemede later became the residence of Mr. William P. Hardenbergh, the nephew of Henry J. Hardenbergh. This view is from the front, while those on the facing page are from the rear. (Bernardsville Public Library Local History Collection.)

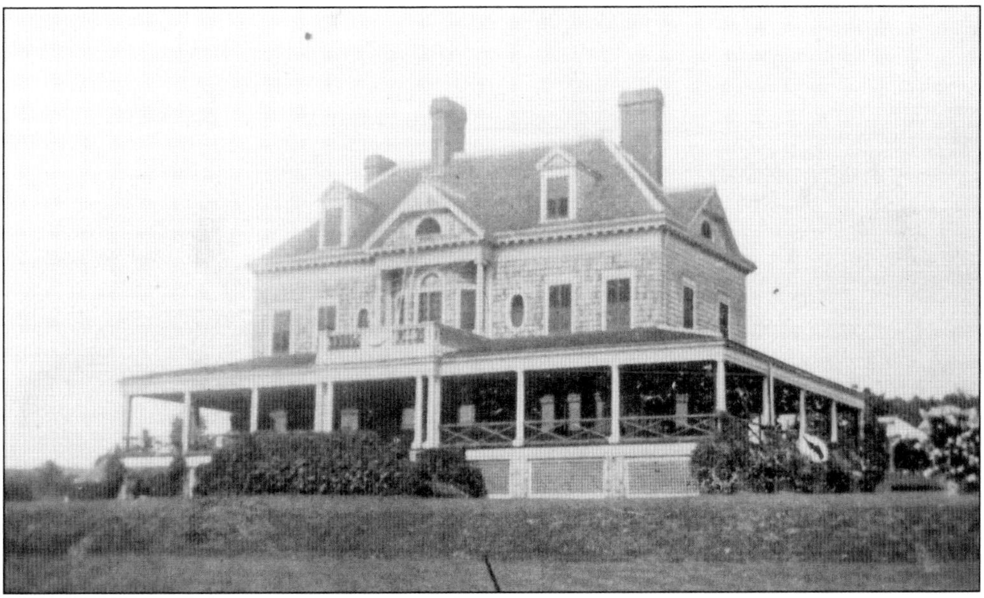

The home of Mr. Frederic P. Olcott, president of the Central Trust Company, in New York. Mr. Olcott donated the school bearing his name, along with twenty-seven acres, to the community. He had Henry Janeway Hardenbergh design the building. He had a private racetrack on his property. In 1915, his estate was purchased to establish a larger course for the Somerset Hills Country Club which had first been located overlooking Ravine Lake. (Bernardsville Public Library Local History Collection.)

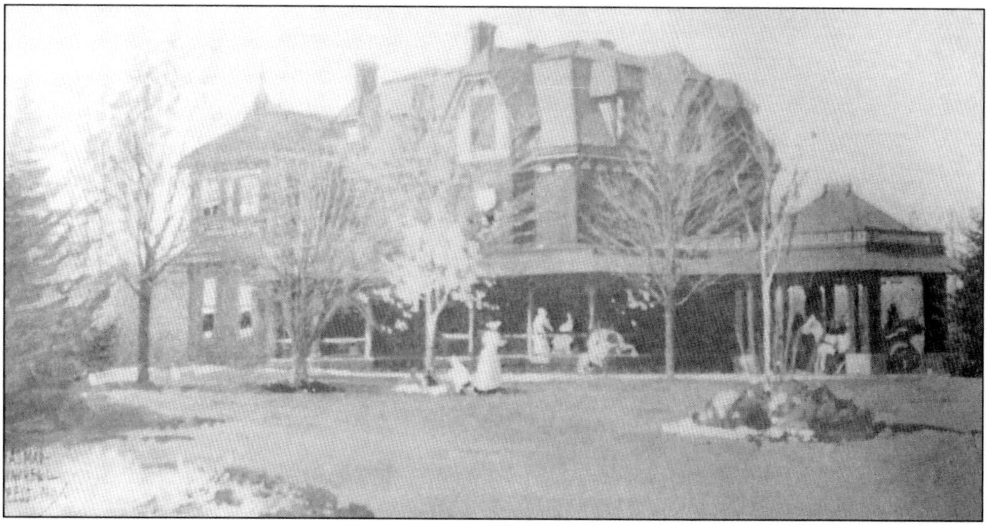

George I. Seney came to Bernardsville about 1873 and built this "cottage." He also built the Somerset Inn which enabled many wealthy New Yorkers to visit the hills, buy land, and build houses. After Mr. Seney built The Maples, Charles Pfizer and others lived in the Seney Cottage while their own homes were under construction. Mr. Pfizer bought the property, and kenneled his fox hounds on the grounds before moving the pack to Gladstone. (Somerset Inn Brochure.)

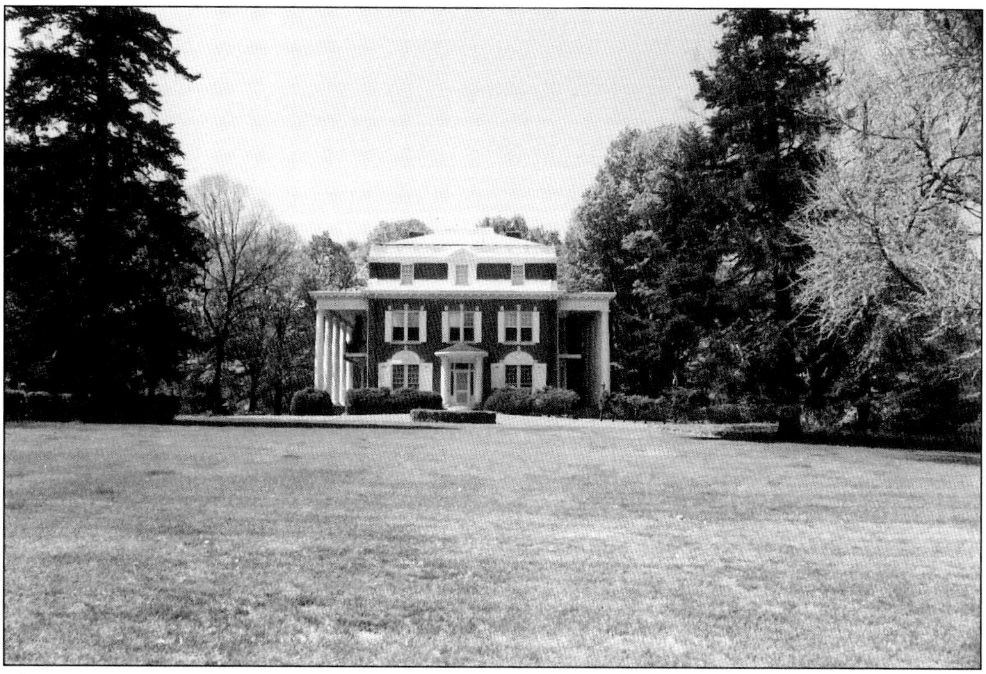

The Maples was the estate of George I. Seney, who came to Bernardsville about 1873. Seney was president of the Metropolitan Bank of New York. Later the estate was owned by Francis G. Lloyd, the president of Brooks Brothers, who gave it the name. (Lorraine Hunt Kopacz, manager of Douglas Elliman Realty.)

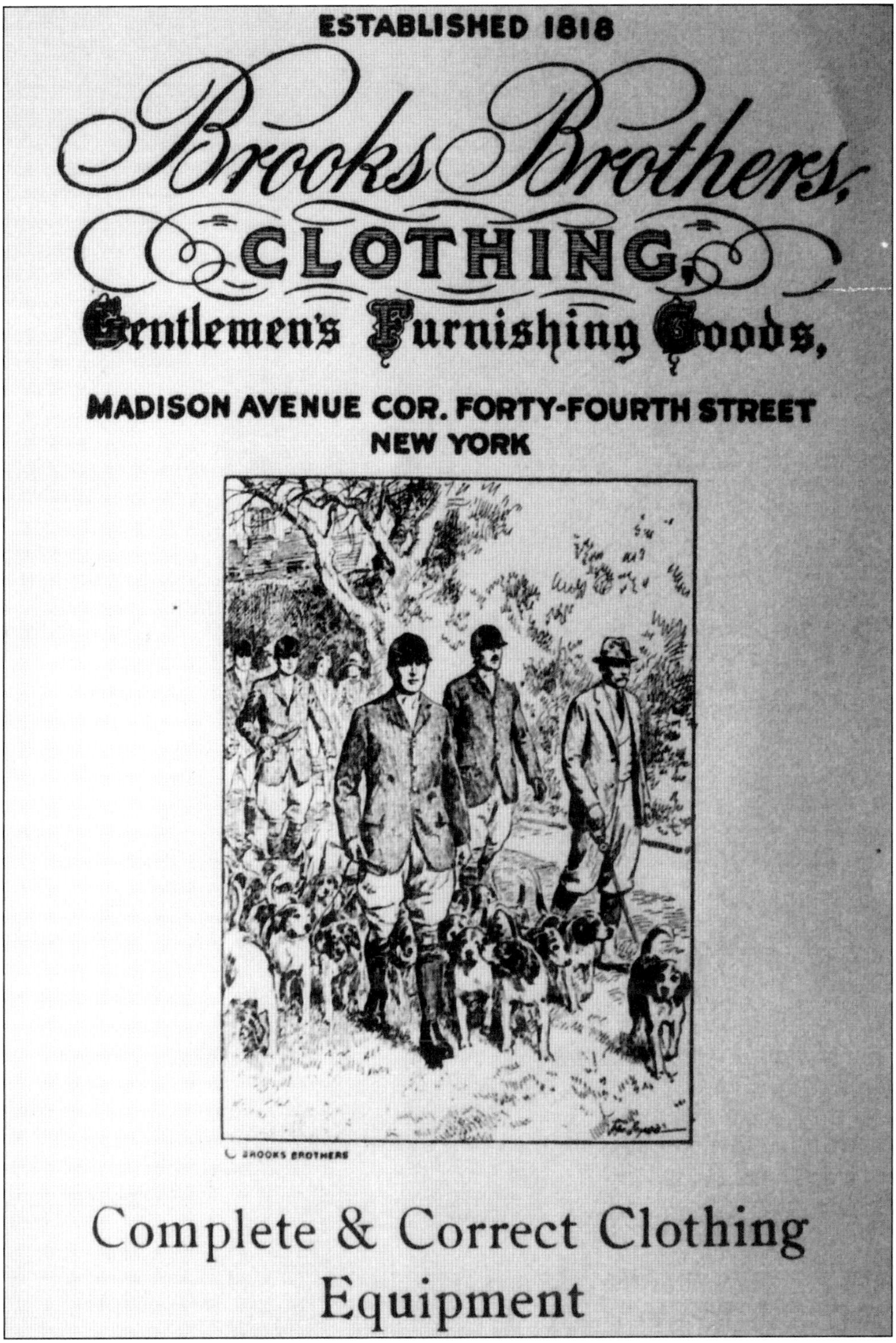

This Brooks Brothers advertisement was featured in the *Somerset Hills Kennel Club Dog Show Catalogue*, Far Hills, on October 15, 1932.

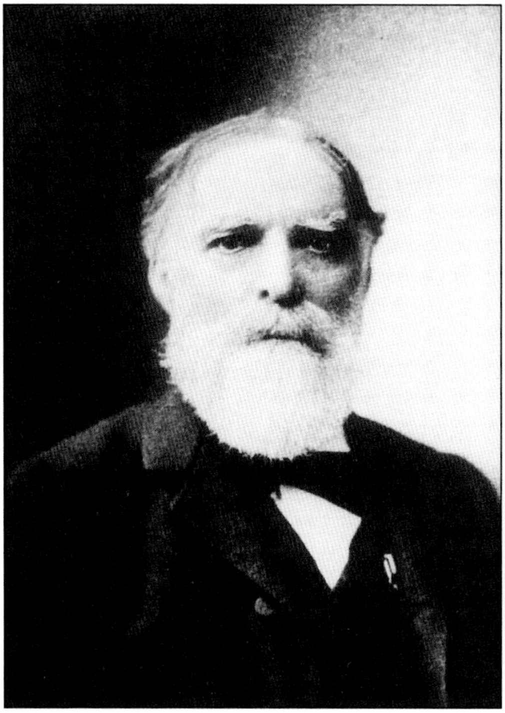
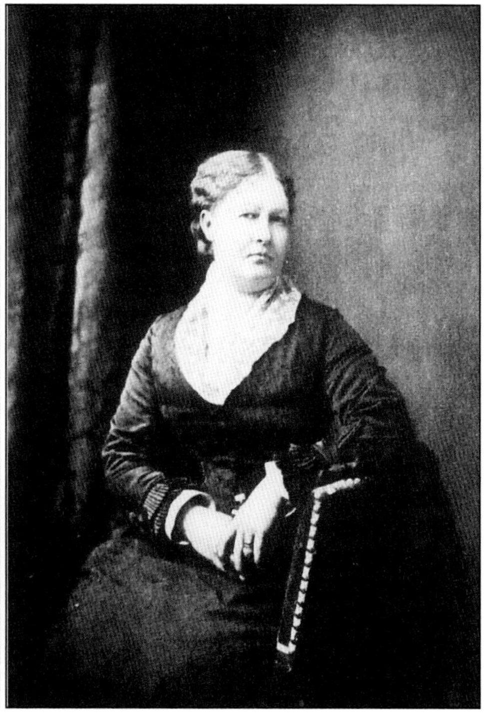

Judge John Forrest Dillon (1831–1914) was personal counsel for Jay Gould, and president of the American Bar Association. This photograph was taken in 1899. On the right is his wife, Mrs. Anna Price Dillon, (1853–1898). (Margery Dillon Turpin.)

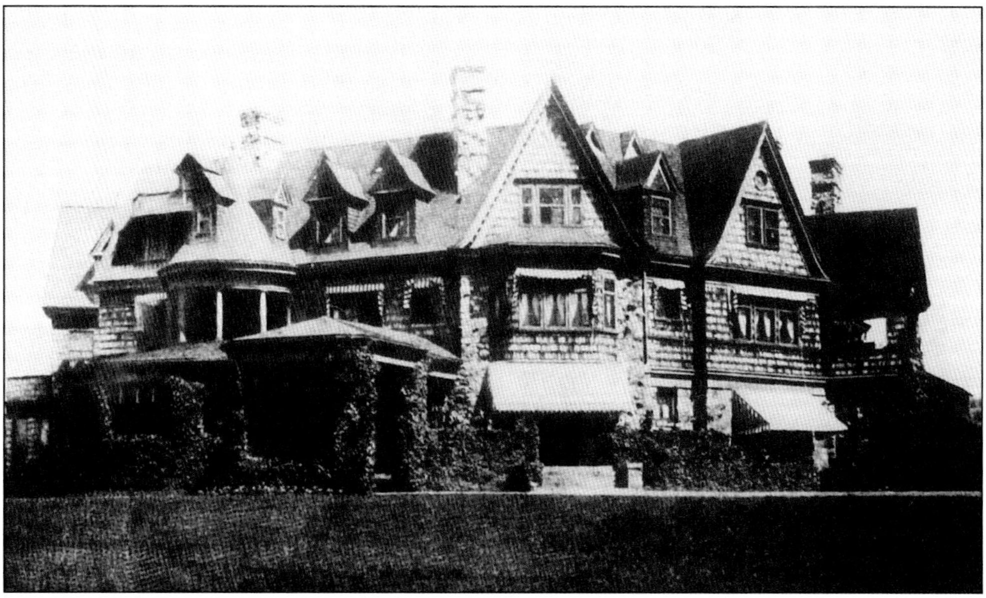

Knollcrest, the estate of Judge John F. and Mrs. Anna Price Dillon, was built in 1895. In 1898 Dillon's wife and daughter perished when the French ocean liner *La Bourgogne* sank off Nova Scotia. He rushed to Halifax, chartered a steamer and hunted the ocean for days in an unsuccessful search for their bodies. In 1919 G. Hermann Kinnicutt bought the property, demolished Knollcrest, and built Mayfields on the site. (Margery Dillon Turpin.)

This 1898 image shows John Milton Dillon, the son of Judge John Forrest Dillon and his wife, Anna. (Margery Dillon Turpin.)

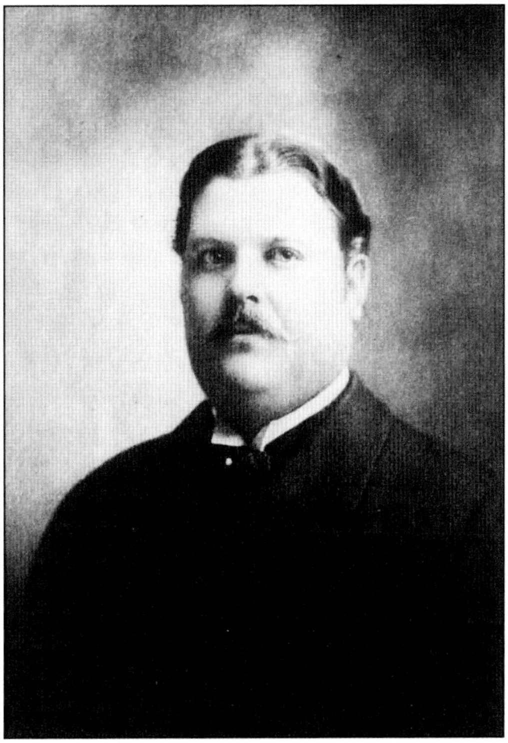

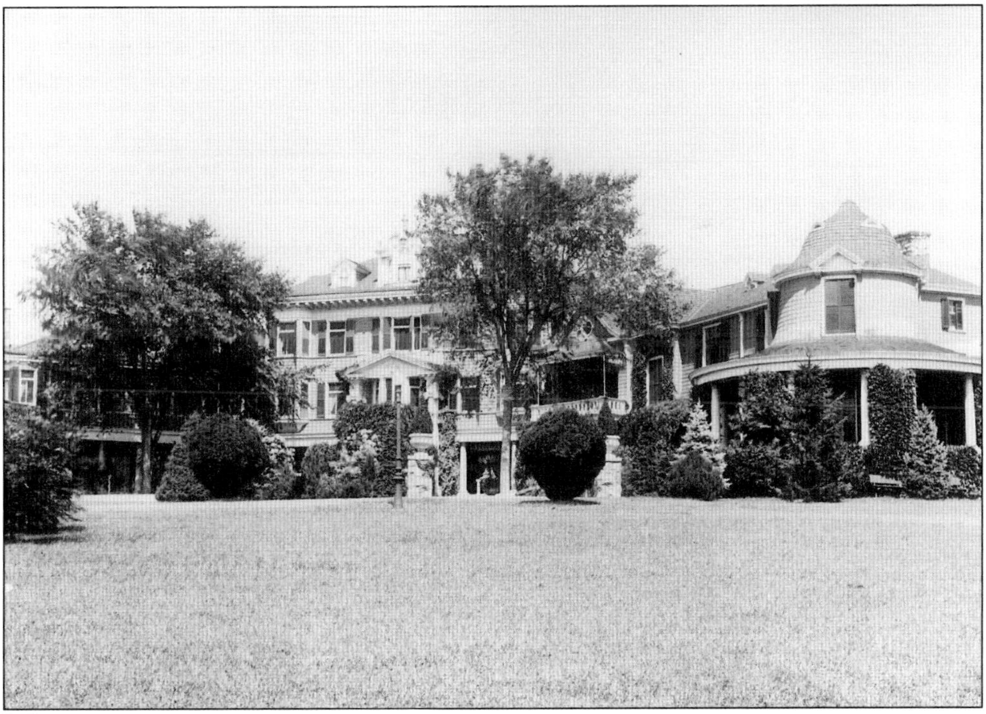

Overleigh, the summer home of Mr. John Milton and Mrs. Lucy Sands Downing Dillon, was located directly across the street from his father, Judge John F. Dillon's, estate "Knollcrest." This view was taken in 1906. (Margery Dillon Turpin.)

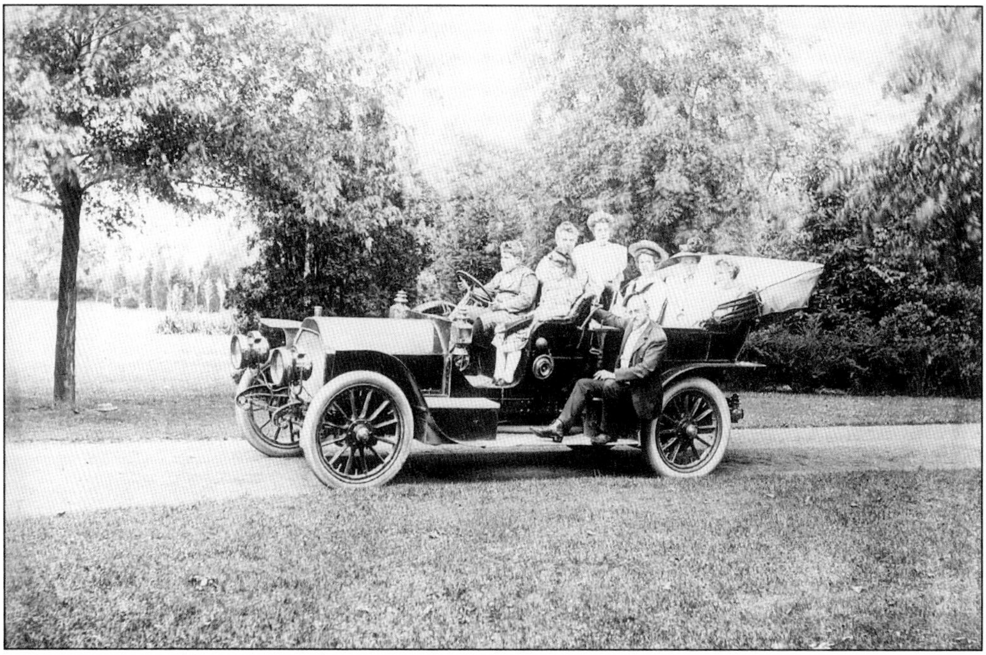

Milton Sands Dillon, sits at the wheel of his father John M. Dillon's 1906 touring car. His sister, Dorothy, sits beside him. The others are members of the Downing family, relatives of the Dillons. (Margery Dillon Turpin.)

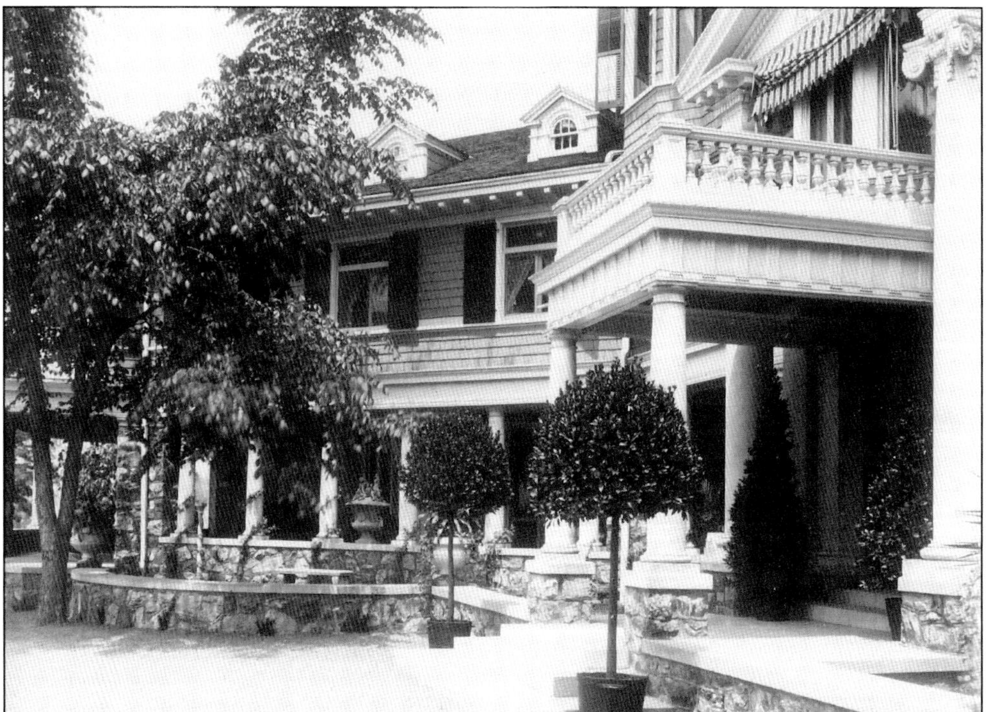

This photograph of the front entrance of Overleigh was taken in 1903. (Margery Dillon Turpin.)

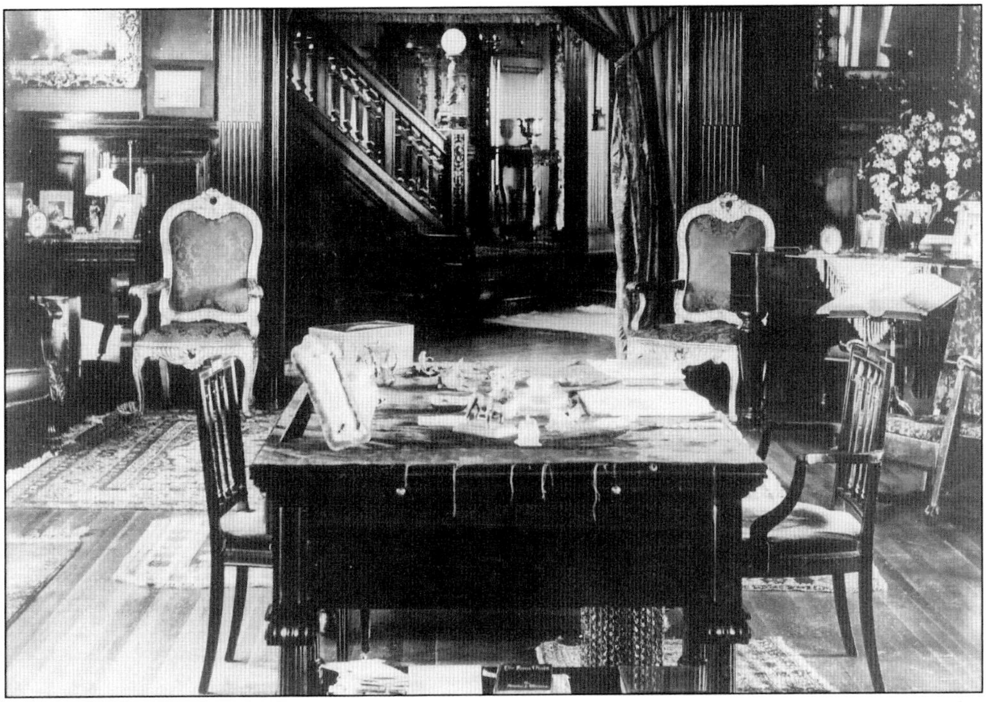

Here we can see a portion of the living room at Overleigh, looking toward the stairs and the music room. (Margery Dillon Turpin.)

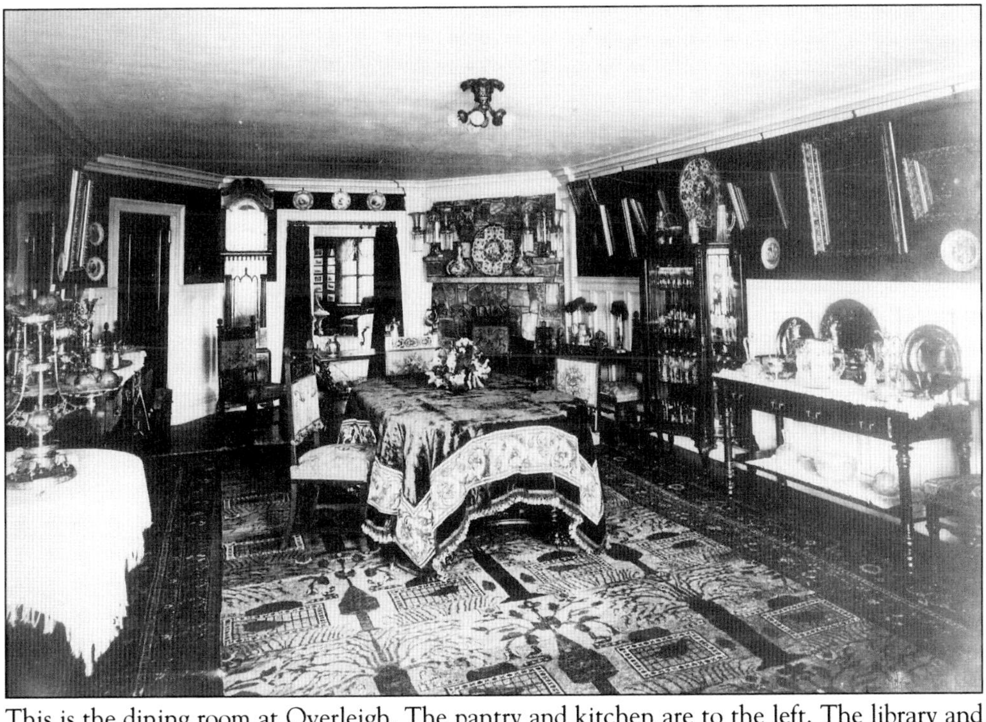

This is the dining room at Overleigh. The pantry and kitchen are to the left. The library and game room are through the door, and the front hall is to the right. (Margery Dillon Turpin.)

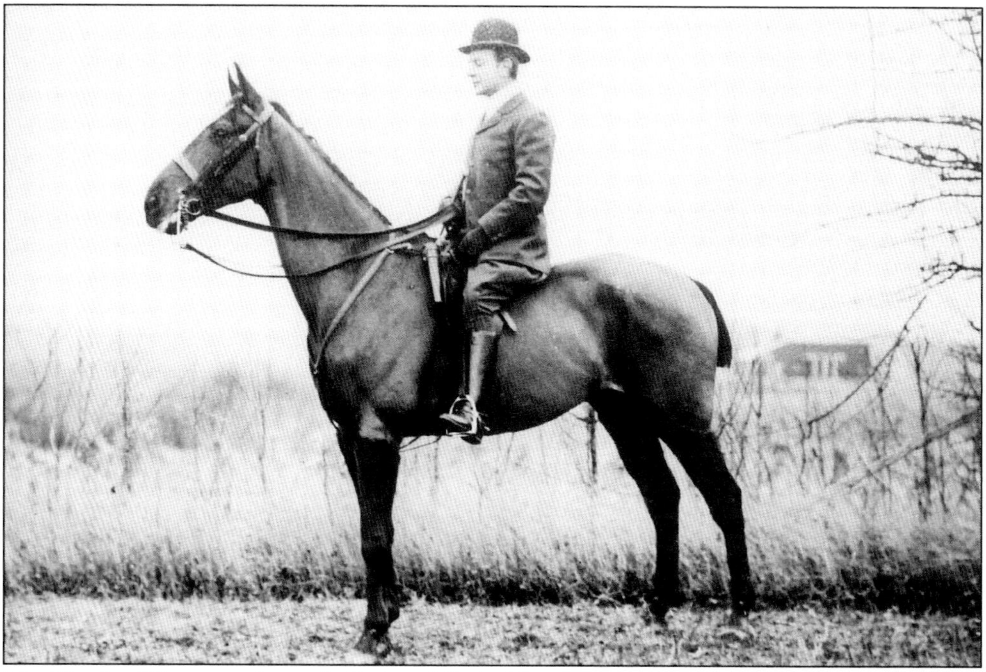

Mr. Charles Pfizer posed astride Duke of York. The log of the Essex Hounds notes that Mr. Pfizer rode Duke of York with the drag on November 22, 1902. The field was composed of twenty guests of Mr. Pfizer, sixteen of whom were mounted on his hunters (horses). Following the hunt, they all had breakfast at the estate of Mr. Charles Squibb, in Bernardsville. Duke of York's hair has been clipped everywhere except for his legs (to protect them from brambles) giving him the appearance of wearing stockings. (James S. Jones.)

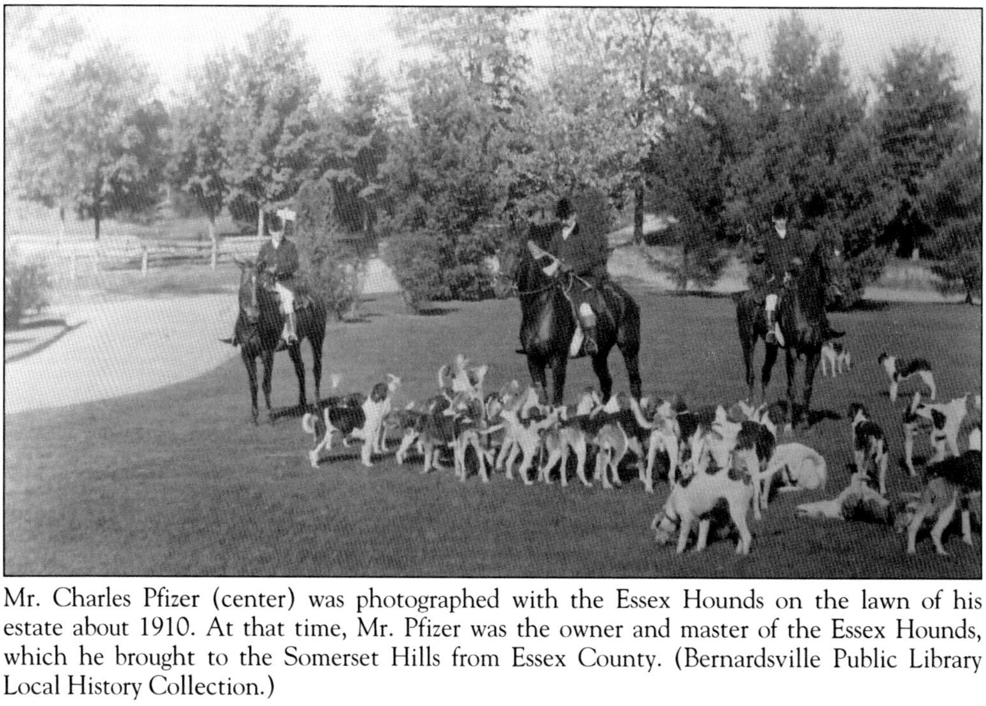

Mr. Charles Pfizer (center) was photographed with the Essex Hounds on the lawn of his estate about 1910. At that time, Mr. Pfizer was the owner and master of the Essex Hounds, which he brought to the Somerset Hills from Essex County. (Bernardsville Public Library Local History Collection.)

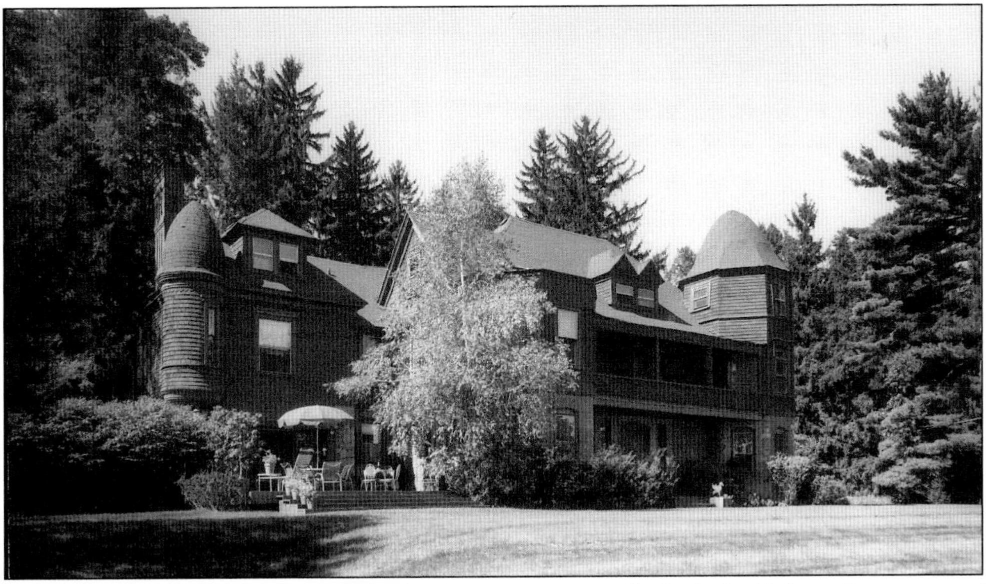

The stone and shingle estate of Charles Pfizer was originally built for Robert Seney, son of George Seney, in 1881. The home was designed by the firm of Lamb and Rich, of New York. Mr. Pfizer, the son of the founder of the Pfizer Pharmaceutical and Chemical Company, bought the estate in 1891 and called it Yademos, which is the word "someday" spelled backwards. (Turpin Real Estate.)

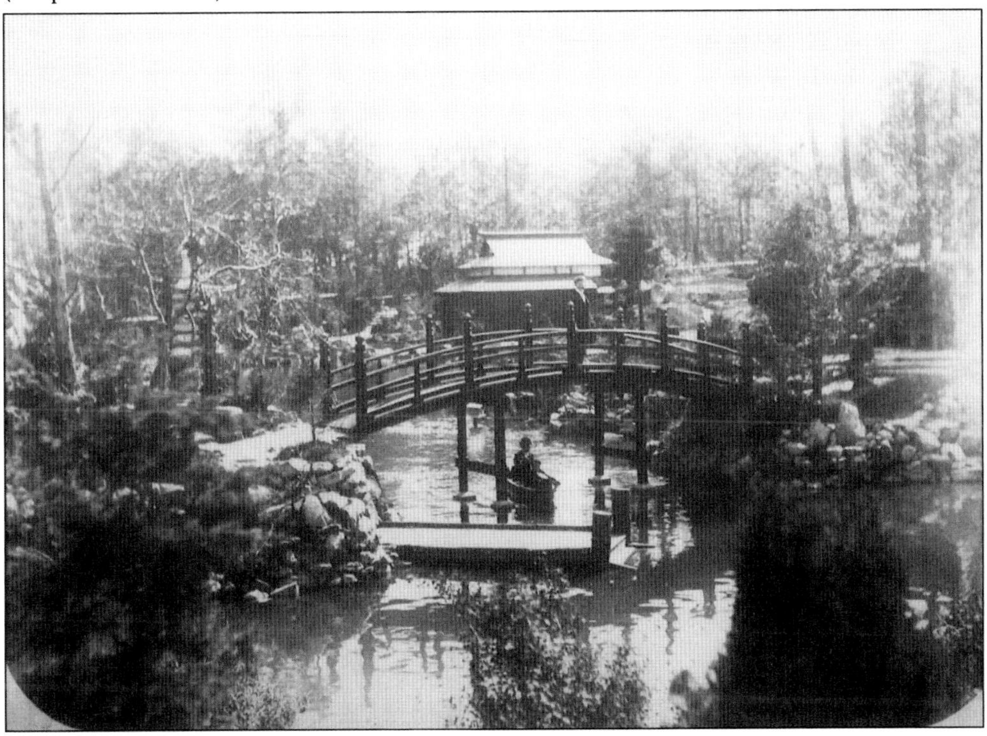

Mr. Pfizer had an elaborate Japanese garden on his estate in 1906. *Madame Butterfly*, with Mary Pickford, was filmed in this garden in 1915. (Bernardsville Public Library Local History Collection.)

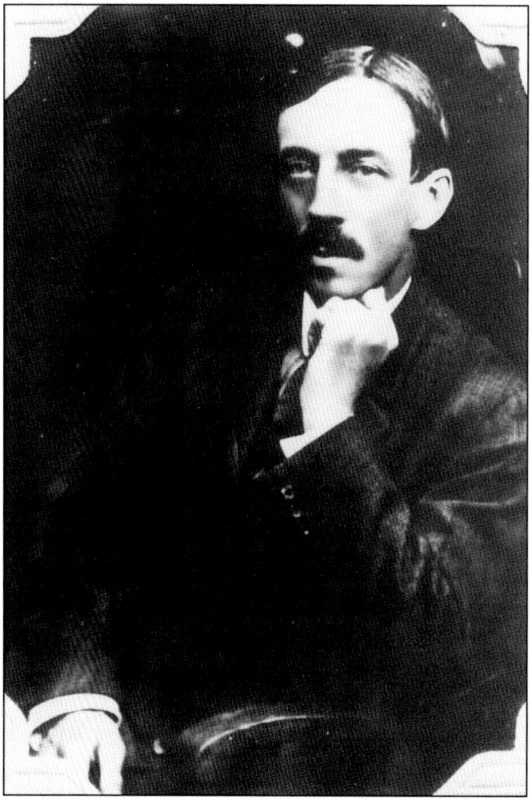

Richard Stevens, one of the sons of the founder of Stevens Institute of Technology, built an estate in Bernardsville in the 1890s. His mansion was later destroyed by fire. (Hugh Fenwick.)

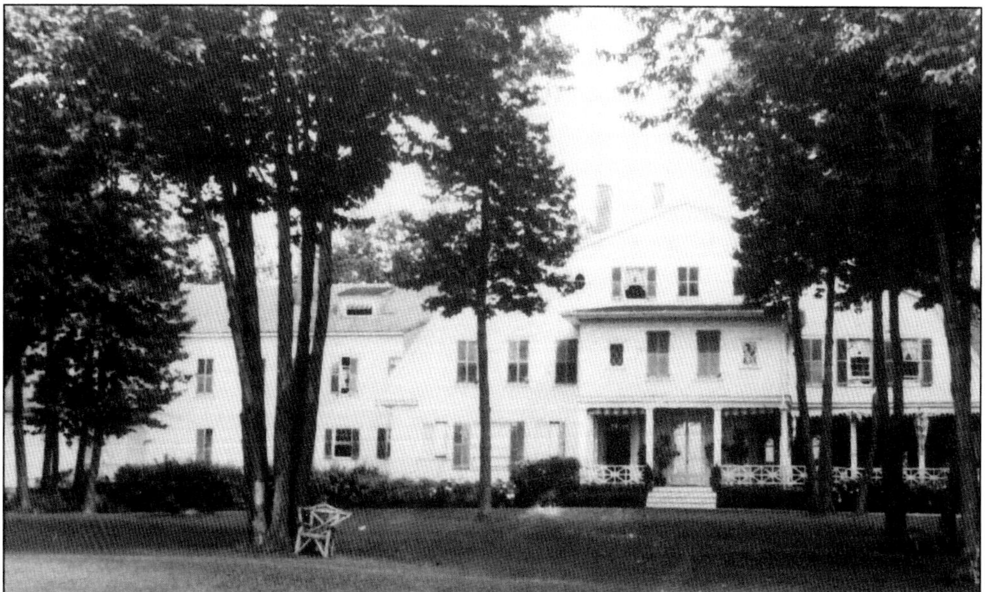

The home of Richard Stevens, built in 1891–92, which was destroyed by fire. A cousin of the family, Lili, who married Charles M. Chapin, later bought the property and built Westover (see p. 33). (Bernardsville Public Library Local History Collection.)

Robert Livingston Stevens was one of the sons of the founder of Stevens Institute of Technology. Here, Mr. Stevens is mounted on his hunter. He frequently rode in fox hunts as the guest of his neighbor, Charles Pfizer. Note that the horse is wearing spats to protect its ankles from fence rails and brambles. (Hugh Fenwick.)

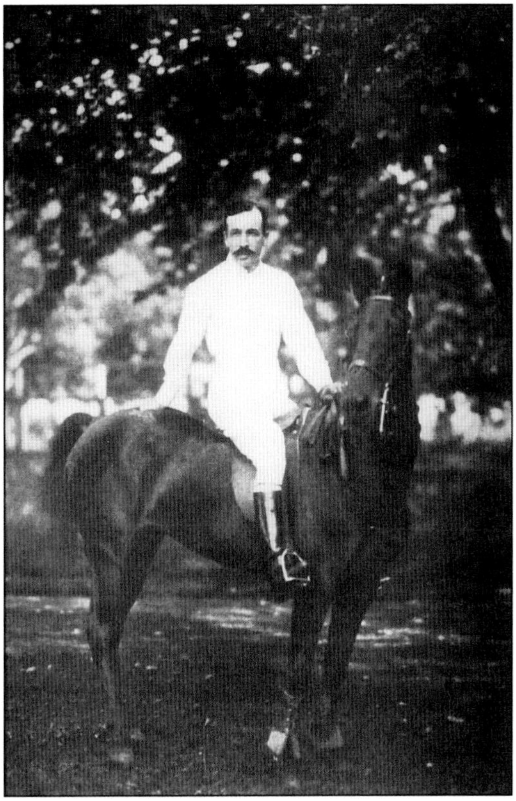

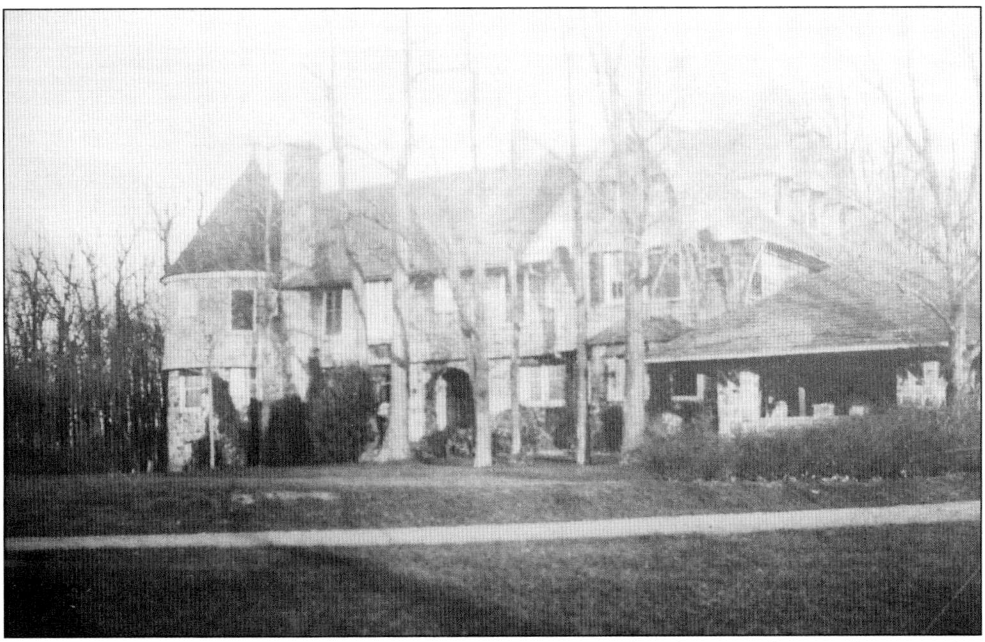

The home of Robert Livingston Stevens was built in 1890. This photograph was taken in 1909. (Hugh Fenwick.)

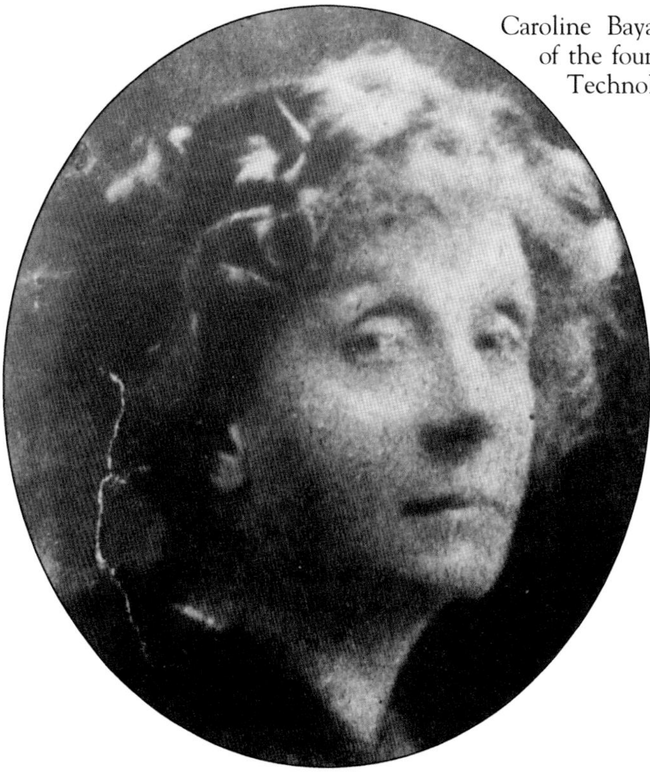

Caroline Bayard Stevens was the daughter of the founder of the Stevens Institute of Technology. (Hugh Fenwick.)

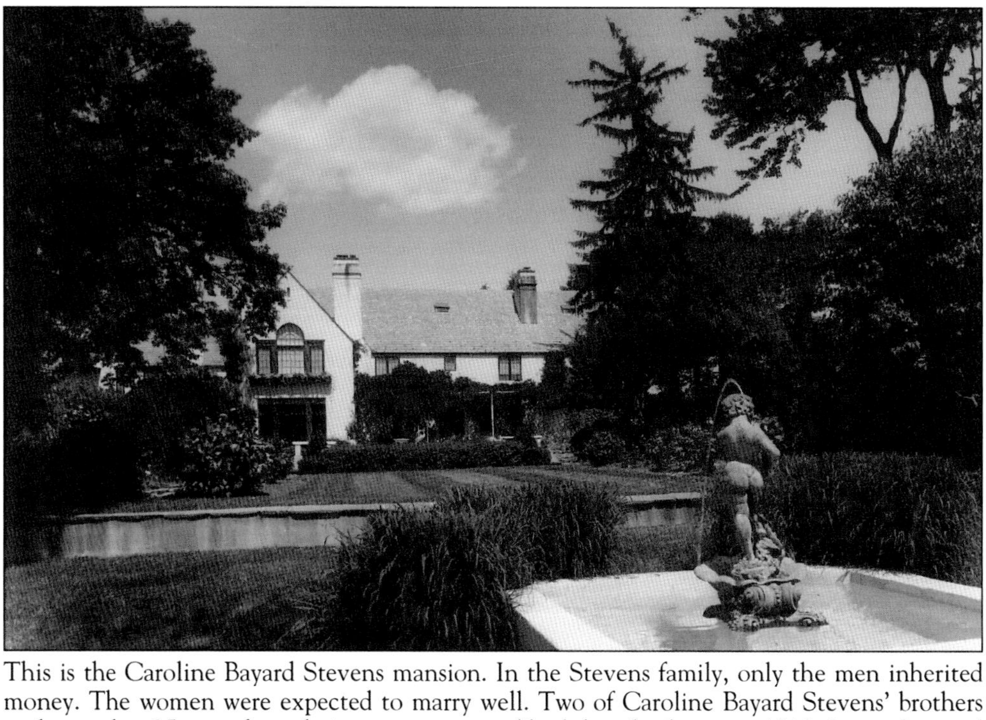

This is the Caroline Bayard Stevens mansion. In the Stevens family, only the men inherited money. The women were expected to marry well. Two of Caroline Bayard Stevens' brothers each gave her 25 acres from their own estates, and built her this house in 1910. It was designed by architect Harry Aldridge. (Turpin Real Estate.)

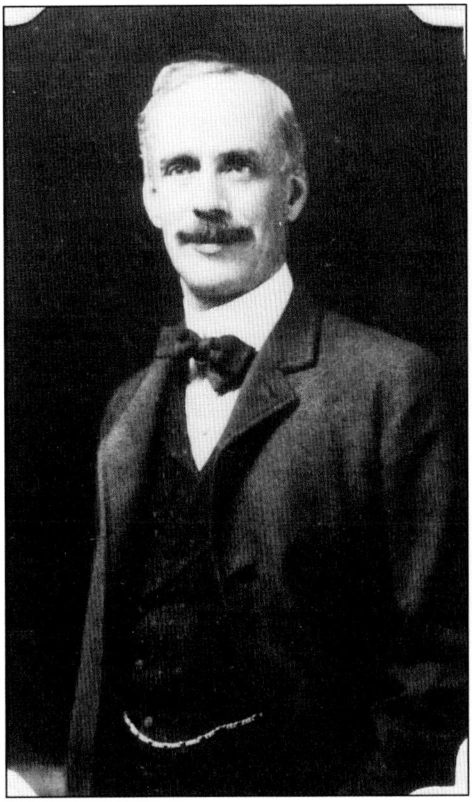

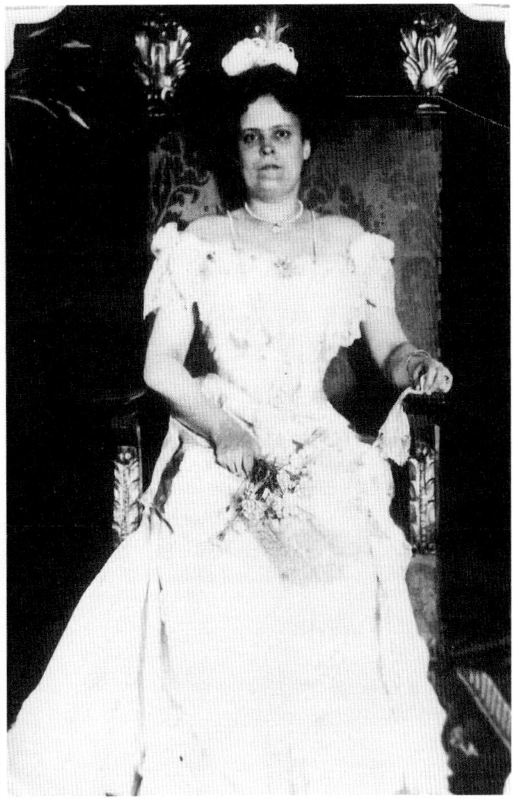

Colonel Edwin A. Stevens, Congresswoman Millicent Fenwick's great uncle, and Emily C. Lewis Stevens, his wife. Colonel Stevens was another son of the founder of Stevens Institute of Technology. (Hugh Fenwick.)

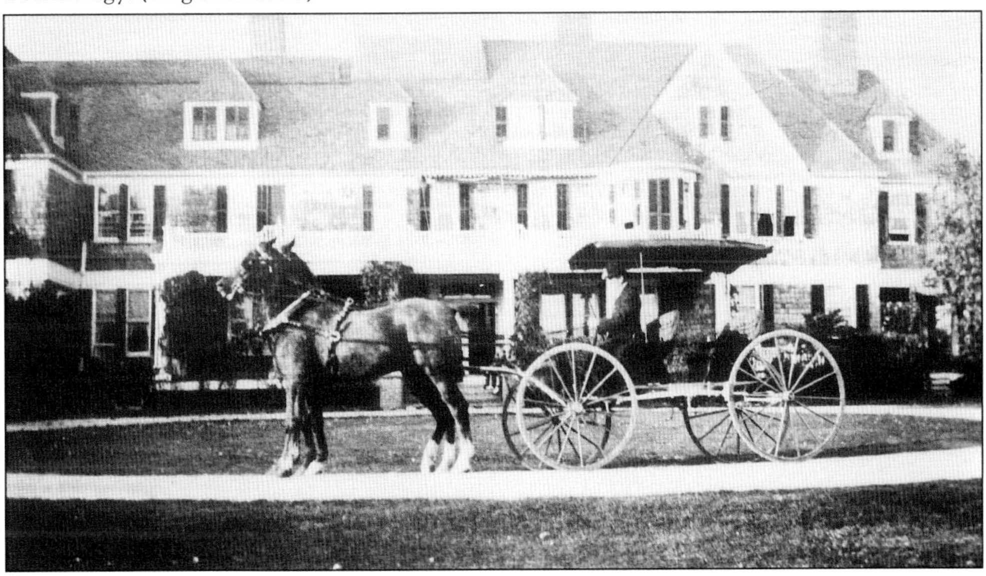

The Colonel Edwin A. Stevens house was built in 1892. This is where Congresswoman Millicent Fenwick grew up. The photograph was taken in 1909, when it was the home of Millicent Fenwick's parents, Mary and Ogden Hammond (Hugh Fenwick.)

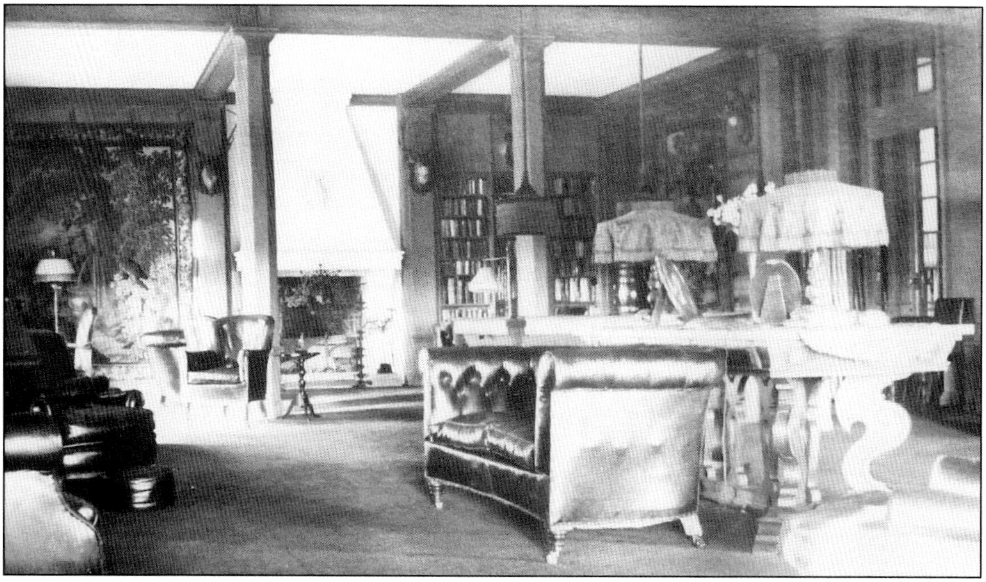

This is the interior of the living room of the Hammond's house in 1909. (Hugh Fenwick.)

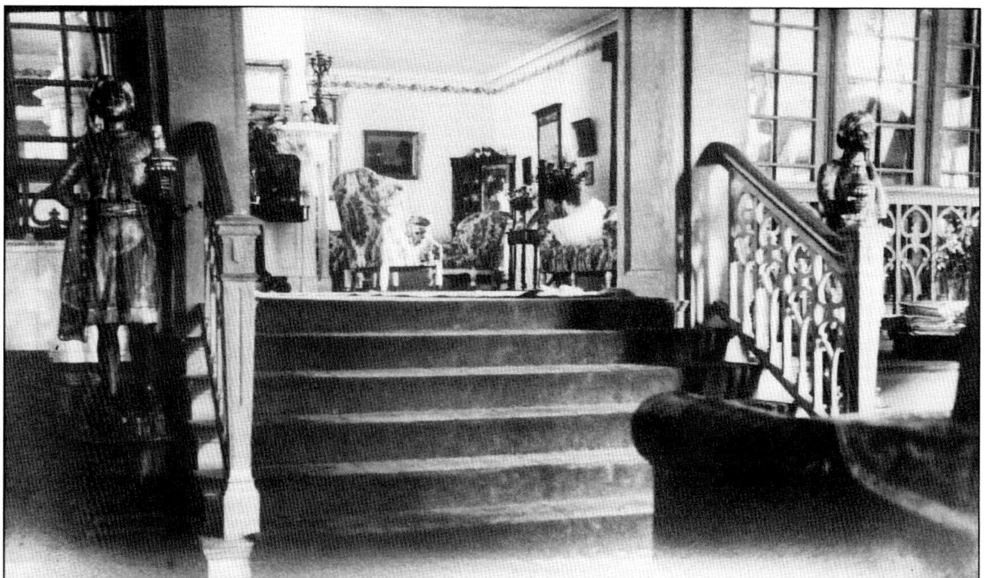

This view shows the interior of the Hammond's house, looking from the living room, in 1909. In 1950, Millicent Fenwick had most of the mansion (everything beyond this door), demolished to save the cost of heat and maintenance. The two Moors still stand guard in the living room of the current house. (Hugh Fenwick.)

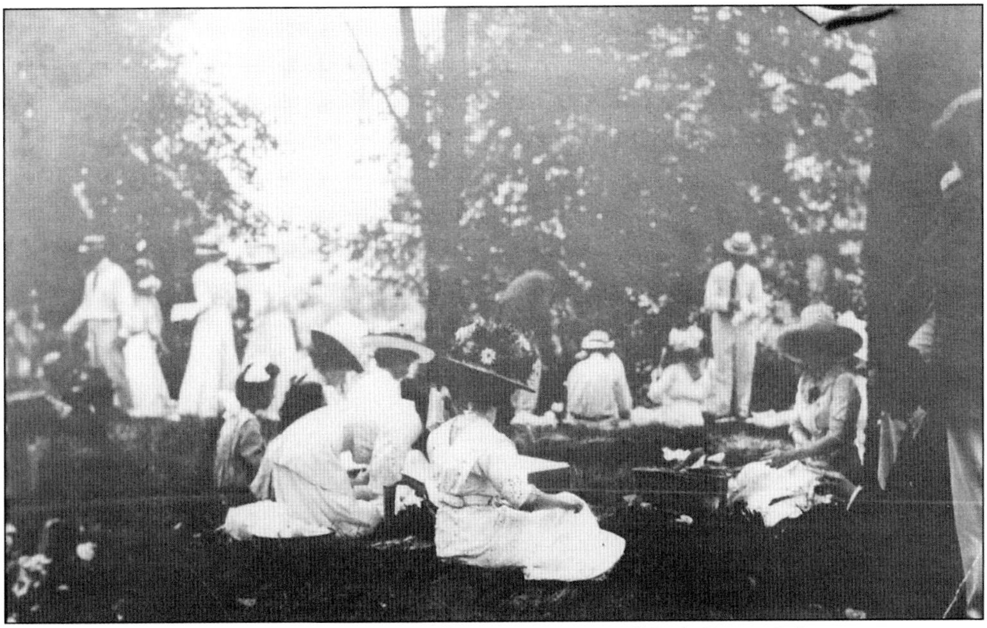

A garden picnic was held at the Hammond's estate in 1911. (Hugh Fenwick.)

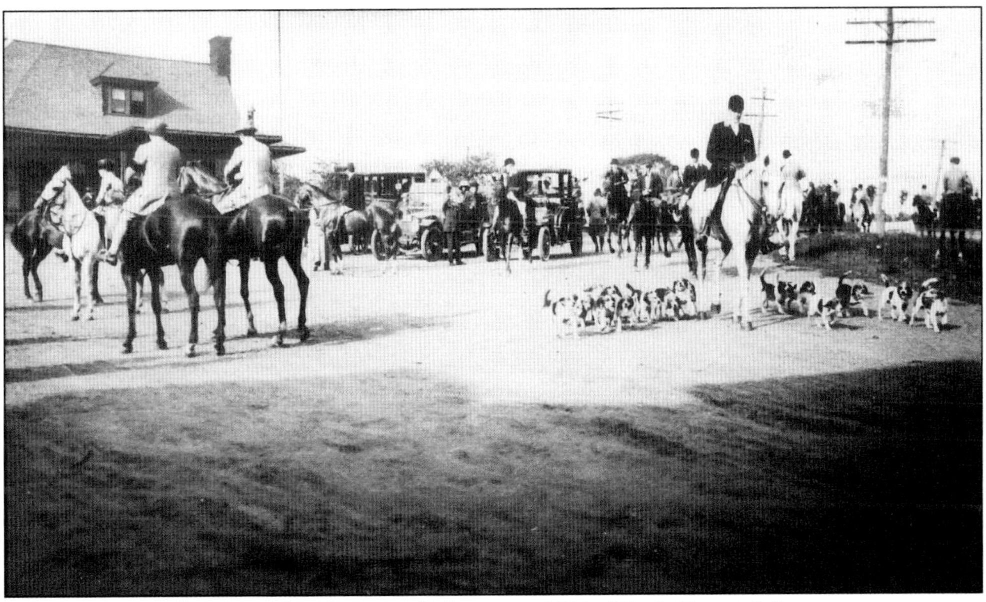

The Essex Hounds met at the Hammond's house in 1911. (Hugh Fenwick.)

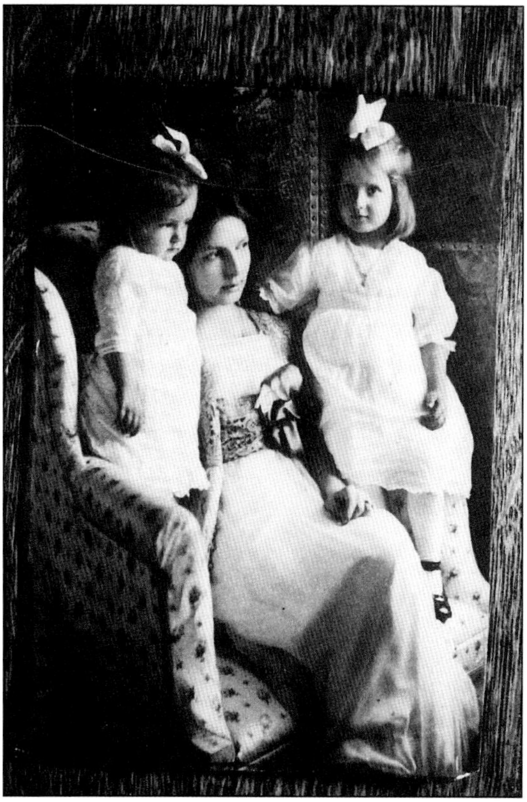

Millicent Fenwick (left) and her sister, Mary Stevens Hammond, posed with their mother, Mary Picton Stevens Hammond, c. 1906. Mrs. Hammond was to die in the sinking of the *Lusitania* in 1915. (Hugh Fenwick.)

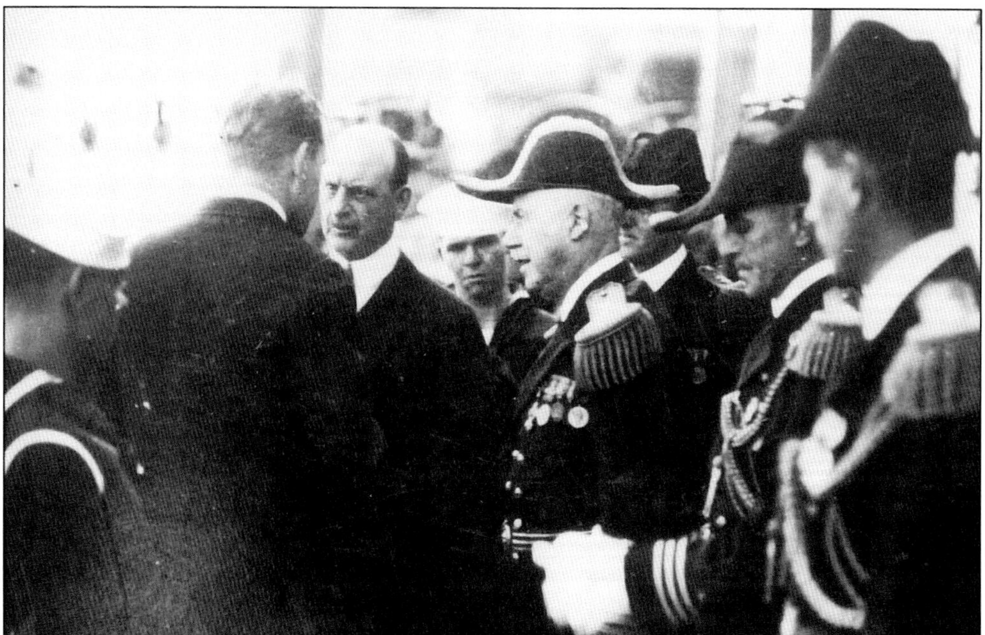

Millicent Fenwick's father, Mr. M. Ogden Hammond, was appointed ambassador to Spain from 1926 to 1929, during the term of President Coolidge. Millicent and her sister lived with their father in Spain and learned diplomacy. (Hugh Fenwick.)

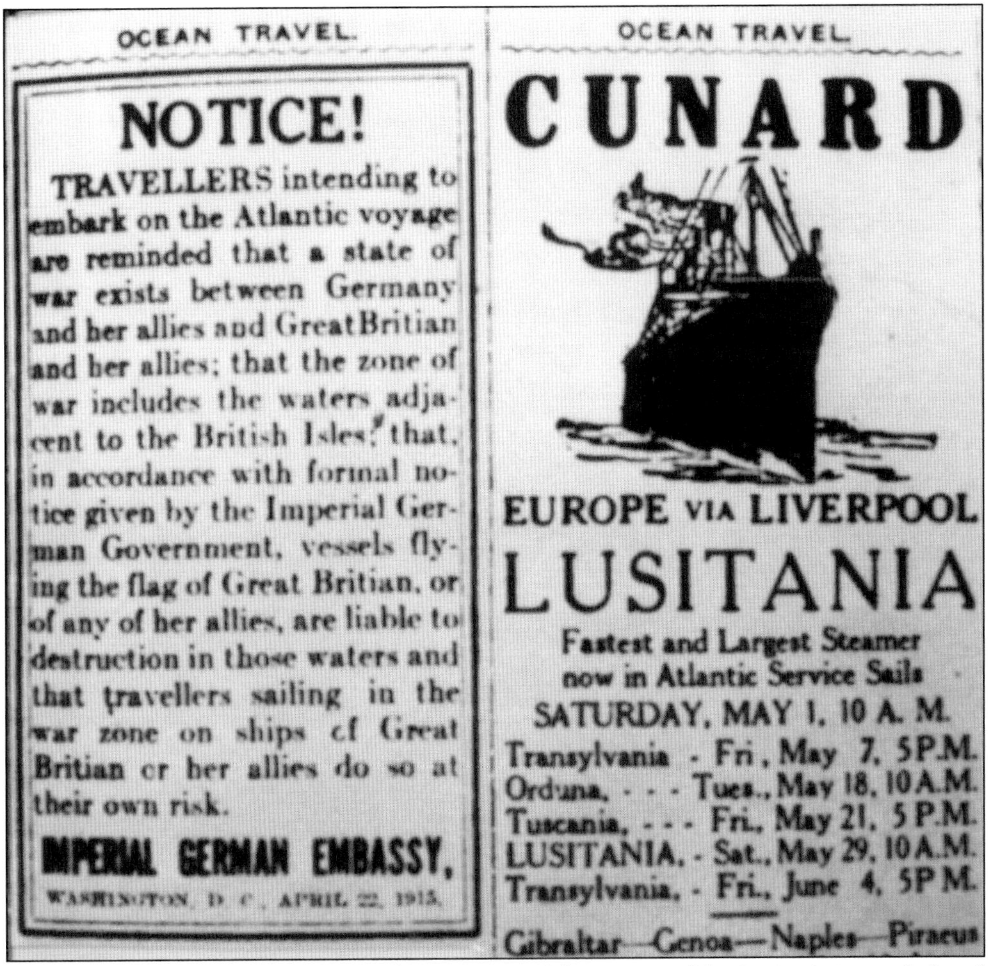

OCEAN TRAVEL.

NOTICE!

TRAVELLERS intending to embark on the Atlantic voyage are reminded that a state of war exists between Germany and her allies and Great Britian and her allies; that the zone of war includes the waters adjacent to the British Isles; that, in accordance with formal notice given by the Imperial German Government, vessels flying the flag of Great Britian, or of any of her allies, are liable to destruction in those waters and that travellers sailing in the war zone on ships of Great Britian or her allies do so at their own risk.

IMPERIAL GERMAN EMBASSY,
WASHINGTON, D. C., APRIL 22, 1915.

OCEAN TRAVEL.

CUNARD

EUROPE VIA LIVERPOOL
LUSITANIA
Fastest and Largest Steamer now in Atlantic Service Sails
SATURDAY, MAY 1, 10 A. M.
Transylvania - Fri., May 7, 5 P.M.
Orduna, - - - Tues., May 18, 10 A.M.
Tuscania, - - - Fri., May 21, 5 P.M.
LUSITANIA, - Sat., May 29, 10 A.M.
Transylvania, - Fri., June 4, 5 P.M.

Gibraltar—Genoa—Naples—Piraeus

Just to the left of the Cunard Line's advertisement of the voyage of the *Lusitania* is an ad placed by the German government noting that the ship was carrying war materials and would be sunk. No one believed that they would actually do it. (Hugh Fenwick.)

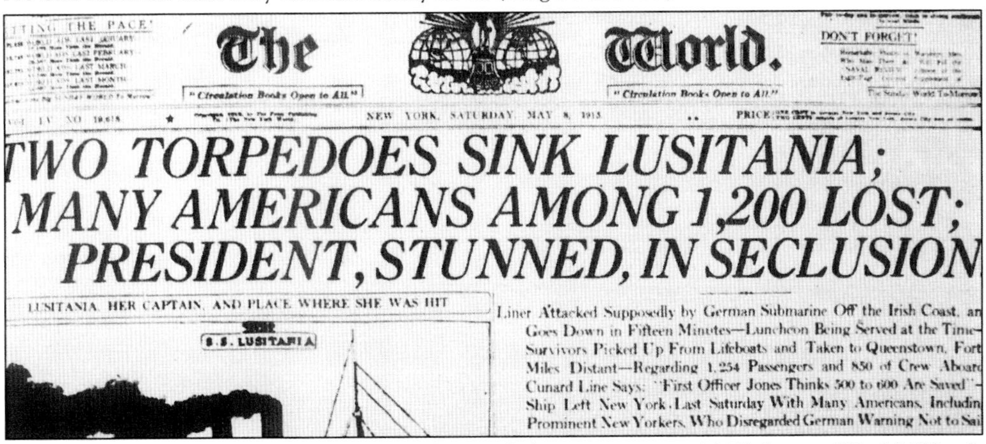

The World.

"Circulation Books Open to All."

NEW YORK, SATURDAY, MAY 8, 1915

TWO TORPEDOES SINK LUSITANIA; MANY AMERICANS AMONG 1,200 LOST; PRESIDENT, STUNNED, IN SECLUSION

LUSITANIA, HER CAPTAIN, AND PLACE WHERE SHE WAS HIT

S.S. LUSITANIA

Liner Attacked Supposedly by German Submarine Off the Irish Coast, an Goes Down in Fifteen Minutes—Luncheon Being Served at the Time— Survivors Picked Up From Lifeboats and Taken to Queenstown, Fort Miles Distant—Regarding 1,254 Passengers and 850 of Crew Aboard Cunard Line Says: "First Officer Jones Thinks 500 to 600 Are Saved"— Ship Left New York Last Saturday With Many Americans, Includin Prominent New Yorkers, Who Disregarded German Warning Not to Sai

Newspaper headlines announced the sinking of the *Lusitania* in 1915 during World War I. Millicent Fenwick's mother, Mary Picton Stevens Hammond, was drowned. (Hugh Fenwick.)

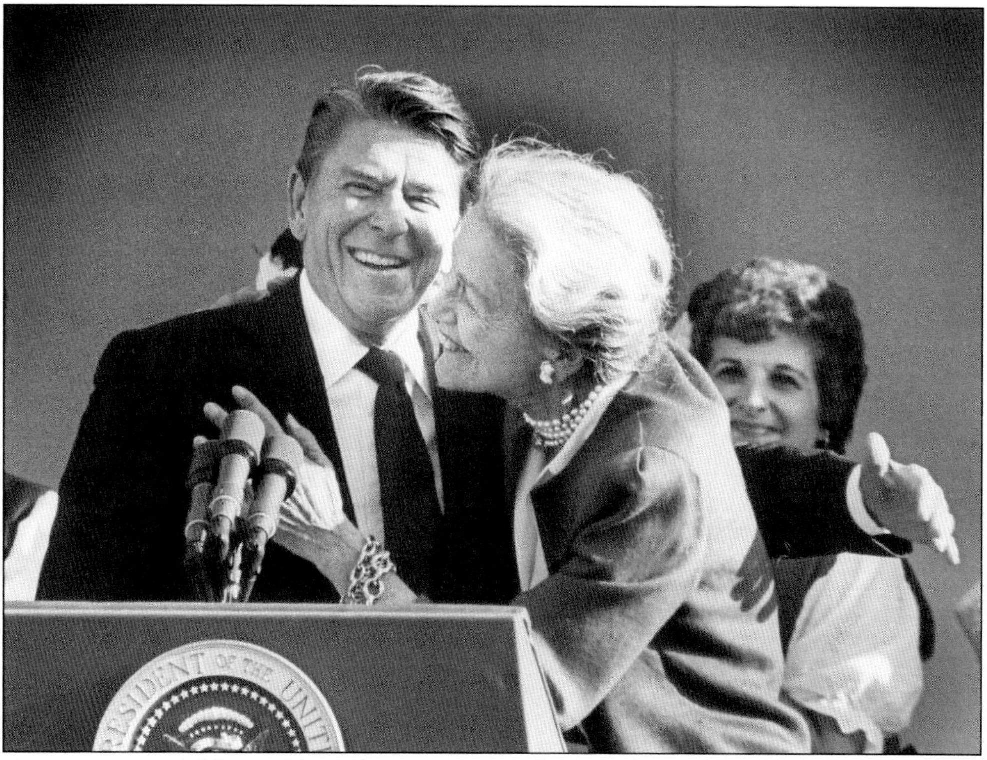

Congresswoman Millicent Fenwick was photographed on the campaign trail with President Ronald Reagan in 1982, at the San Genaro Fair in Flemington. (*The Somerset Messenger Gazette*, K. John.)

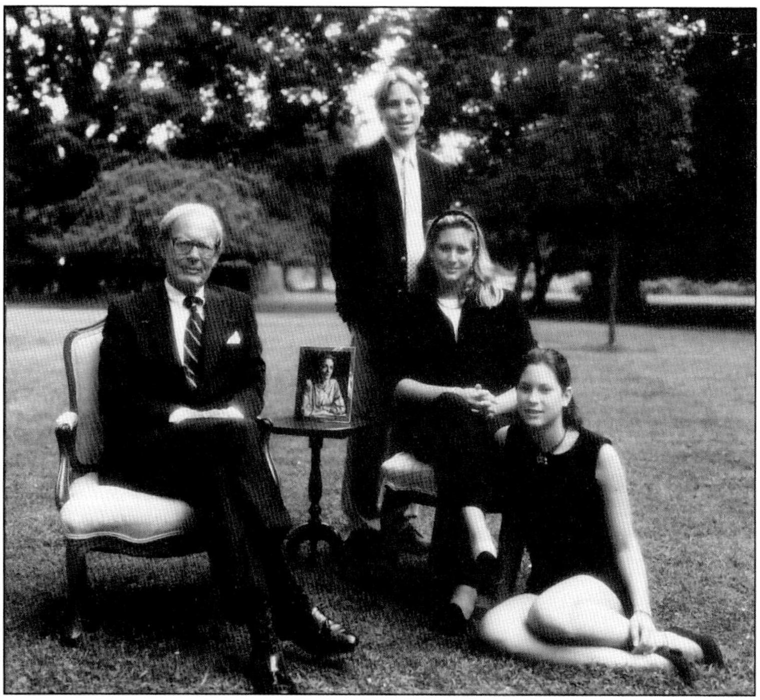

Continuing the long family tradition of public service, Hugh Fenwick became mayor of Bernardsville on January 1, 1995. Here he is pictured with his son Bayard, and daughters Sibyl and Leigh. (Hugh Fenwick.)

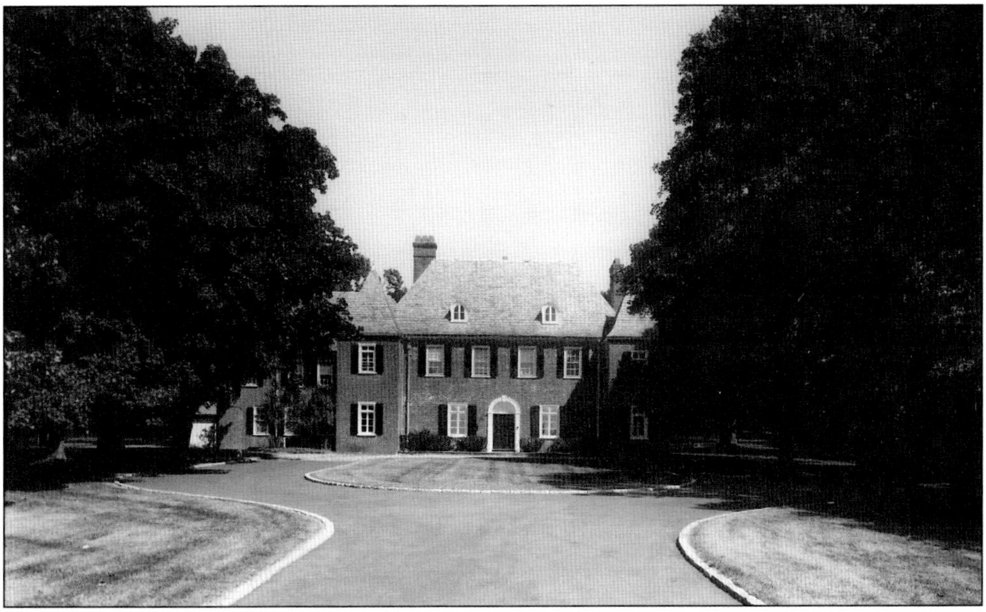

After the Richard Stevens house burned down (see photograph on p. 24) the property was purchased by Mr. and Mrs. Charles M. Chapin, who built Westover on the site. Mrs. Chapin is Richard Stevens' grandniece. The French chateau-style country manor was designed by prominent New York architect, Arthur C. Jackson, and built in 1938. (Turpin Real Estate.)

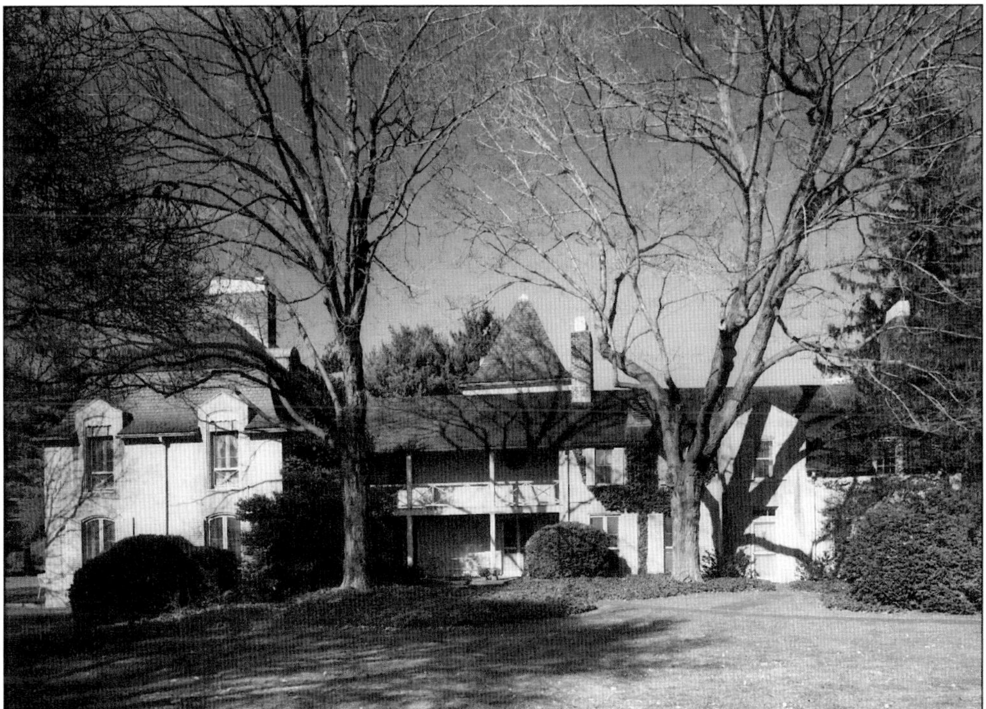

Sherwood Farm is the 297-acre estate of Mr. Charles M. Chapin II. The French chateau-style manor house was designed by Eugene Mason, and built in 1937 around an 1850s farm house. (Turpin Real Estate.)

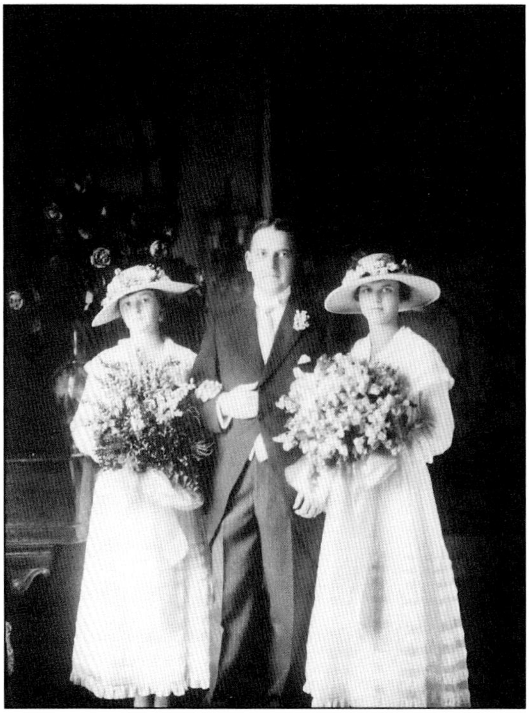

C. Ledyard Blair was photographed with two of his daughters, Edith (left) and Marise (right), at the wedding of his daughter Florence in 1916. Clinton Ledyard Blair founded the investment banking firm of Blair and Company with his father and grandfather in 1890, the year he graduated from Princeton. He was involved with the Gould railroad interests. At the outbreak of World War I, C. Ledyard Blair was on the North German Lloyd ocean liner *Kronprinzessin Cecille*. The ship had set sail from New York, but turned back when it was learned of the outbreak of war. Mr. Blair took the helm of the ship and safely piloted it through New England waters to safety at Bar Harbor, Maine, as a squadron of British warships gave chase. Blair had memorized the charts of the Maine coast while yachting there as a youth. The ship was carrying $10 million in gold and $3.5 million in silver in the hold. (Anthony Villa.)

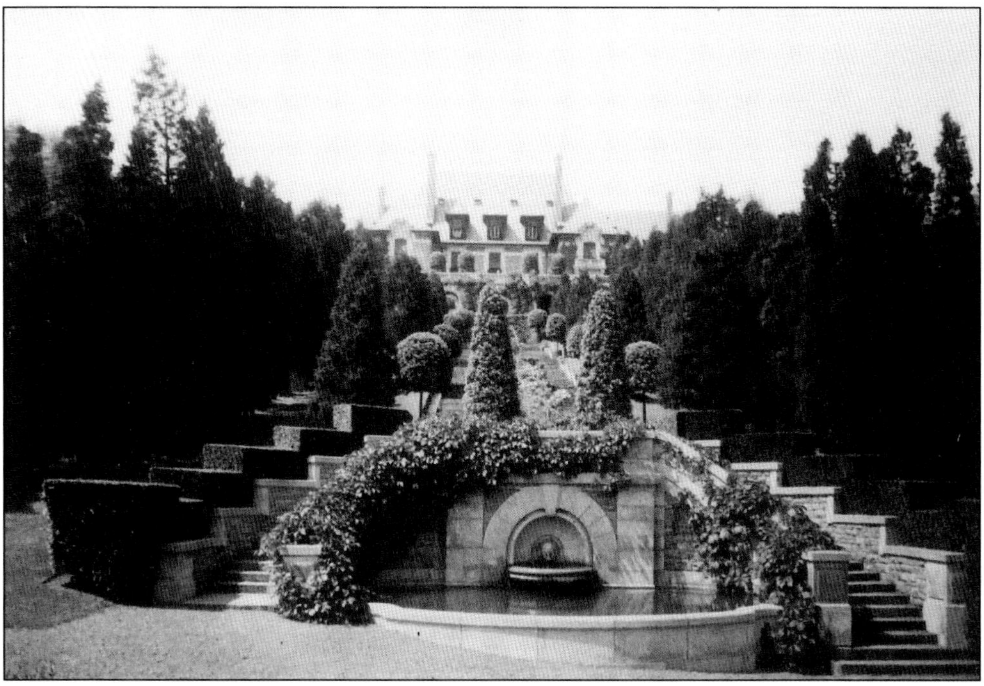

Blairsden, the mansion of C. Ledyard Blair was constructed between 1898 and 1903. To build Blairsden, Mr. Blair had the top of the mountain leveled off. A funicular railway was constructed to bring materials up the mountain from the ravine below. When completed, the estate required twenty-two household servants and fifty more to maintain the 423-acres of grounds. (Anthony Villa.)

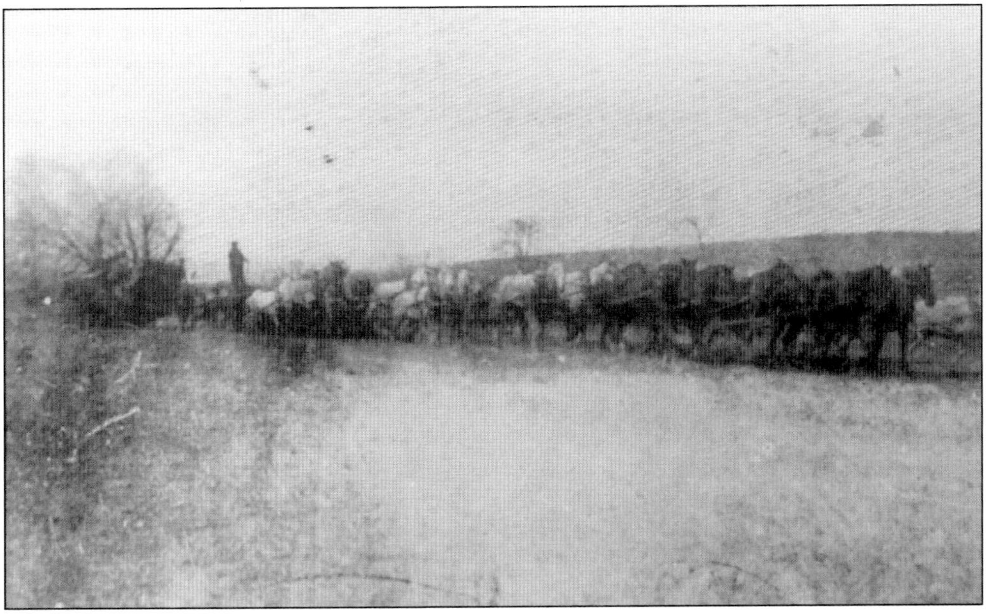

Not wanting to wait for things to grow, Mr. Blair bought every twenty-five to fifty-year-old boxwood tree within 50 miles, to plant around the reflecting pool. One hundred full grown maple trees were brought in to create a forest around the estate. Teams of twenty-two horses were used to move the trees, with giant balls of earth, to the estate. The weight of these trees collapsed many of the county's wooden bridges, which had to be replaced by Mr. Blair. (Bernardsville Public Library Local History Collection.)

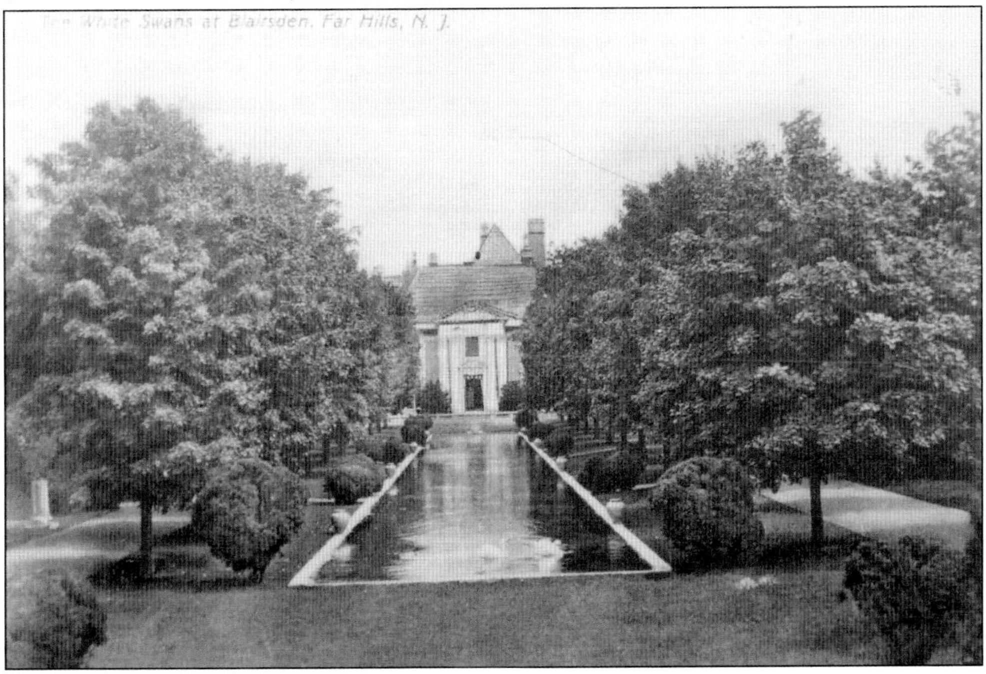

A 300-foot rectangular reflecting pool was constructed at the entrance to Blairsden. It was flanked with busts of the Roman Emperors. Here, swans swim in the reflecting pool. (Bernardsville Public Library Local History Collection.)

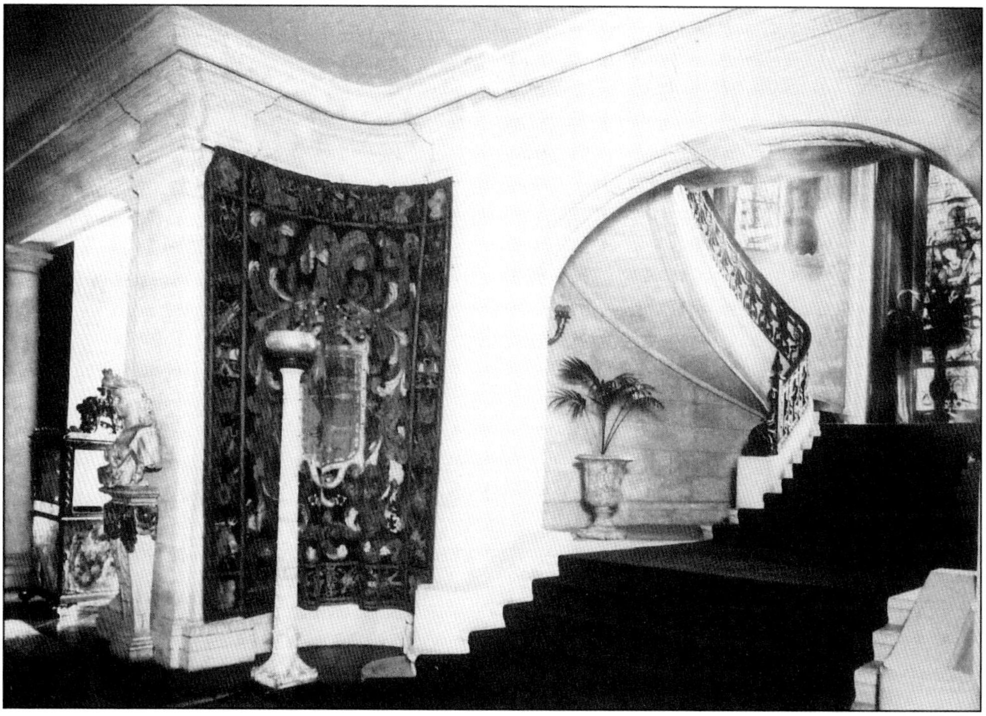

In 1909, the two senators from each state were asked to choose the handsomest man in their state. The single handsomest man from each state would form an escort of honor for President Taft to the inaugural ball. Senators Kean and Briggs were in agreement that the honor should go to C. Ledyard Blair. This is the main staircase in Blairsden. (Anthony Villa.)

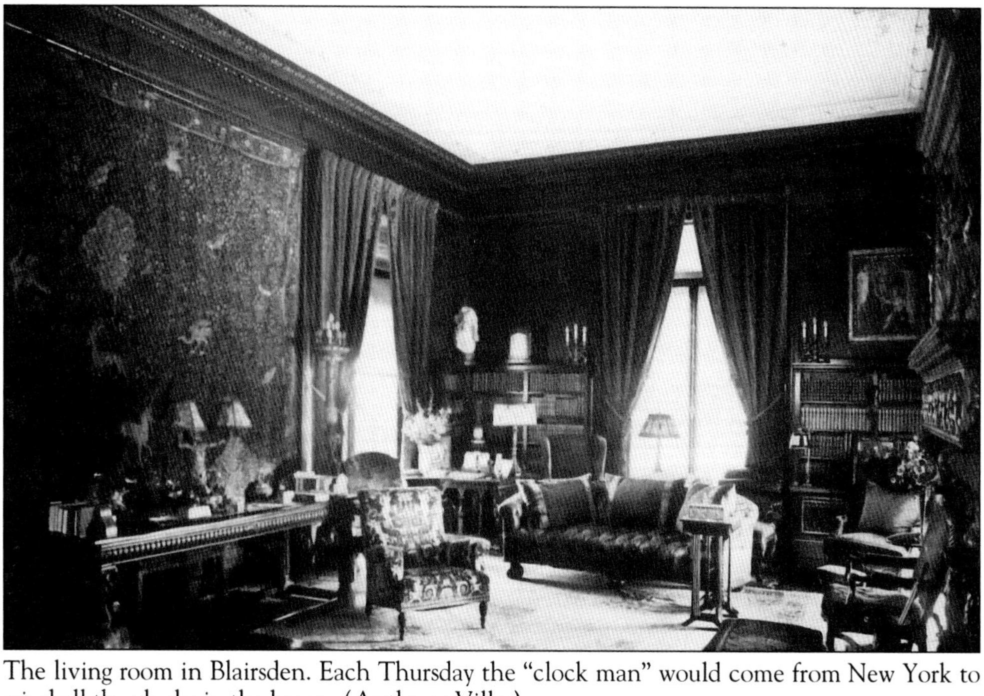

The living room in Blairsden. Each Thursday the "clock man" would come from New York to wind all the clocks in the house. (Anthony Villa.)

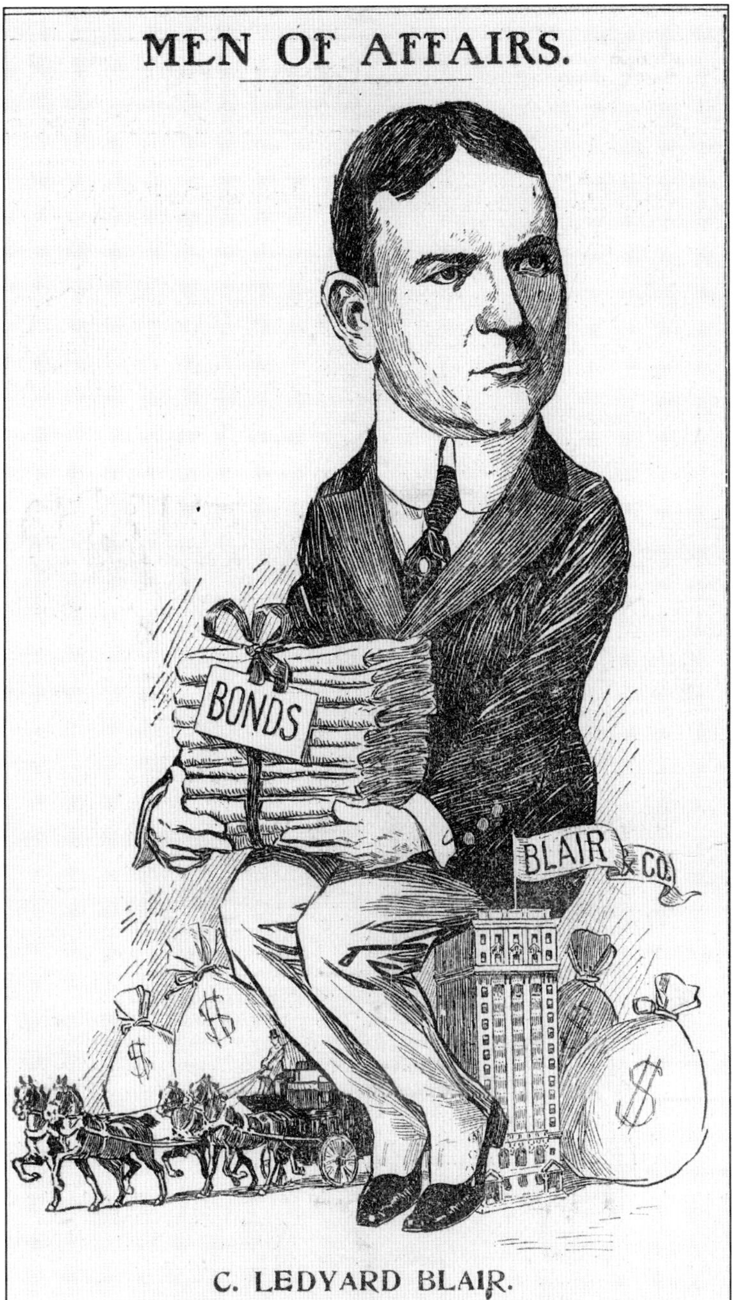

This cartoon was taken from the *Evening Mail*, January 21, 1903. (Bernardsville Public Library Local History Collection.)

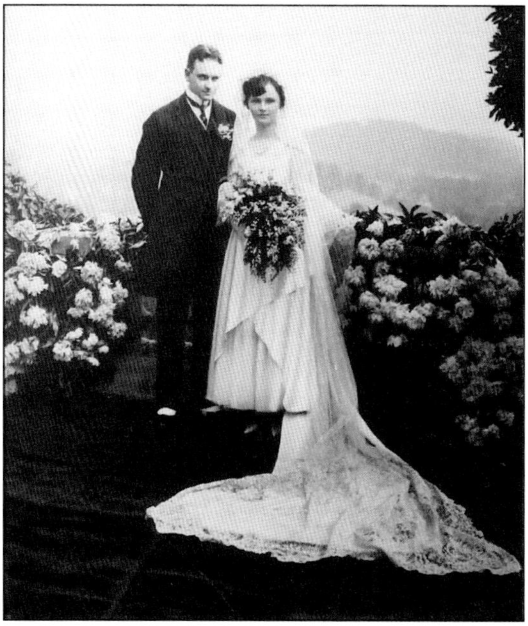

Edith Blair, daughter of C. Ledyard Blair, wed Mr. Richard Van Nest Gambrill at Blairsden on June 21, 1917. (Anthony Villa.)

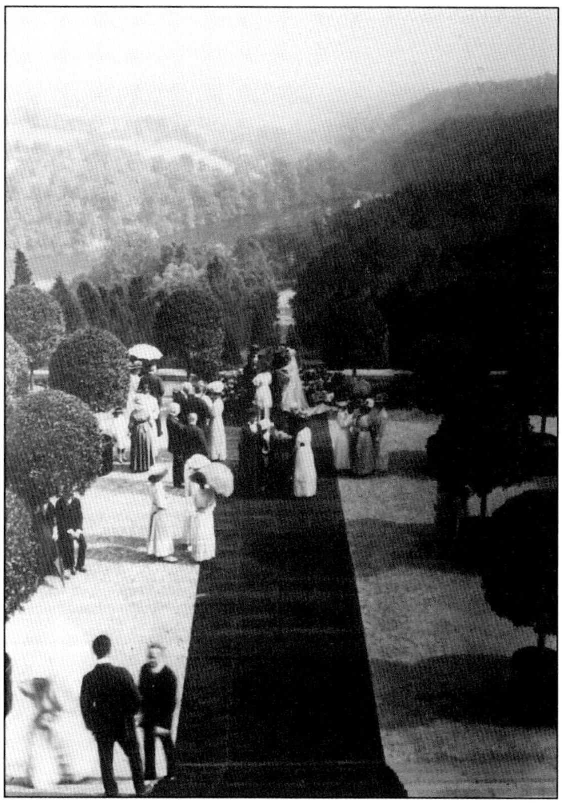

The reception for the Blair-Gambrill wedding was held on the terrace at Blairsden, overlooking Ravine Lake. To the left, Mrs. Percy R. Pyne (under a parasol) talks with C. Ledyard Blair. To the right, Charlote Fowler is also under a parasol (on the carpet), and Mrs. Hellard (in black) talks to Osborn Baker. The date is June 21, 1917. (Anthony Villa.)

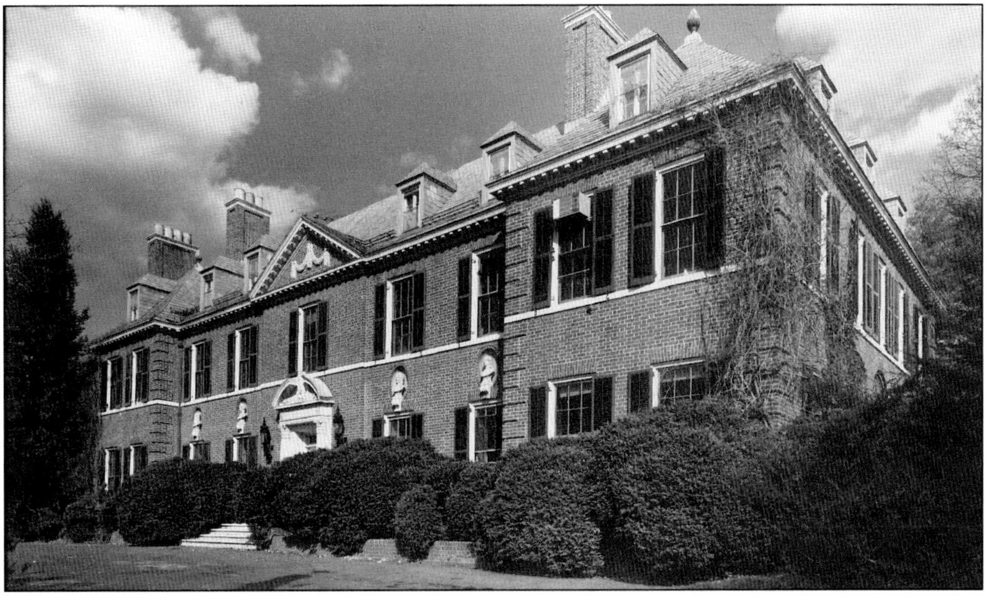

Richard Gambrill bought land in 1927 from John Sloane on the top of a hill adjacent to Blairsden and built Vernon Manor. The house was designed by James C. Mackenzie. Mr. Gambrill enjoyed hunting and horsemanship. He maintained his own pack of beagles to hunt hare on foot. He also served as Master of the Essex Fox Hounds in the 1940s. (Turpin Real Estate.)

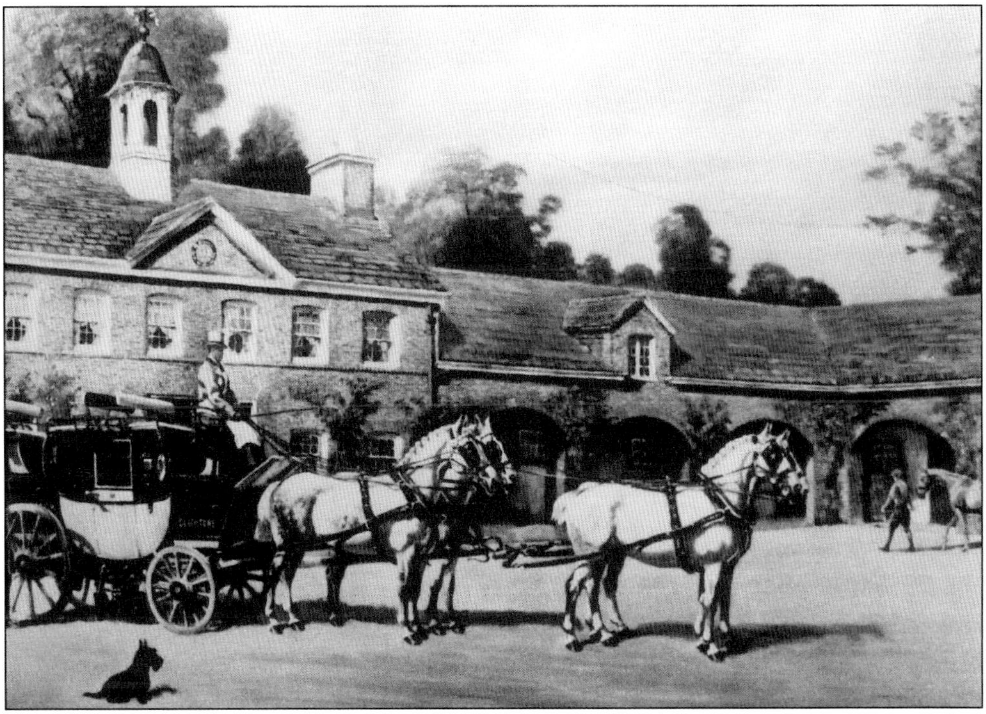

A painting signed "Voss" and dated 1934 shows Richard Gambrill with his coach-and-four in the courtyard of his stables at Vernon Manor. This may be the coach Defiance, which had formerly belonged to his father-in-law, C. Ledyard Blair. (Anthony Villa.)

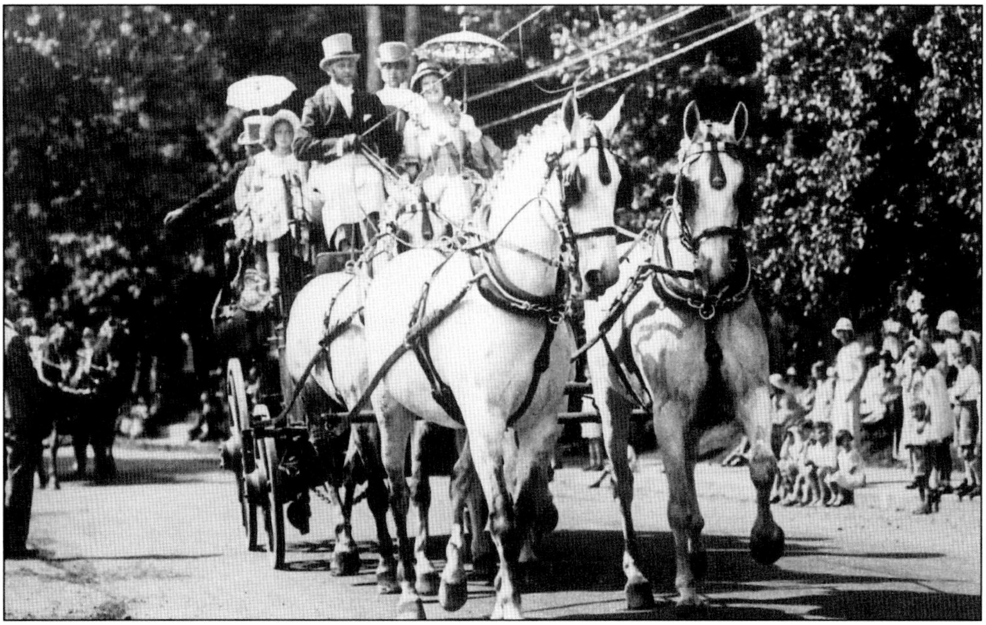

Richard Gambrill is driving his coach-and-four in a parade celebrating Washington's bicentennial in Peapack. Beryl Robertson is sitting beside Mr. Gambrill. His daughter, Diana, may be seen sitting behind him. (Anthony Villa.)

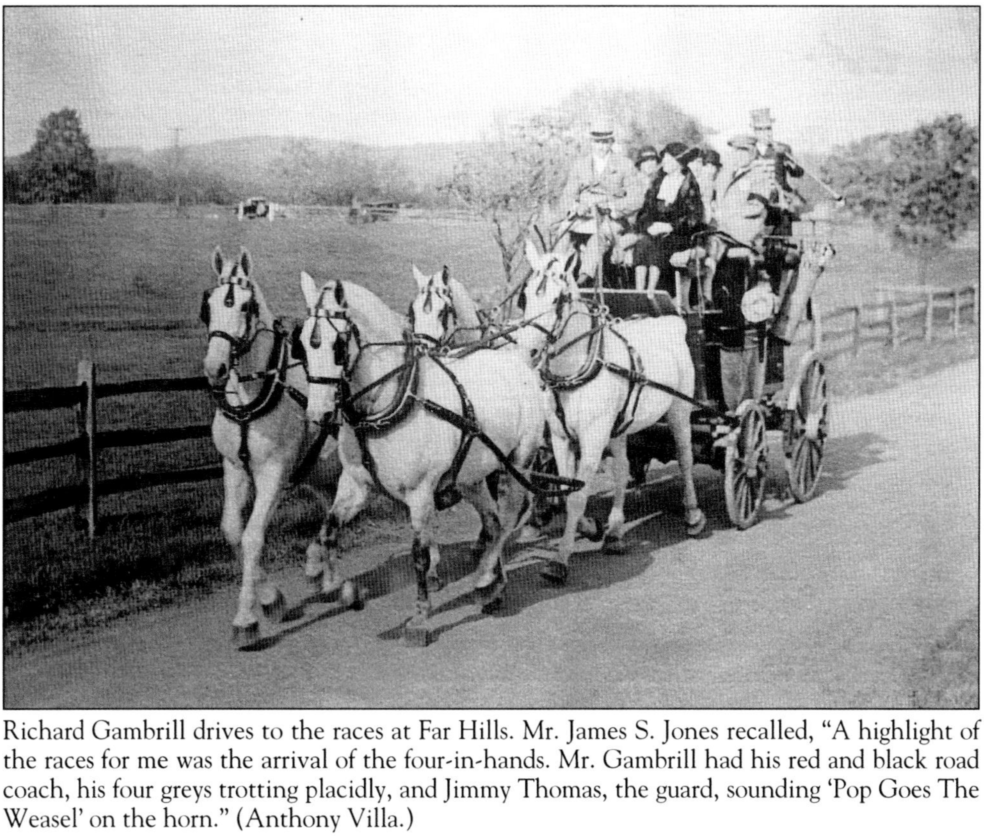

Richard Gambrill drives to the races at Far Hills. Mr. James S. Jones recalled, "A highlight of the races for me was the arrival of the four-in-hands. Mr. Gambrill had his red and black road coach, his four greys trotting placidly, and Jimmy Thomas, the guard, sounding 'Pop Goes The Weasel' on the horn." (Anthony Villa.)

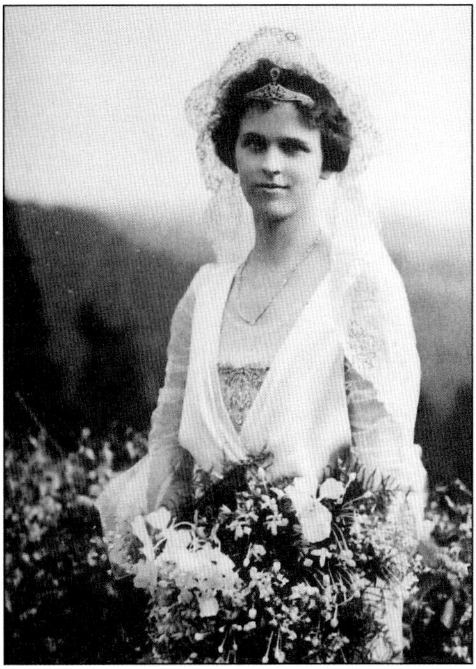

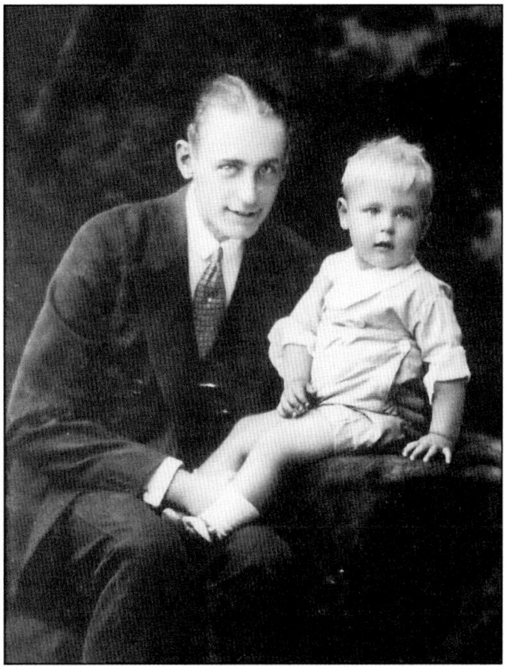

LEFT: C. Ledyard Blair's daughter, Marise, posed at her wedding to Pierpont Morgan Hamilton on September 11, 1919. She is wearing the same veil that her sister Edith wore at her wedding in 1917. (Anthony Villa.)
RIGHT: Marise's husband, Pierpont "Pier" Morgan Hamilton, and their son, Phillip, were photographed in 1922. (Anthony Villa.)

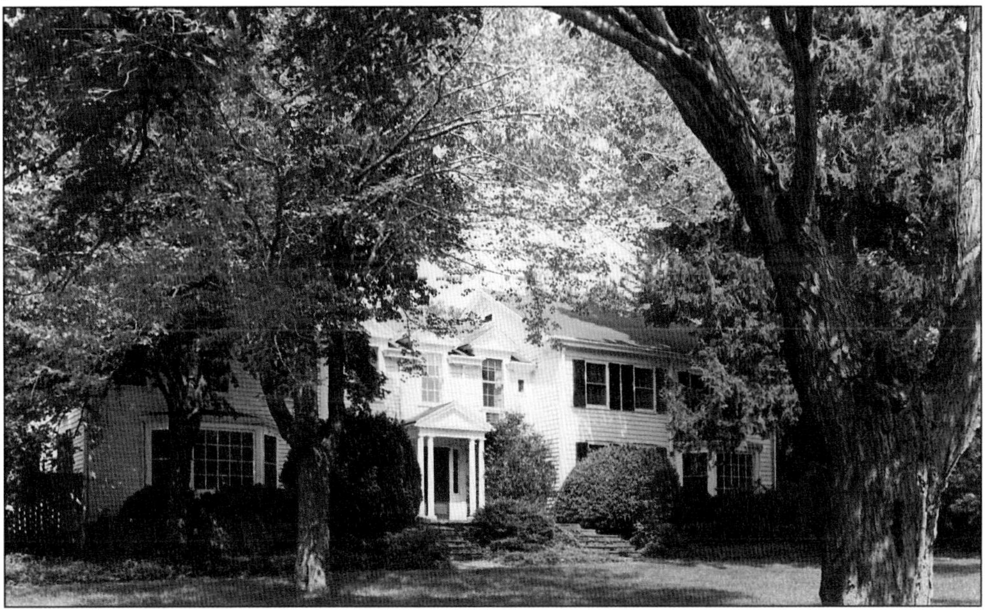

Windfall was the estate of Pierpont Morgan and Marise Blair Hamilton following their marriage in 1919. The property later became the residence of Percival "Dobie" Keith, who designed the Oak Ridge Project, which refined the plutonium needed to make the first atomic bombs. (Turpin Real Estate.)

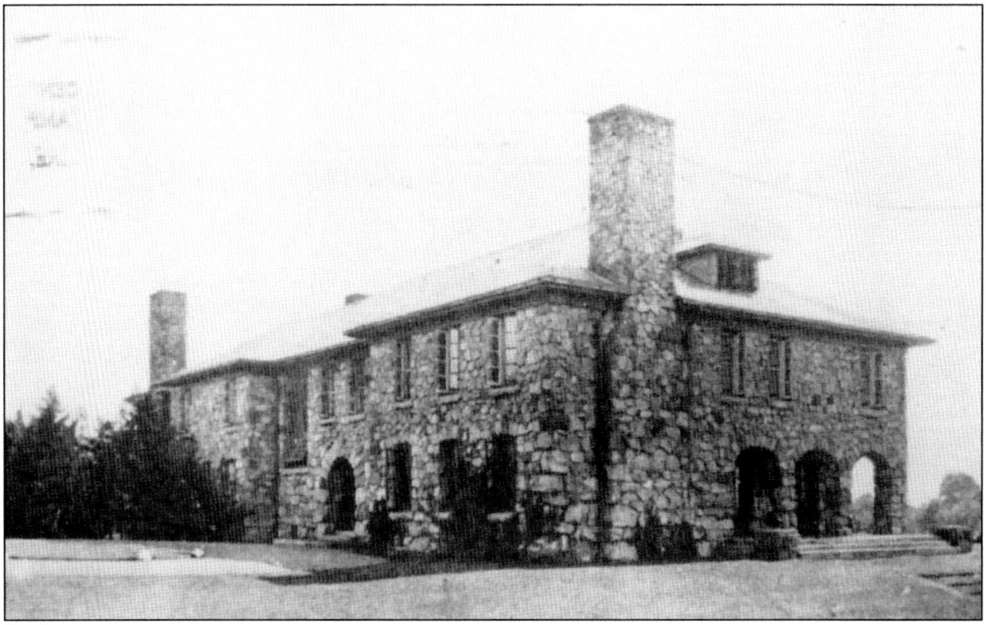

Peachcroft was the imposing fieldstone estate of J. William Clark, the president of the Clark Thread Company of Newark. The American branch of the family firm from Paisley, Scotland, was established in this country by Mr. Clark's father, William Clark. (Bernardsville Public Library Local History Collection.)

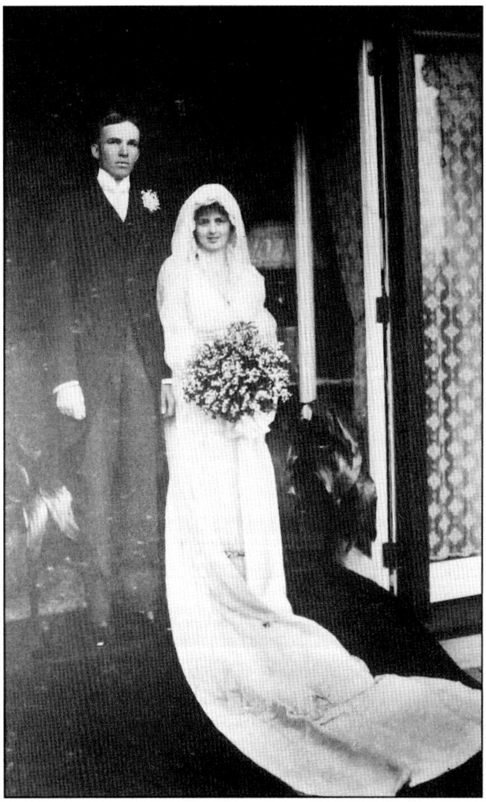

William Clark, the son of J. William Clark wed Marjory Blair, daughter of C. Ledyard Blair on September 20, 1913. Eight hundred guests were invited. A special train was chartered to bring guests from Hoboken to Peapack, and return them there after the celebration. Clark became a judge and served as Presiding Judge at the Nuremberg war crimes trials. (Anthony Villa.)

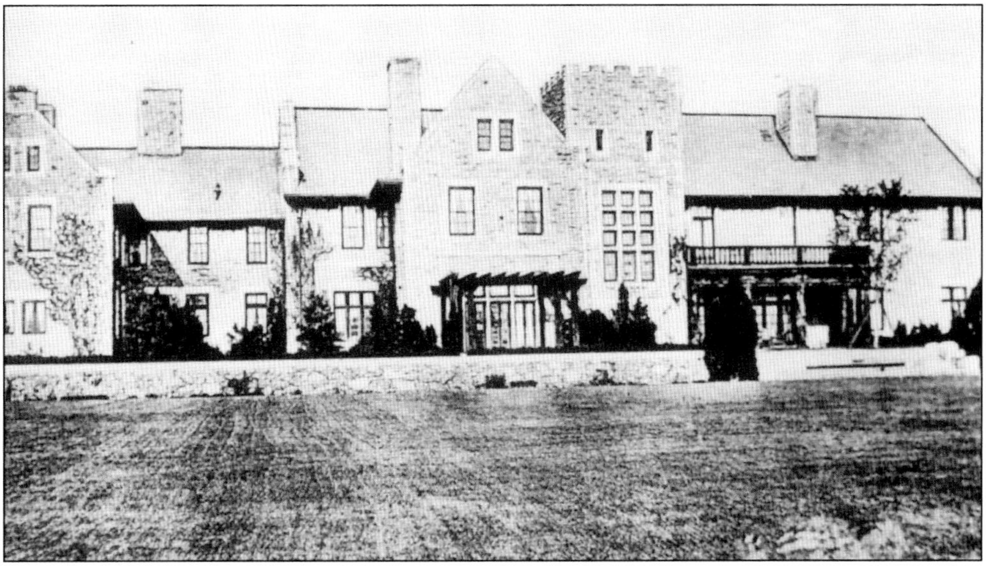

New York financier Percy R. Pyne built Upton Pyne in 1899, naming it after the home of his English ancestors. Lawrence Aspinwall was the architect who designed the structure. It was the largest mansion in the area until it was torn down in 1982. (Bernardsville Public Library Local History Collection.)

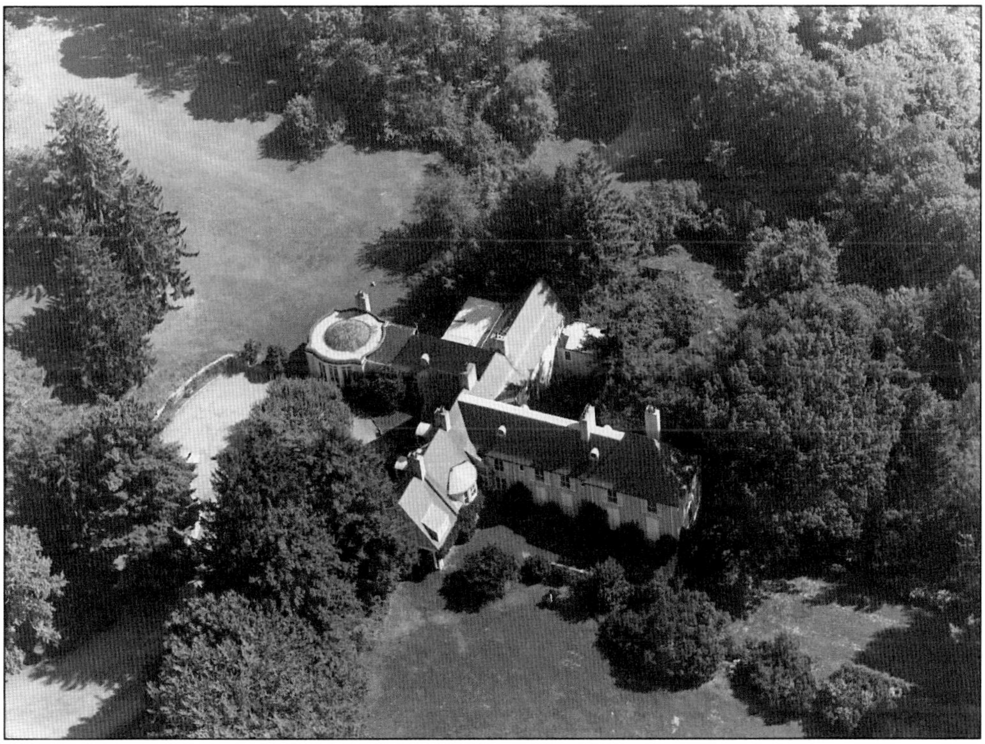

Upton Pyne's thirty-room coachman's cottage has been converted into a mansion in its own right, and is presently the dwelling of German film producer Bernd Schaefers and his wife, Karin. (Turpin Real Estate.)

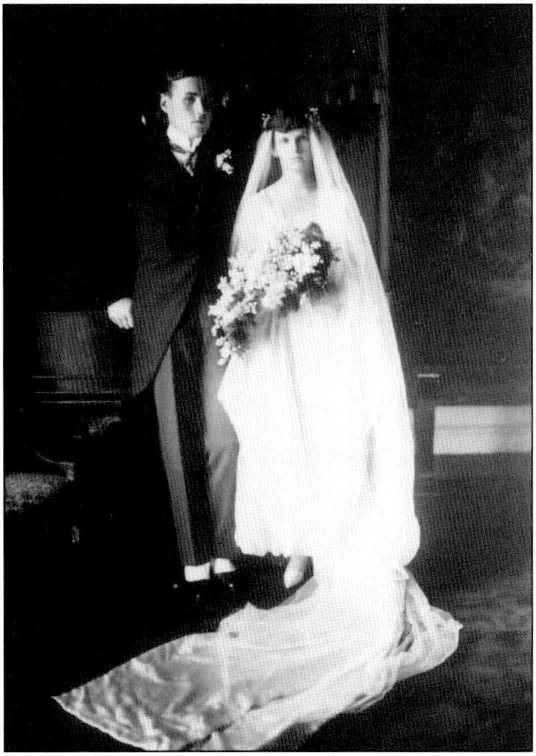

H. Rivington Pyne, son of Percy Pyne, and Florence Blair, daughter of C. Ledyard Blair, were united in marriage on June 16, 1916 in St. Bernard's Church. Following the service, there was a large reception at Blairsden. Mr. Pyne served as private secretary to American Ambassador James W. Gerard in Berlin from 1914 until the outbreak of World War I. During the war he served in the Army Air Corps. (Anthony Villa.)

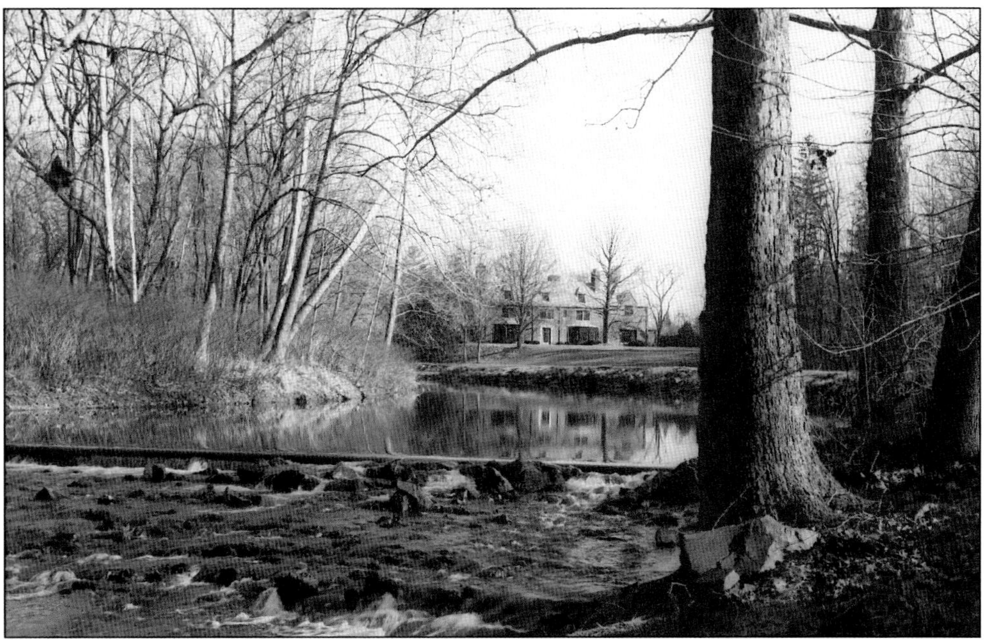

Shale, was the estate of Mr. and Mrs. Rivington Pyne. While in residence here he was elected to the New Jersey Assembly and the State Senate. He also served as chairman of the Republican party. Later this home belonged to John McGraw, a descendant of the founder of the McGraw-Hill publishing empire. Mr. McGraw called the estate River Run Farm. (Turpin Real Estate.)

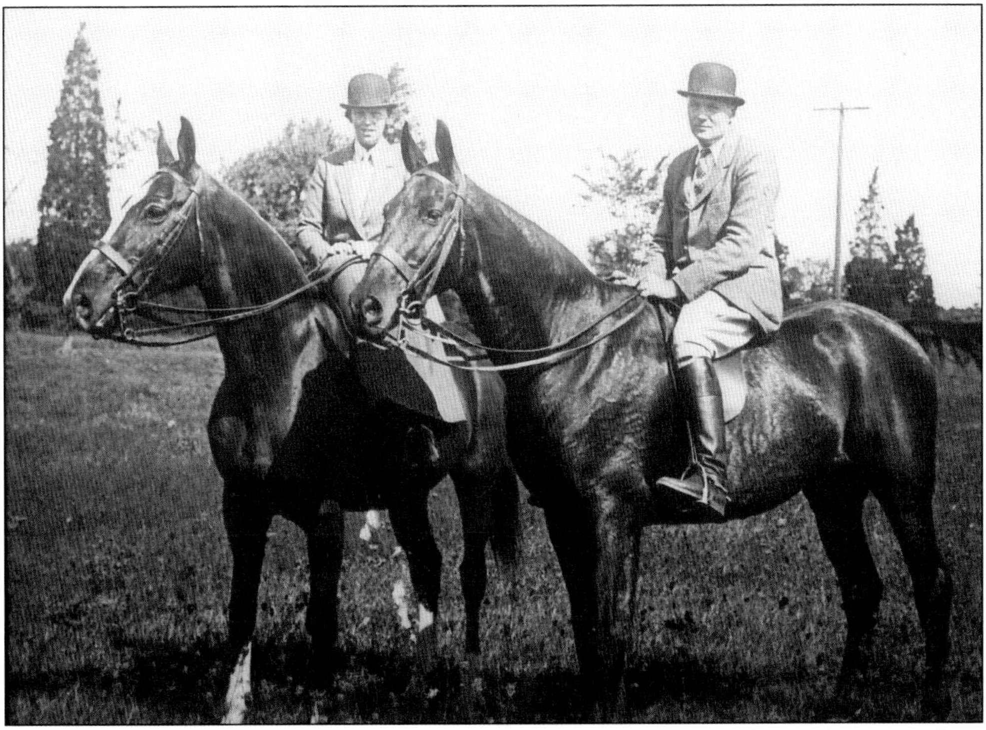

Senator and Mrs. Rivington Pyne were members of the Essex Hunt Club, and are seen here participating in the 1930 fox hunt at their estate. Mrs. Pyne is riding side-saddle. (Masters of the Essex Fox Hounds.)

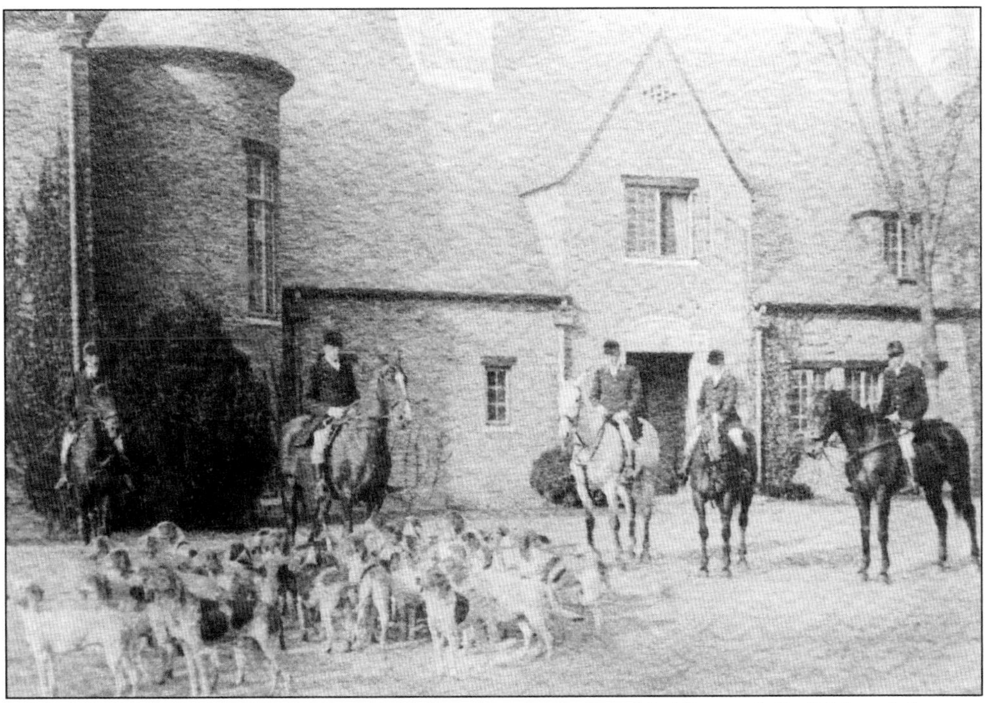

The Essex Fox Hounds are shown at the Pyne mansion in 1930. (Kenneth B. Schley, Jr.)

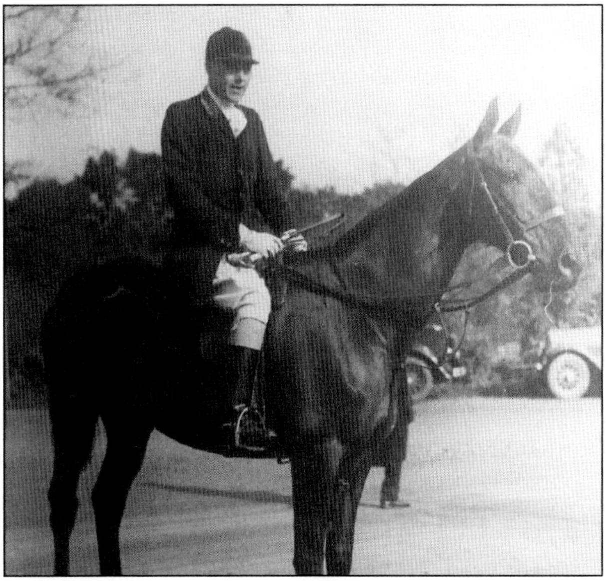

Grafton Howland Pyne was another son of Percy Pyne. He is seen here riding with the Essex Fox Hounds. (Masters of the Essex Fox Hounds.)

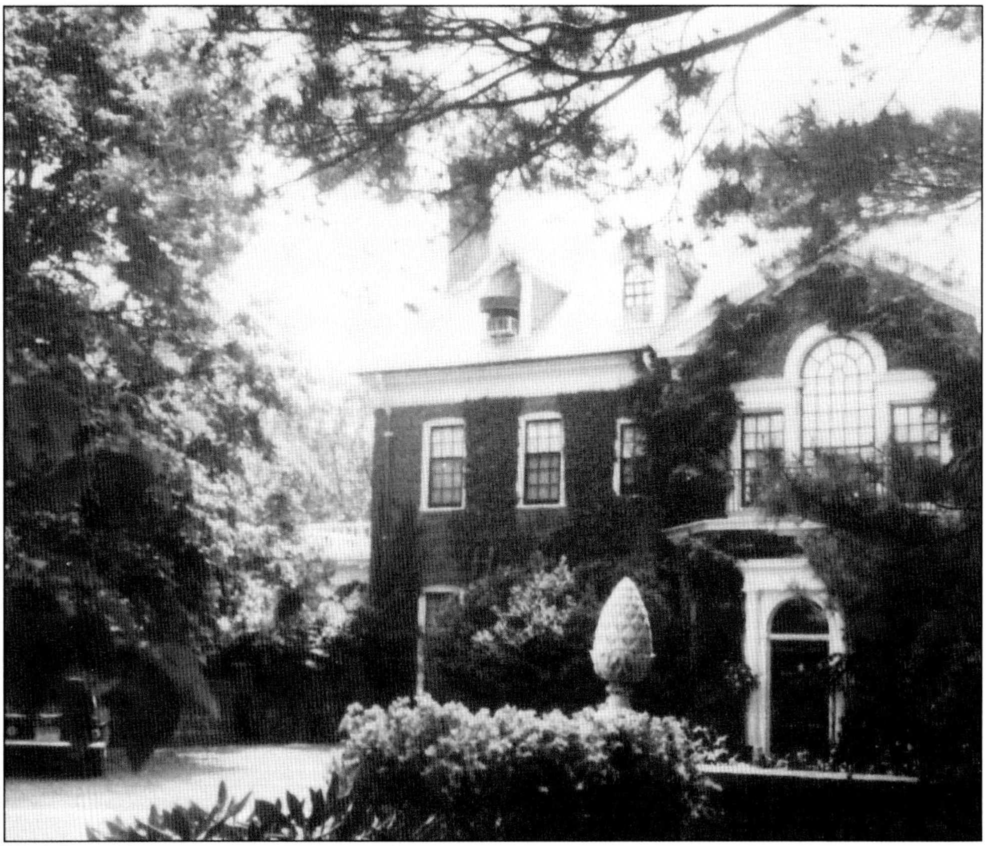

Cragwood, built on land cut off from Upton Pyne, was the home of Mr. and Mrs. Grafton Pyne. John Wright Pyne and Alison Pyne (Mrs. John Ewing) are children of Grafton Pyne. Cragwood was later purchased by Mr. and Mrs. Charles Engelhard. Another view of the property follows under Engelhard (see p. 73). (Bernardsville Public Library Local History Collection.)

John H. Ewing was formerly the president of Abercrombie & Fitch, and is presently a state senator from Somerset County. He served in World War II as an airborne infantry officer, making combat jumps in Okinawa, Corrigedor, the Philippines, and Dutch New Guinea. He served again during the Korean War, earning a Bronze Medal for valor. In 1951 he married Alison Pyne, the daughter of Grafton Pyne. (*The Somerset Messenger Gazette*.)

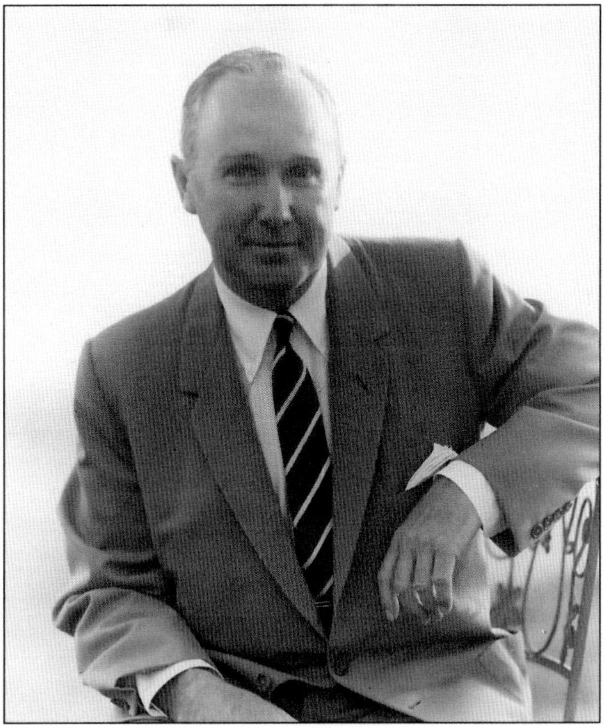

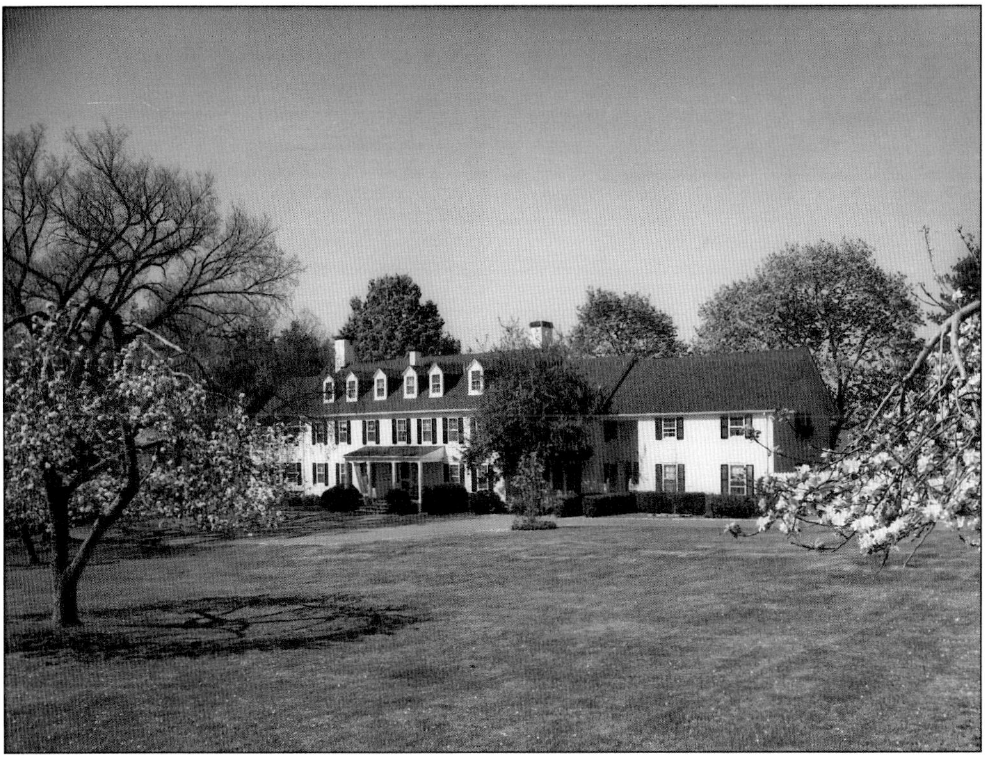

The former Bedminster estate of Senator John H. and Mrs. Alison Pyne Ewing. The property now includes a private polo field, added by a subsequent owner. (Turpin Real Estate.)

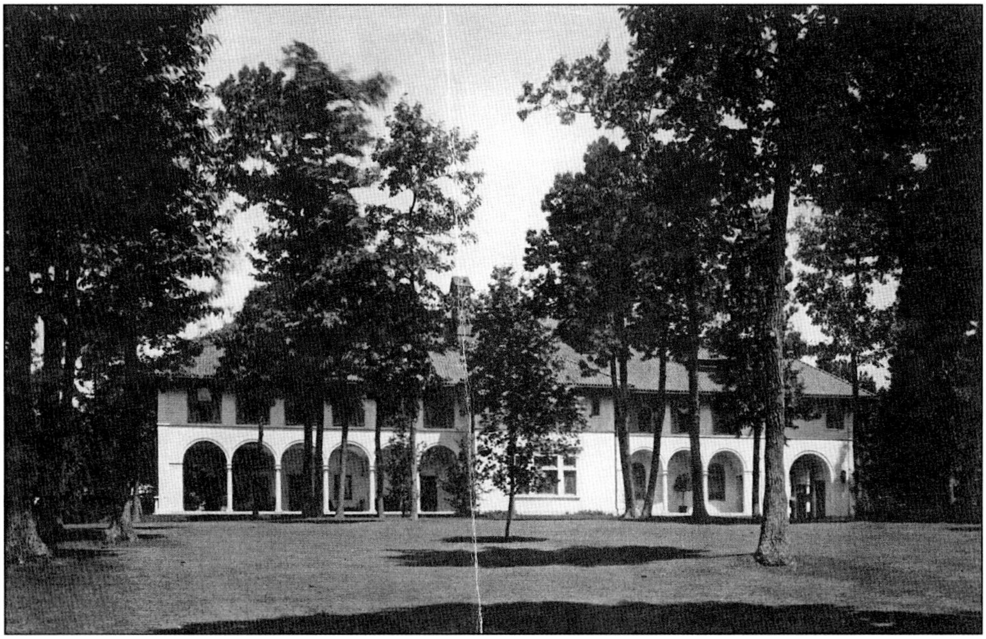

Blythewood was built by Henry R. Kunhardt in 1899. The brick and stucco Italian villa has a red tile roof and a stone foundation. The estate was artfully landscaped with gardens, hedges, and streams. A 2-mile private road connected two lodges on the property. The estate was later owned by the Kuser family. (Bernardsville Public Library Local History Collection.)

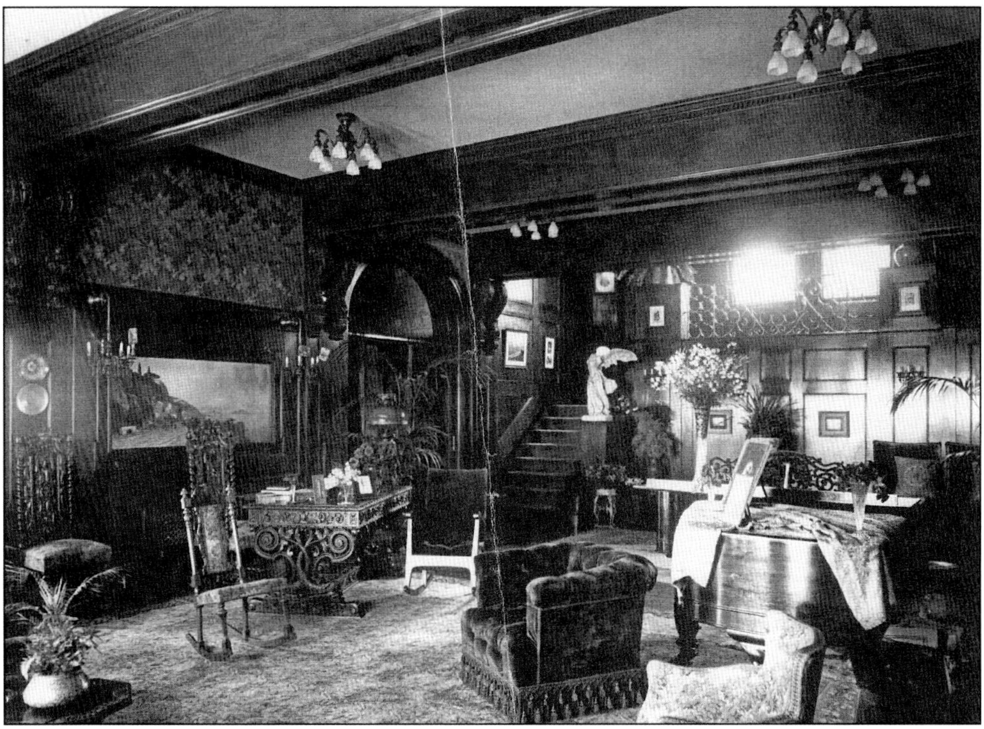

This image shows the interior of Blythewood at the turn of the century. Someone wrote on the picture "Our Dear Home." (Bernardsville Public Library Local History Collection.)

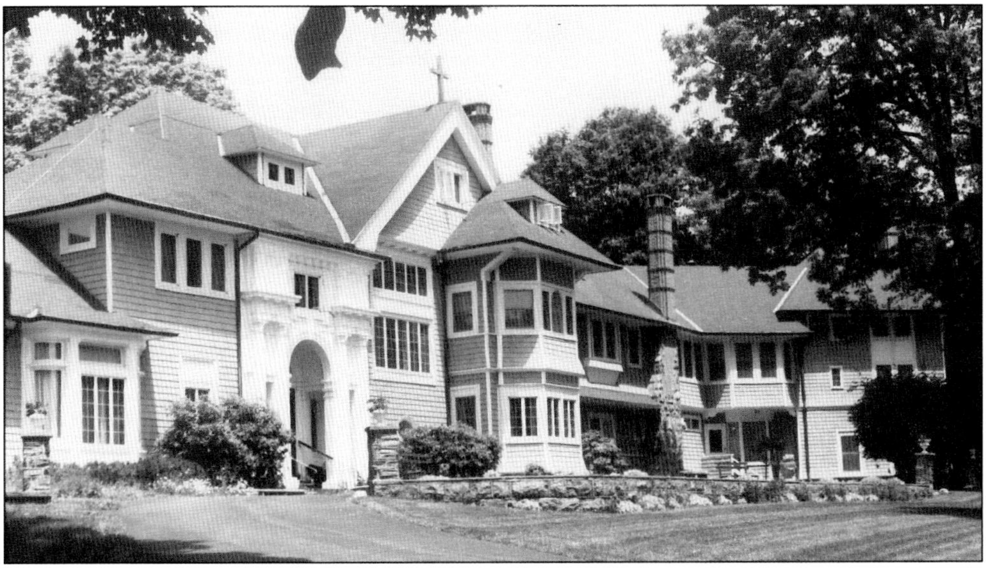

In 1892 Frederic Cromwell built this forty-seven-room Georgian mansion as a gift for his son, Seymour. Seymour Cromwell was the president of the New York Stock Exchange. In 1924, Mr. Cromwell was killed in a fall from a horse. His wife, Agnes Whitney Cromwell, was overwhelmed with grief from the loss of her husband, and couldn't bear to live in the house with all of its memories. In 1927 she sold the house and 112 acres of land to the Sisters of Christian Charity. Today it is a retreat and guest home. (Sisters of Christian Charity.)

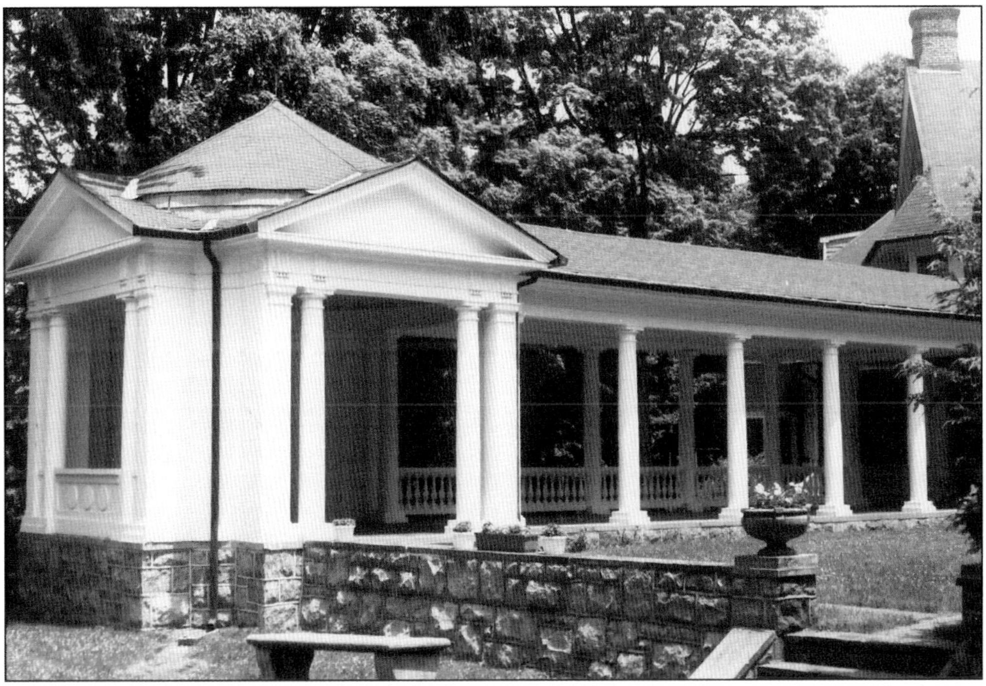

The colonnade of the Seymour Cromwell estate is viewed here from the perspective of the formal Italian garden. When the Cromwells entertained, the musicians played from the enclosure on the end of the colonnade. There is a beautiful view of the hills of Mendham from the back porch. (Sisters of Christian Charity.)

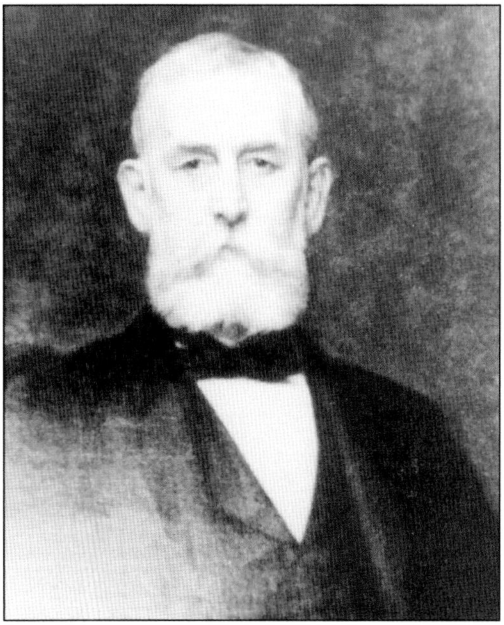

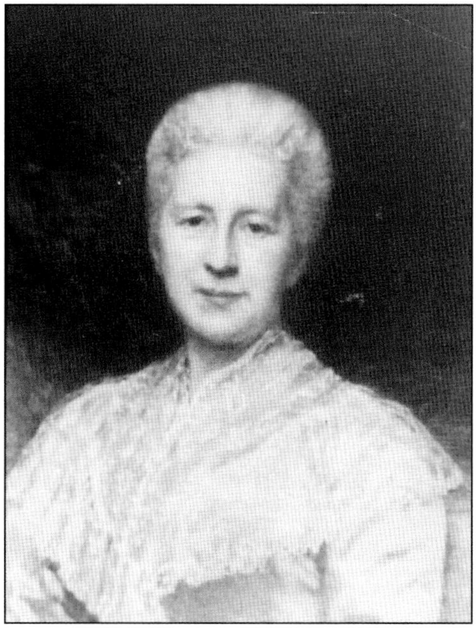

John F. Dryden, founder of the Prudential Insurance Company, established his summer residence in Bernardsville in 1899. In 1901 he was elected to the United States Senate, and he served until 1907. With a silvery beard and mustache and snow white hair, he must have looked very much the elder statesman. On the right is his wife, Mrs. Cynthia Jennings Fairchild Dryden. (Gill St. Bernard School.)

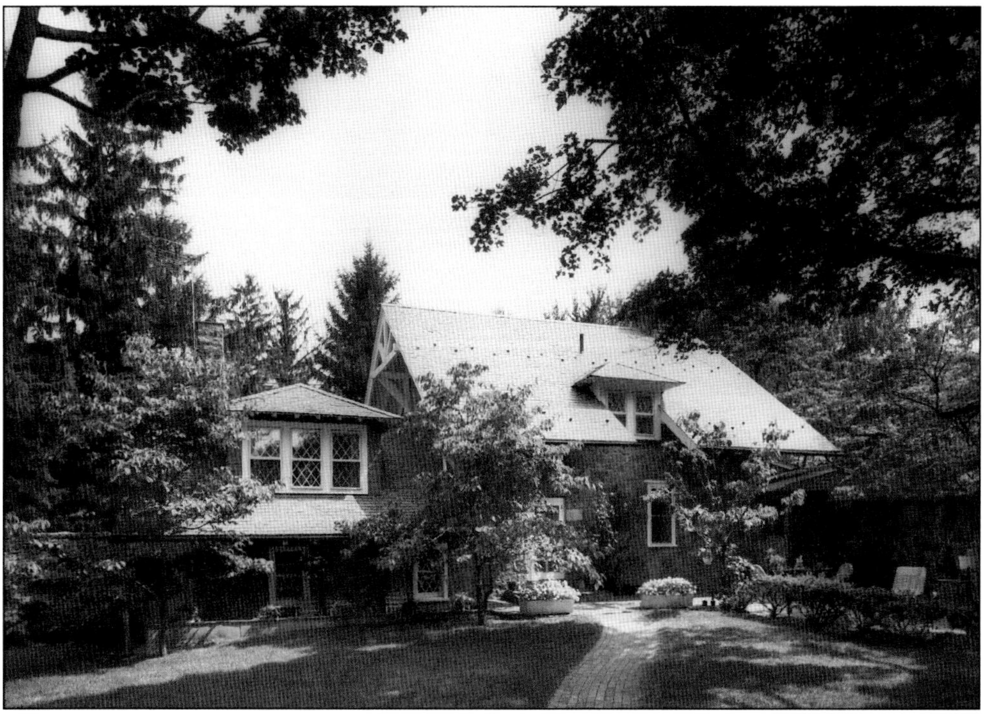

This charming house named Honeyfield, was formerly a gate house to Stronghold, the Dryden estate. (Turpin Real Estate.)

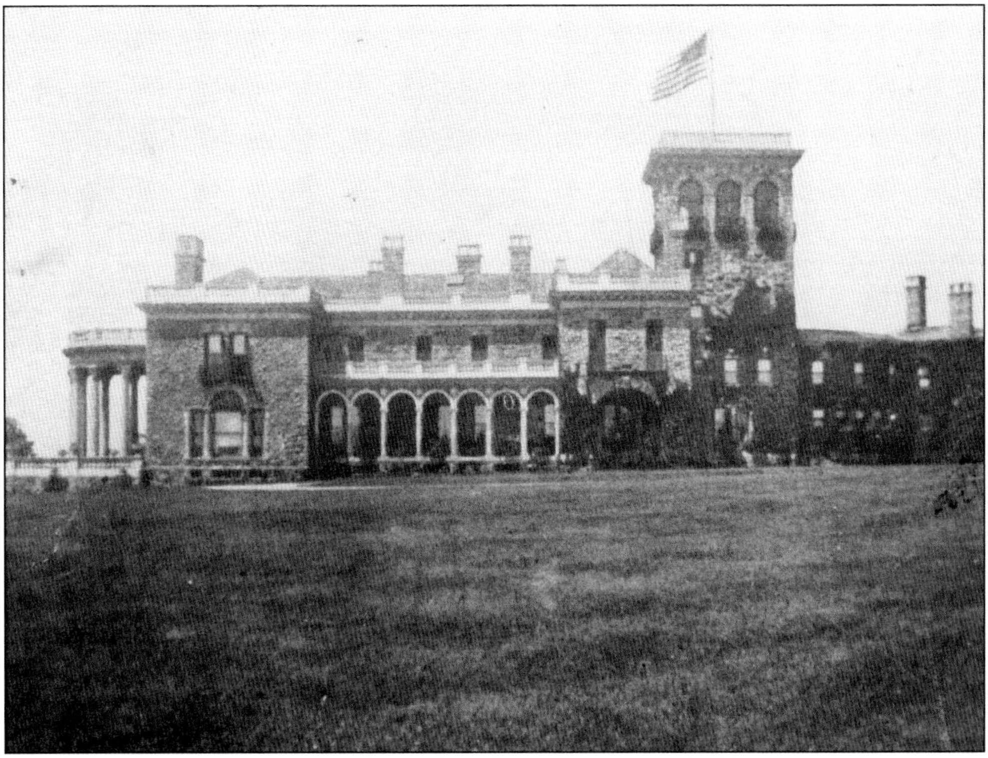

Stronghold, also called The Castle, is the home built by Prudential founder John F. Dryden in 1899. It is constructed of rough brownstone. An elevator in the tower provided Mr. and Mrs. Dryden with a spectacular view from the tower lookout. (Bernardsville Public Library Local History Collection.)

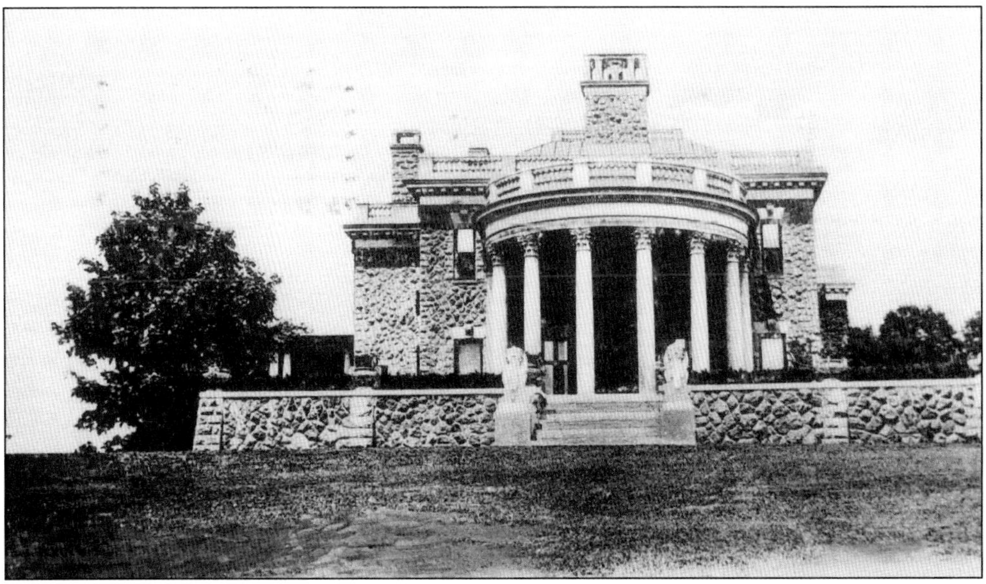

This view shows Stronghold from the south end. The estate was later home to their son Forrest Fairchild Dryden, who succeeded his father as president of Prudential. (Bernardsville Public Library Local History Collection.)

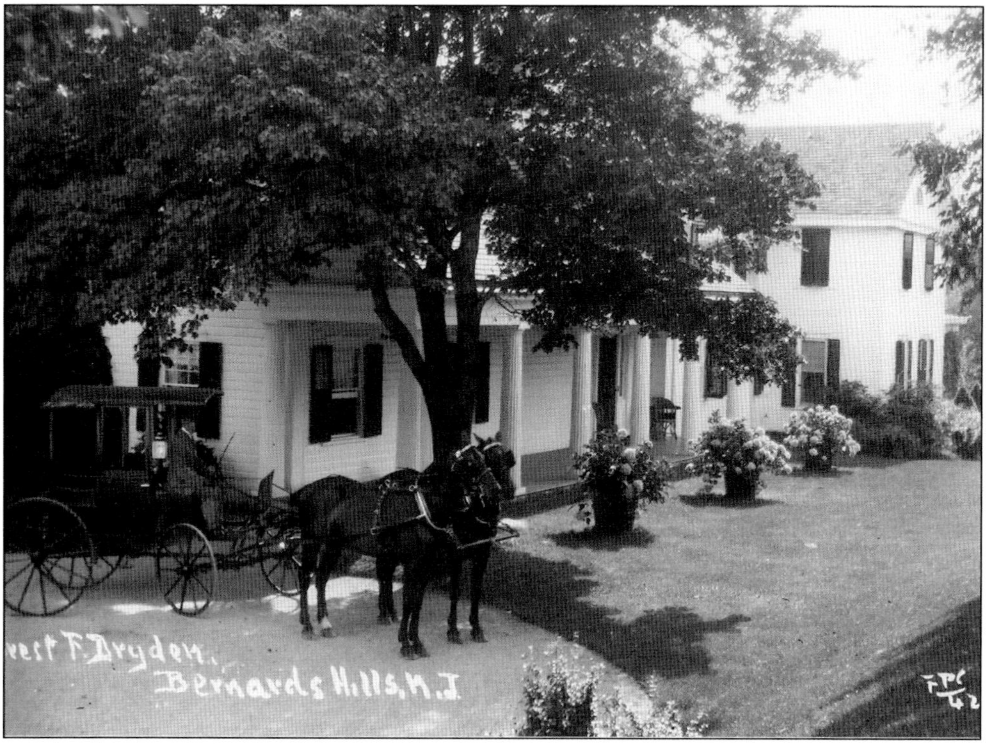

Mr. Forrest Fairchild Dryden, the second president of Prudential Insurance Company, is shown in this *c.* 1901 picture. Mr. Dryden also served as director of the Union National Bank, the National Bank of Commerce, the South Jersey Gas Company, the Electric and Traction Company, the United States Casualty Company, the American Insurance Company, the People's Gas Improvement Company of Trenton, and the Public Service Corporation of New Jersey. (Bernardsville Public Library Local History Collection.)

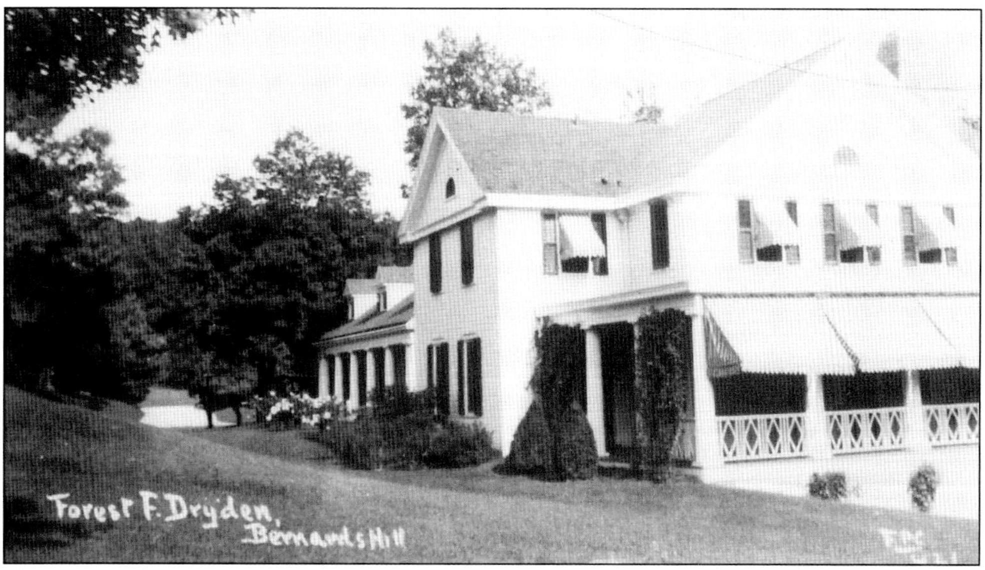

The estate of Forrest Fairchild Dryden prior to his inheriting Stronghold from his father. (Bernardsville Public Library Local History Collection.)

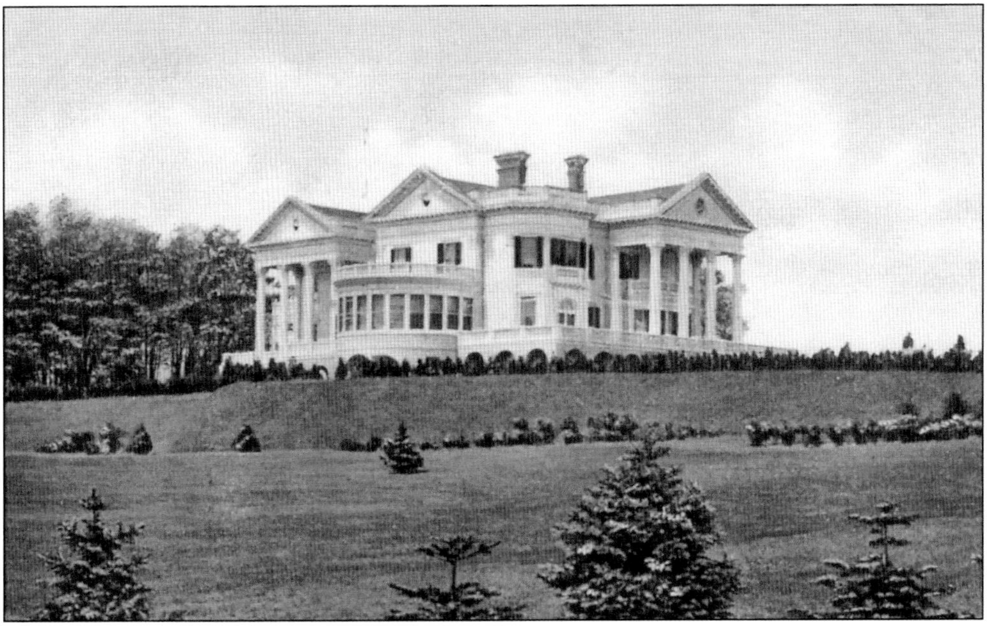

The estate of Colonel Anthony B. Kuser was named Faircourt. Mrs. Kuser was the daughter of John Dryden, and their son was named Dryden Kuser. Colonel Kuser donated High Point State Park to the people of New Jersey. He died in 1929, the year before the park officially opened. (Bernardsville Public Library Local History Collection.)

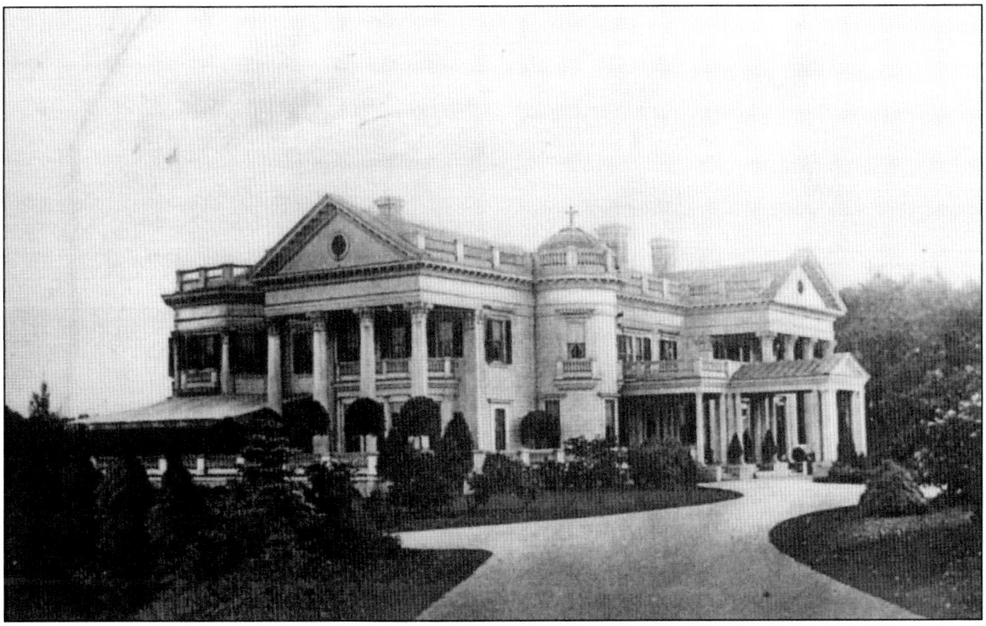

Here is another view of Faircourt. Colonel Kuser maintained an aviary with the finest pheasants in the world. The mansion no longer stands, and all that remains is the wrought iron fence. (Bernardsville Public Library Local History Collection.)

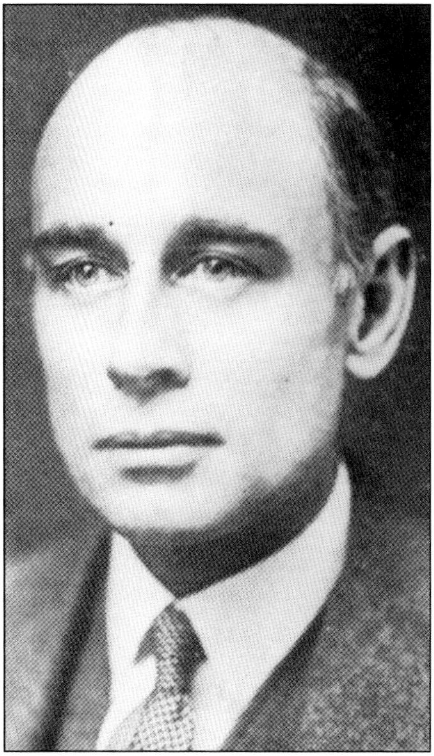

Dryden Kuser was the son of Anthony R. Kuser and Susie F. Dryden, the daughter of Senator John F. Dryden of Stronghold. (Rutgers University New Jersey Special Collection.)

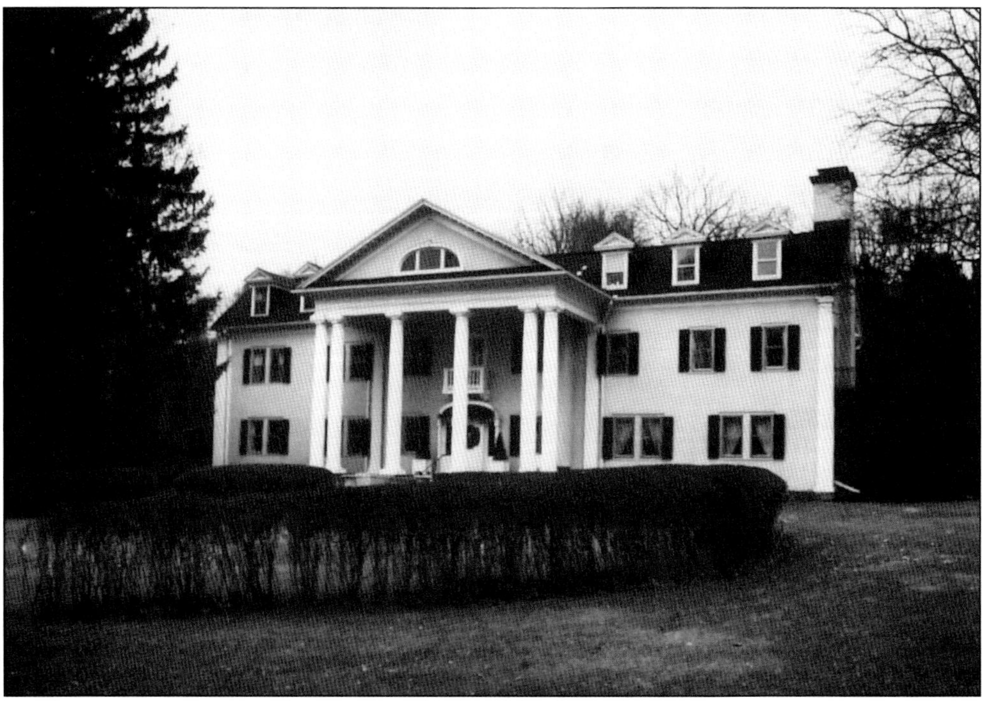

This is the home of Dryden Kuser and Brooke Russell Kuser, his wife. Her father was Marine Corps General John H. Russell, who served as American High Commissioner to Haiti. (Turpin Real Estate.)

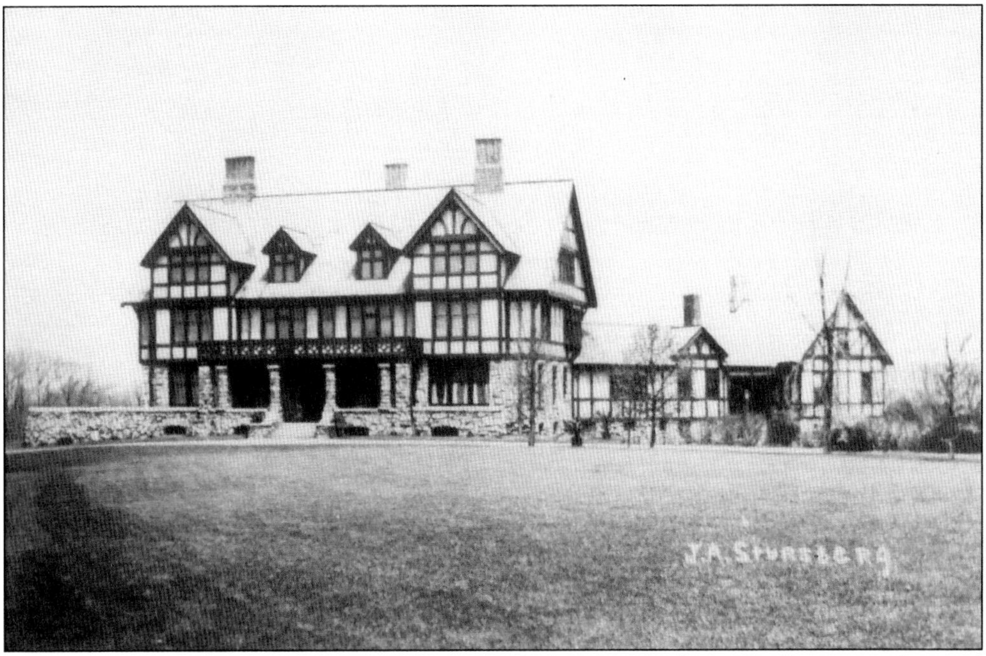

Stonehyrst is the name of the half-timber estate of Julius A. Stursberg. The house was designed by Schicktel and Bettmars, and was built in 1893. There is a stone water tower on the property. (Bernardsville Public Library Local History Collection.)

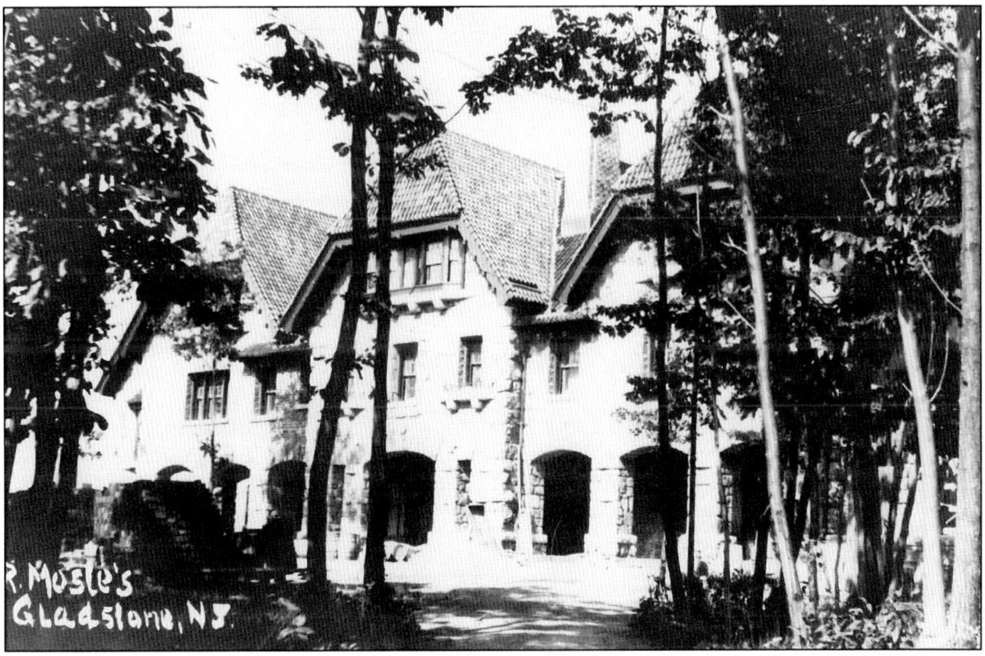

Hillandale, the estate of George R. Mosle, was built in 1910. Mr. Mosle made his fortune shipping sugar from Cuba to the United States. In 1926 the estate was sold to the Sisters of St. John the Baptist, and was used as an orphanage and convent. The sisters founded an elementary school in the 1930s, and a high school in 1949. The school closed in 1992. (Bernardsville Public Library Local History Collection.)

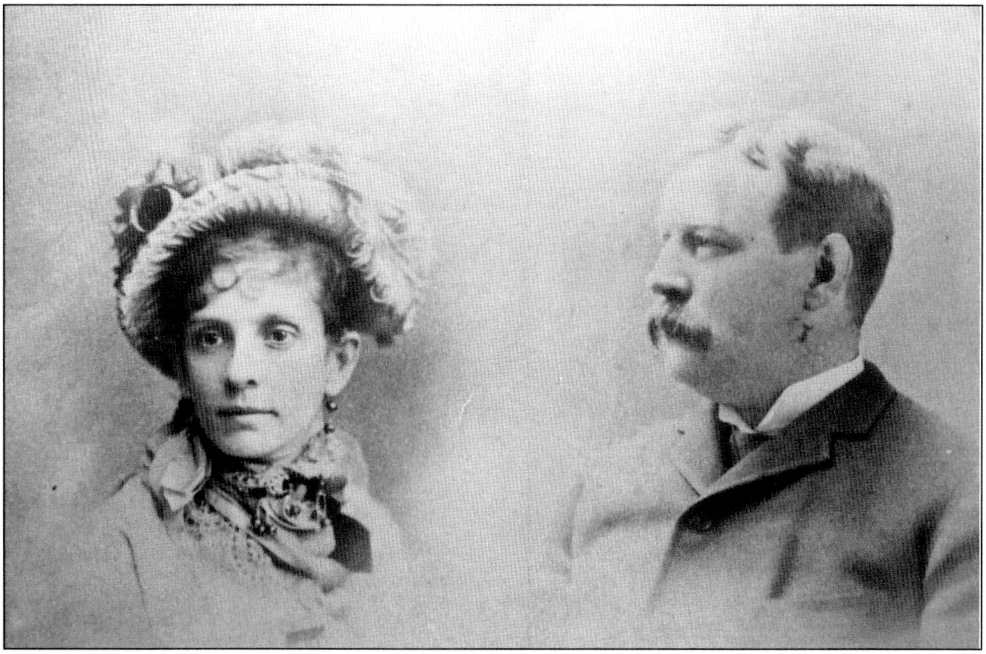

Grant Barney Schley and his wife, Elizabeth, were the builders of Fro Heim, which means happy home. (Bernardsville Public Library Local History Collection.)

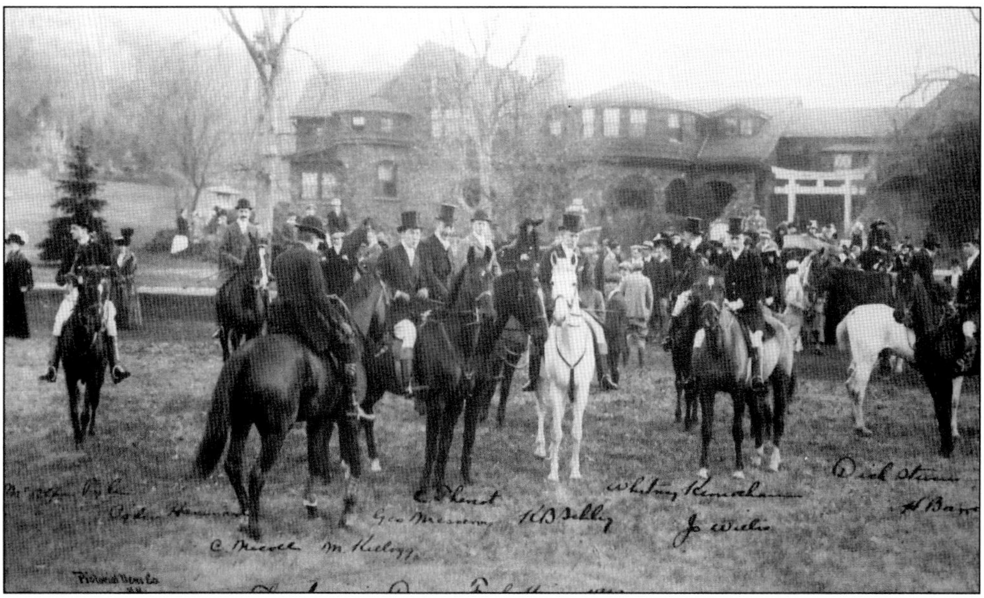

The Essex Fox Hounds hunt at Fro Heim on Thanksgiving day in 1910. The following can be identified in the photograph: Mc Alpen Pyle, Ogden Hammond, C. Nicoll, M. Kellogg, George Messeny, C. Thenot, Ken B. Schley, and Richard Stevens, among others. (Masters of the Essex Fox Hounds.)

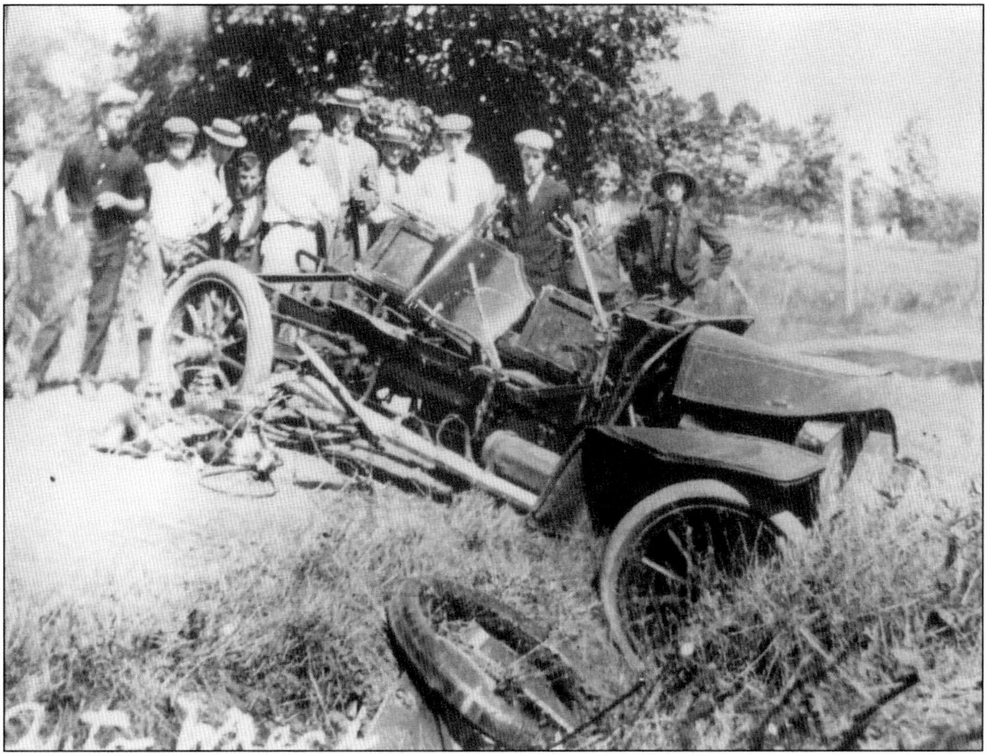

According to the *Bernardsville News*, a "reckless Chauffeur" took Grant B. Schley's car for an unauthorized joy ride with some friends and lost control of the car after attaining the "frightful speed" of 40 to 50 miles per hour. The car hit a telegraph pole. The chauffeur and two friends were killed. This took place in 1907. (Chatfield's.)

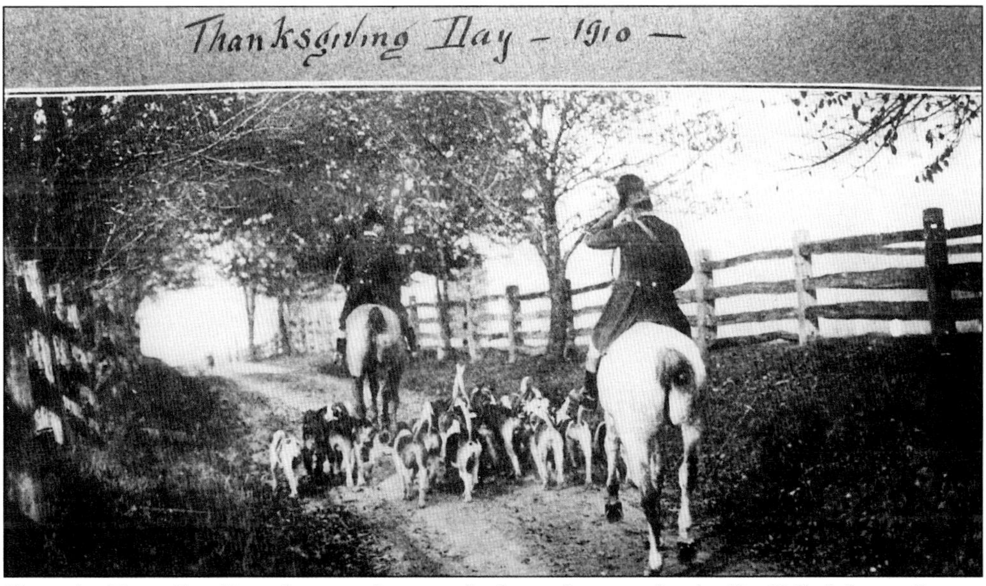

Here, the Essex Fox Hounds were photographed on what may be the Far Hills-Liberty Corner Road on Thanksgiving Day 1910. (James S. Jones.)

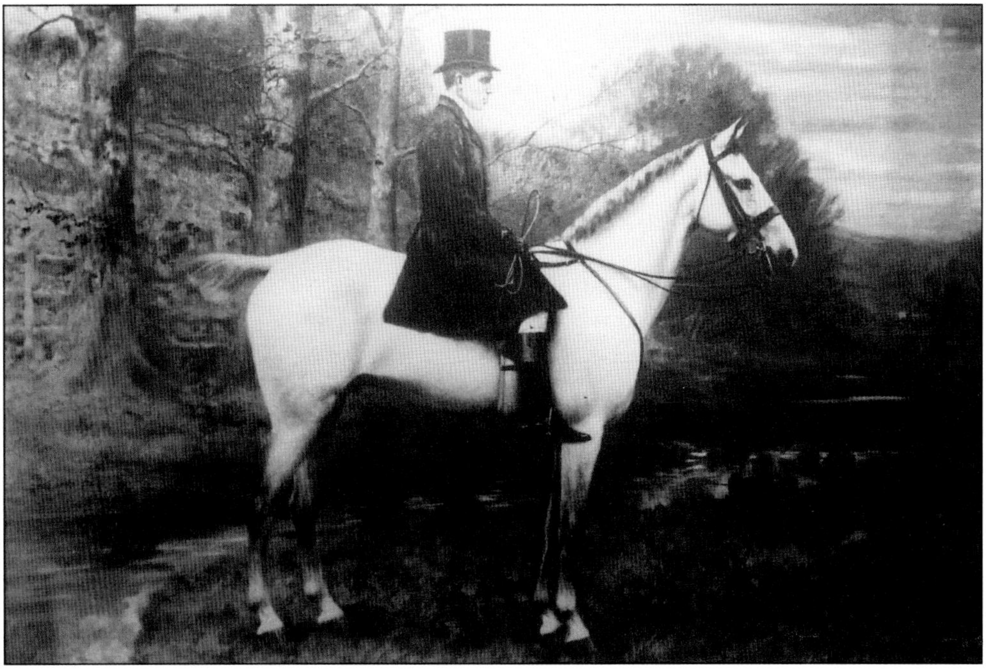

Kenneth B. Schley, son of Grant and Elizabeth Schley, was photographed on Mendoza about 1916. Kenneth graduated from Yale in 1902 and soon entered the world of Wall Street. He became prominent as a stock broker with the firm of Moore & Schley. He served as a member of the board of directors of many important companies. He entertained the Duke and Duchess of Windsor at his home in October 1941. (Kenneth B. Schley Jr.)

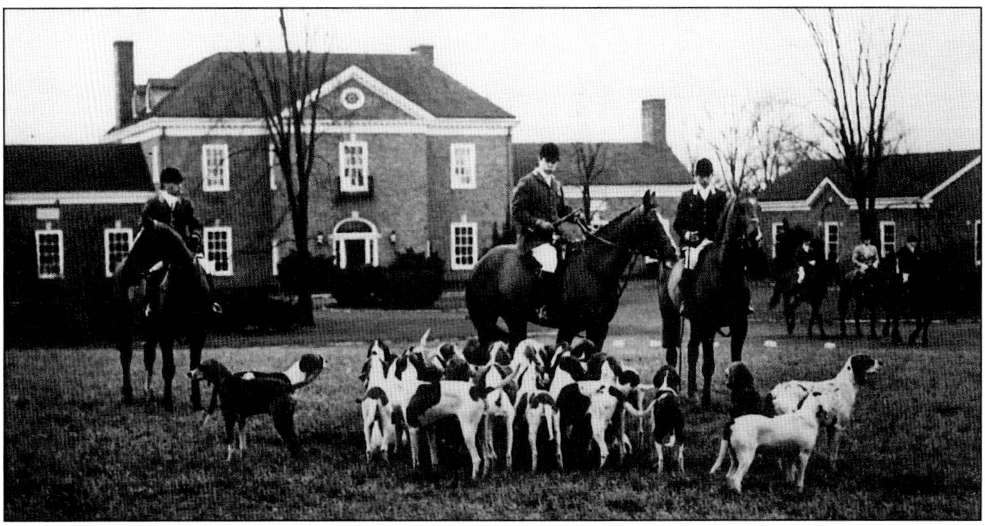

Kenneth B. Schley bought the Field farm along the Lamington River and built this house, which was modeled after the governor's mansion at Williamsburg, Virginia. John D. Rockefeller provided the bricks and roofing shingles (which are terra-cotta, but they look like cedar shakes) from the same batches as those that were being used to restore the governor's mansion. The opening meet of the Essex Fox Hounds 1936 hunting season was held here. At that time, Mr. Schley was a joint master of the Essex Fox Hounds with James Cox Brady. (Kenneth B. Schley Jr.)

At age seventeen, Anne Caroline Schley, the daughter of Kenneth B. Schley, was one of the youngest female pilots to ever get a license. This photograph was taken c. 1929. (Kenneth B. Schley Jr.)

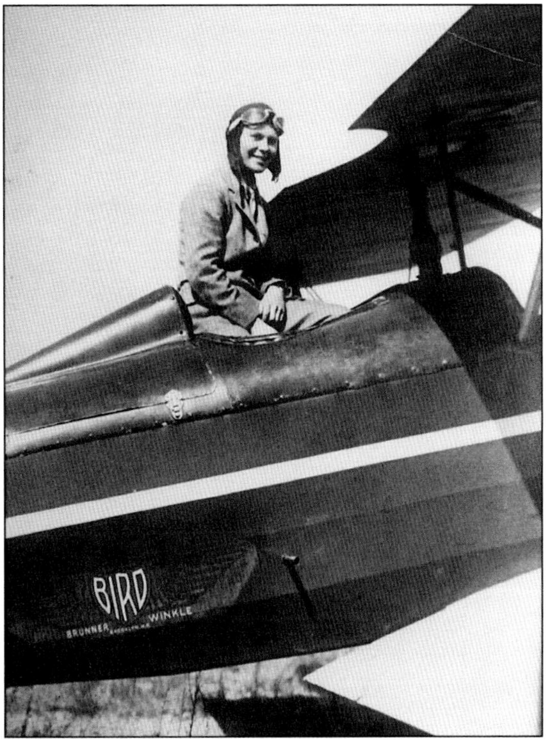

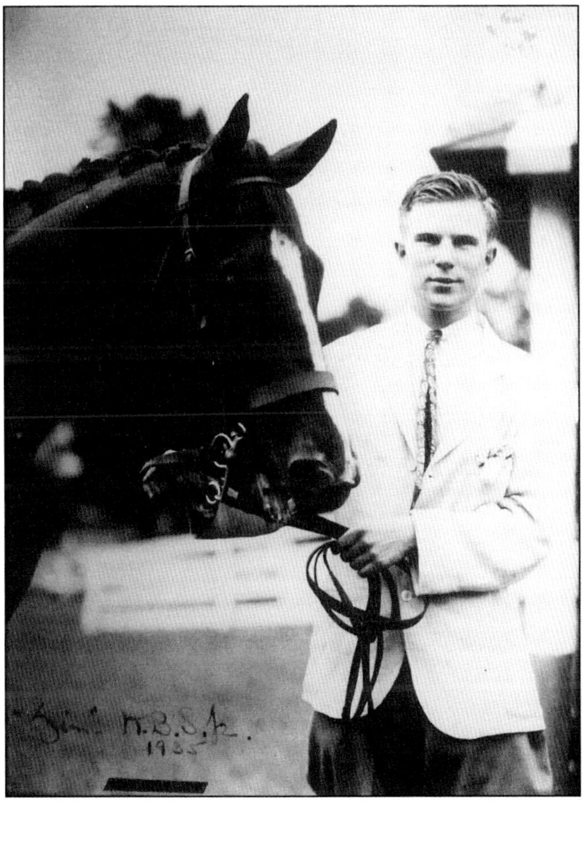

Kenneth B. Schley Jr. was photographed in 1935 with Jim at the Far Hills Race Meeting. During World War II, Mr. Schley flew a Piper Cub airplane as an artillery observer in Europe. He flew over German lines at night to deliver penicillin to the surrounded soldiers of the 101st Airborne Division at Bastogne. Schley had to make his landing between two rows of flashlights held by members of the 101st. He was awarded a Silver Star for his bravery. (Kenneth B. Schley Jr.)

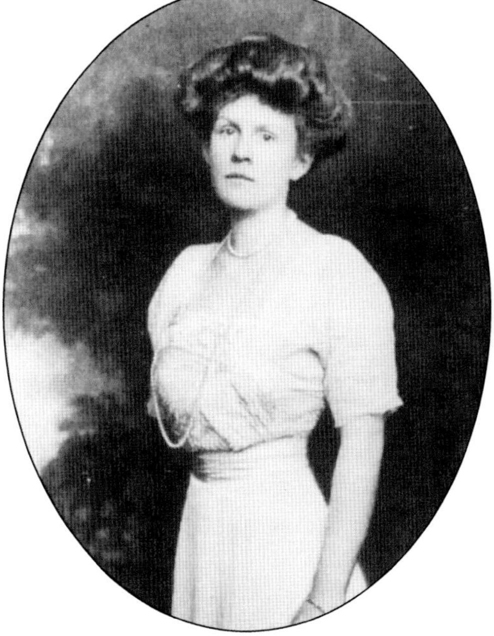

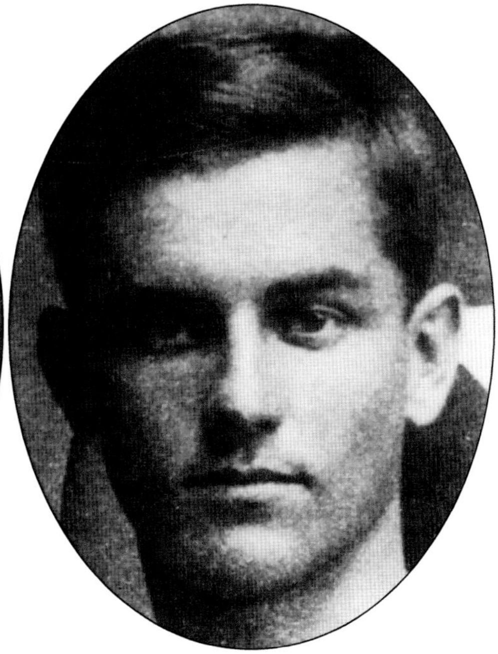

LEFT: Evelyn Schley, the daughter of Grant and Eleanor Schley, is shown in 1906, the year she was married. She died in 1919 from the Spanish Influenza at the age of thirty-two.
RIGHT: Max Behr was photographed in 1905, the year before his marriage to Evelyn. (Behr family.)

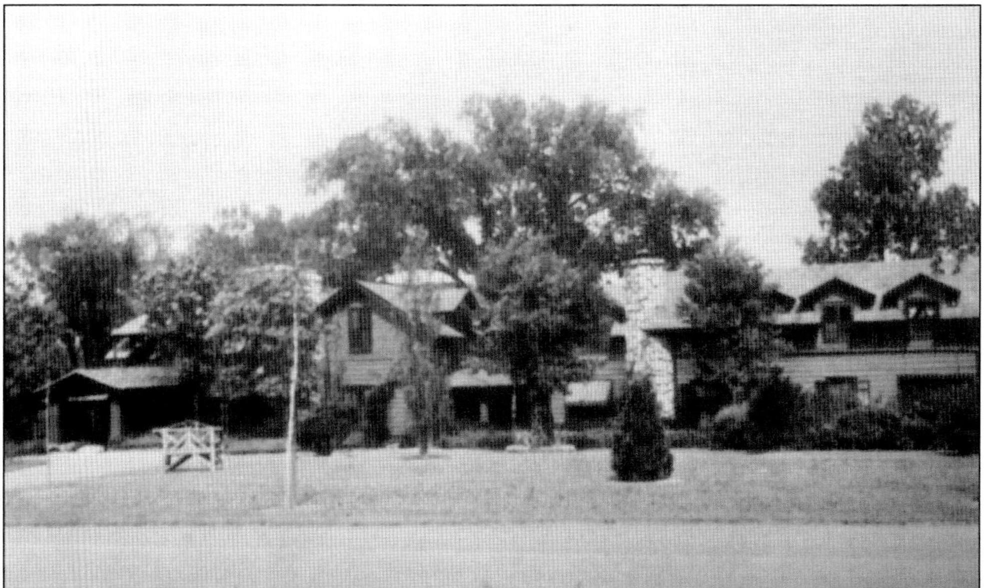

Grant Schley built this stone home that forms a bridge across the brook as a wedding present for his daughter, Evelyn, when she married Max Behr in 1906. The unique home was called the Brook Cottage. (Behr family.)

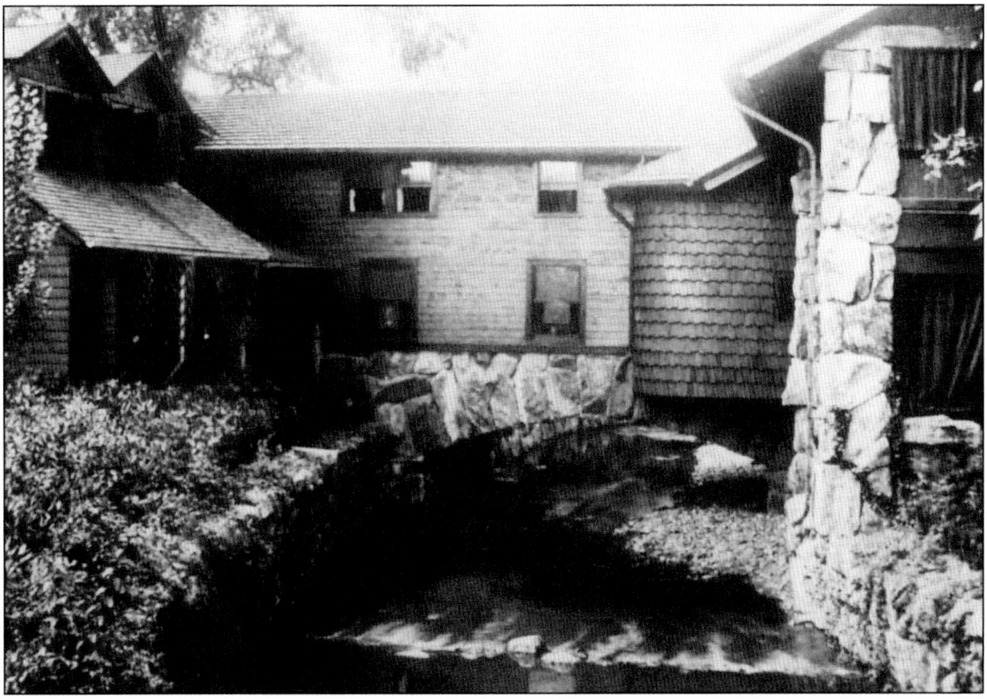

Another view shows how the Brook Cottage forms a bridge over the Mine Brook. (Behr family.)

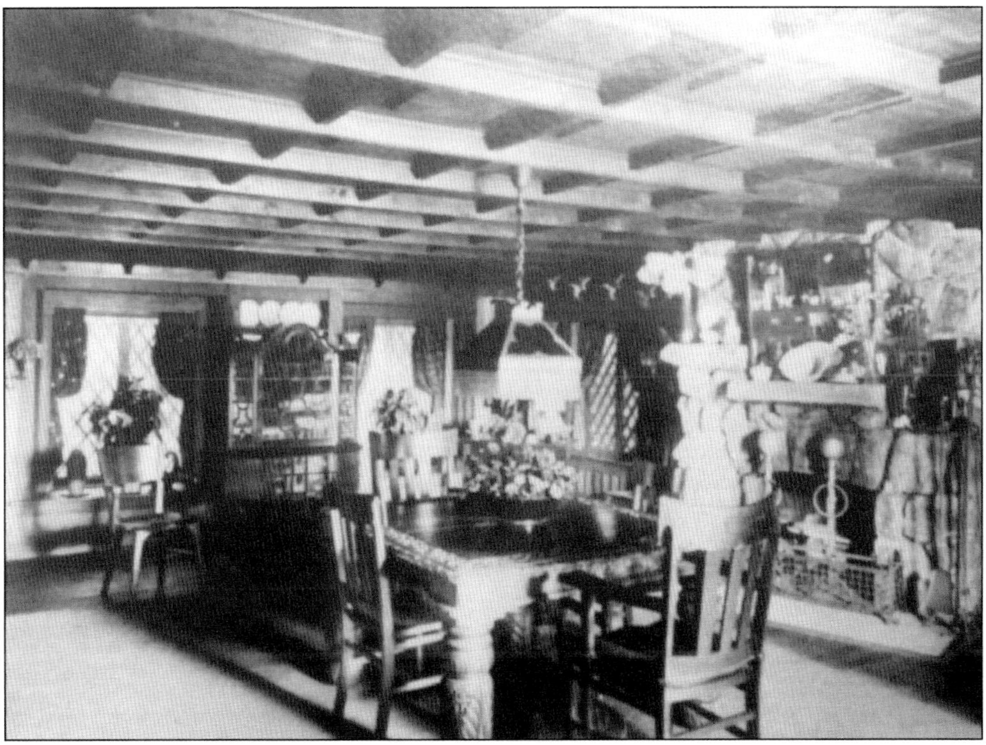

This is the dining room at the Brook Cottage. (Behr family.)

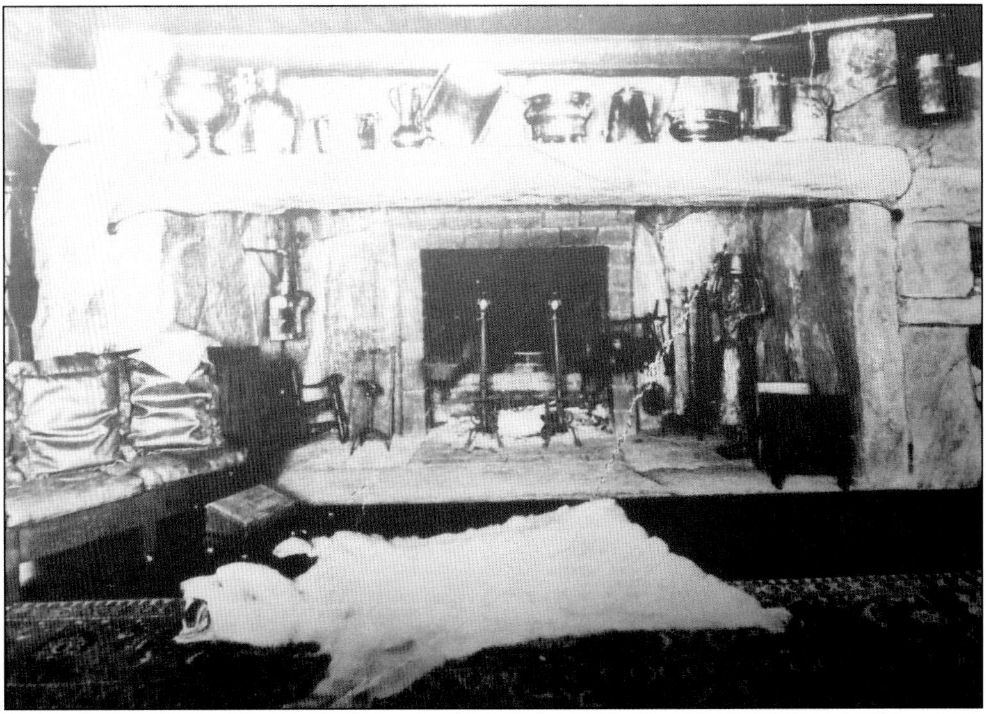

The living room of the Brook Cottage had a lovely fireplace. The stones holding up the mantle were 7 feet tall. The mantle itself measured 20 feet long by 5 feet wide. It came from 20 miles away, and caused three bridges to collapse as it was being brought to the estate. (Behr family.)

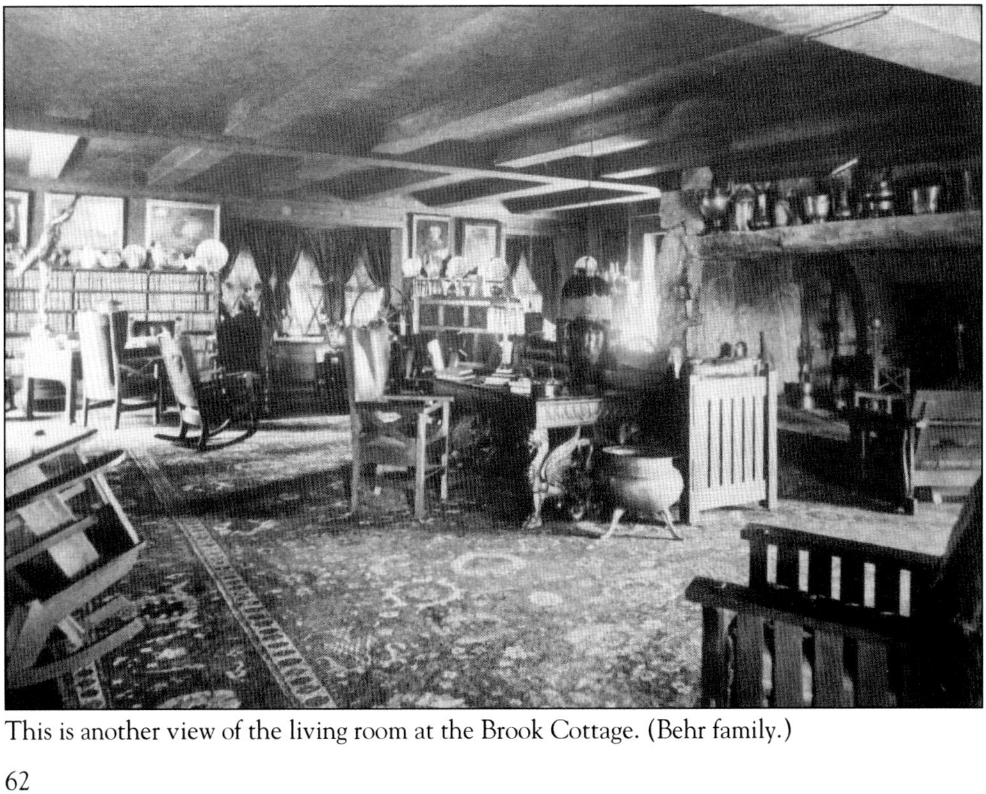

This is another view of the living room at the Brook Cottage. (Behr family.)

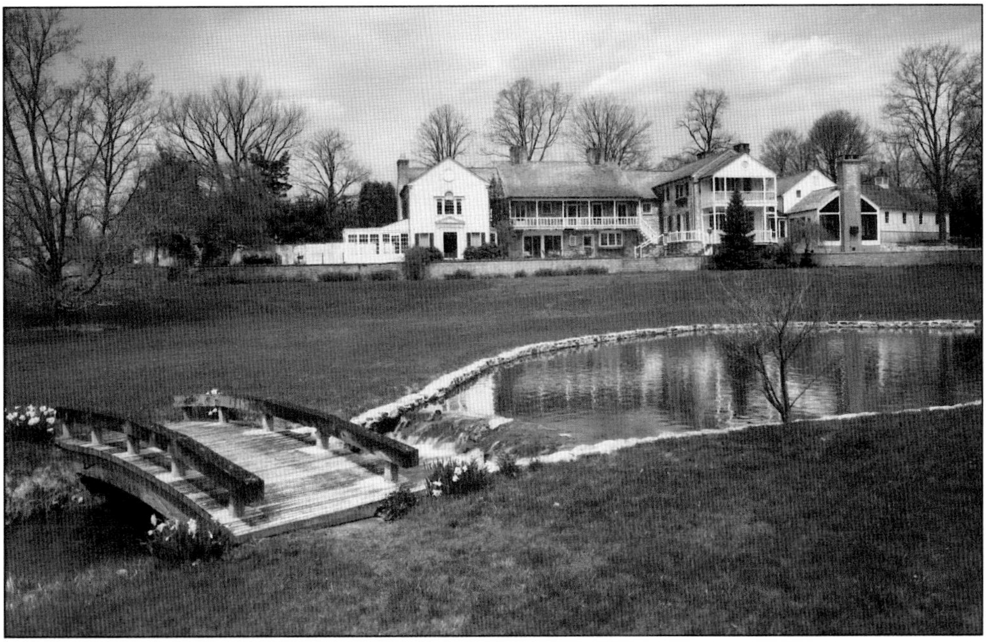

Grant Schley built homes for each of his children. This estate, Rippling Brook Farm, was built by Mr. Schley as a gift for his nephew, Reeve Schley. At the core of the structure is an 1760 tavern that was moved to the site in 1931 from Rocky Hill, Connecticut. It was enlarged with stone from three Revolutionary-era homes nearby. Reeve Schley became a senior vice president of the Chase Bank in New York. (Turpin Real Estate.)

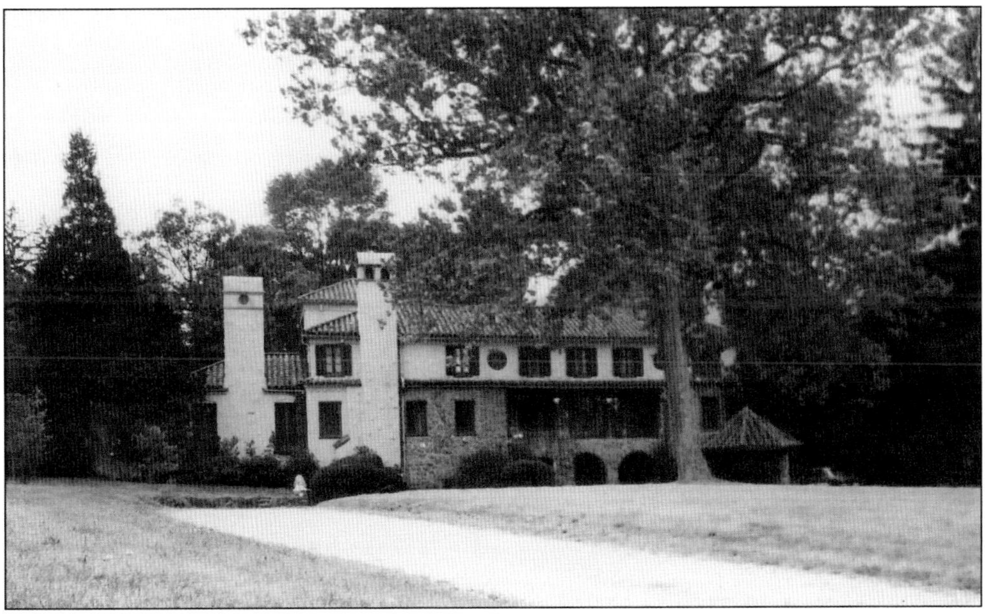

Fro Heim, the estate of Grant Barney Schley, was assembled beginning in 1882 from forty farms and eventually reached 5,000 acres, of which 1,500 acres were kept in cultivation. The house required a live-in staff of thirty-six servants. In the 1930s, after the death of Grant Schley, his son Evander Schley tore down Fro Heim and built this red-tiled roof, Spanish-style house that he named Moorland Farm. (Turpin Real Estate.)

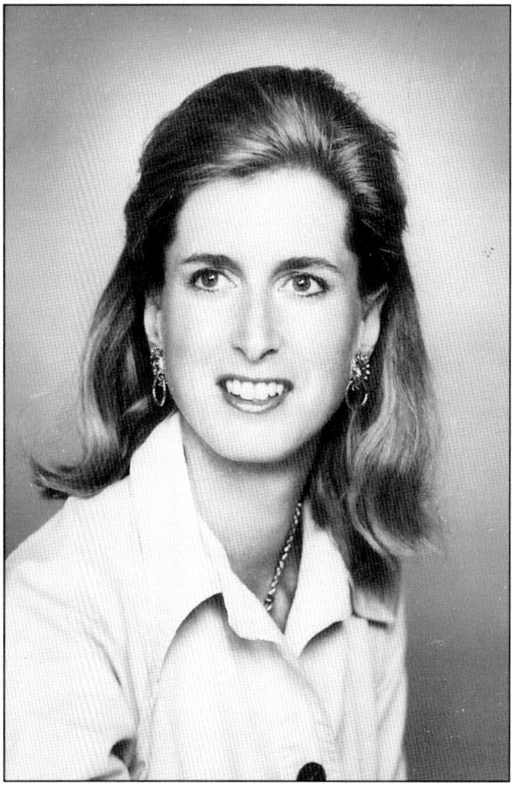

The great-grandniece of Grant Schley, Christine Todd Whitman is shown in 1982 when she became a Somerset County freeholder. She was elected governor of New Jersey on January 18, 1994. (*The Somerset Messenger Gazette*.)

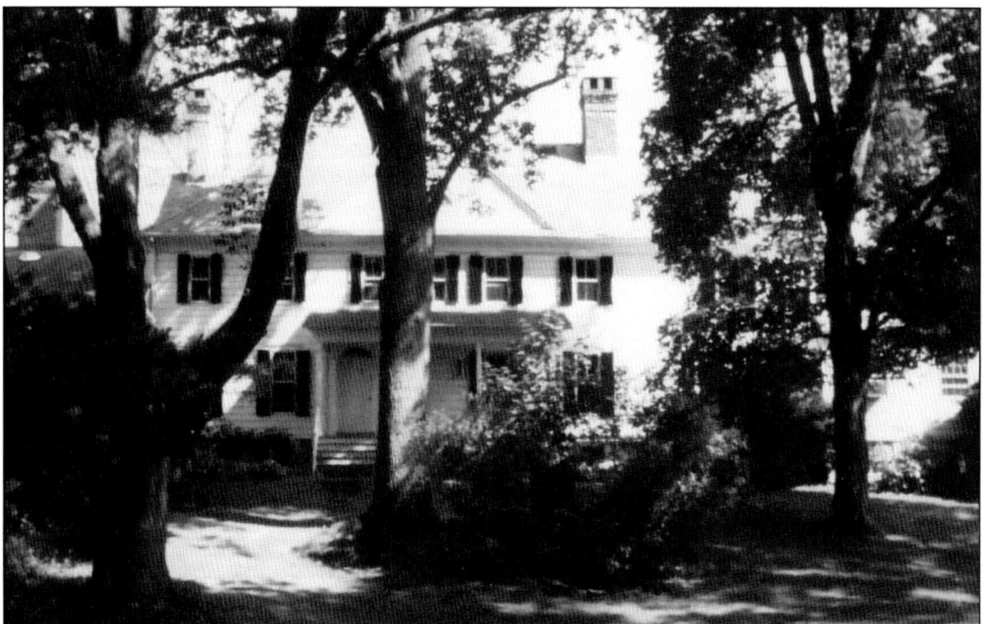

Pontefract, the estate of Webster and Eleanor Schley Todd, is located in Tewksbury and is now the home of Governor Christine Todd Whitman. Eleanor Schley Todd was the daughter of Reeve Schley.

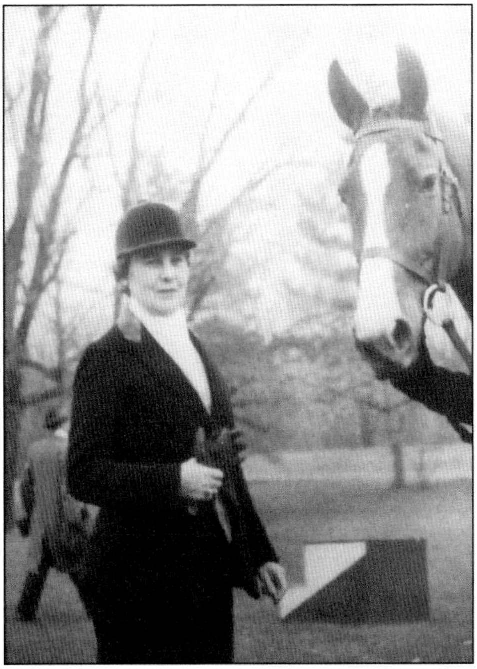
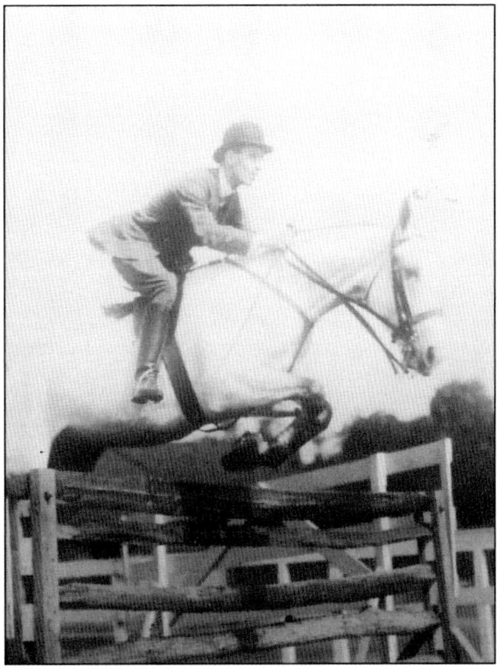

Being master of the Essex Fox Hounds was not an honor reserved only for men. Many women have also held the position. Here is Mrs. Charles (Vera) Scribner as master of the Essex Fox Hounds. Mrs. Scribner always rode (and jumped) side-saddle. On the right is Mr. Charles Scribner on Moonshine at the Essex Hunt Club's 1916 Farmer's Day event. (Masters of the Essex Fox Hounds.)

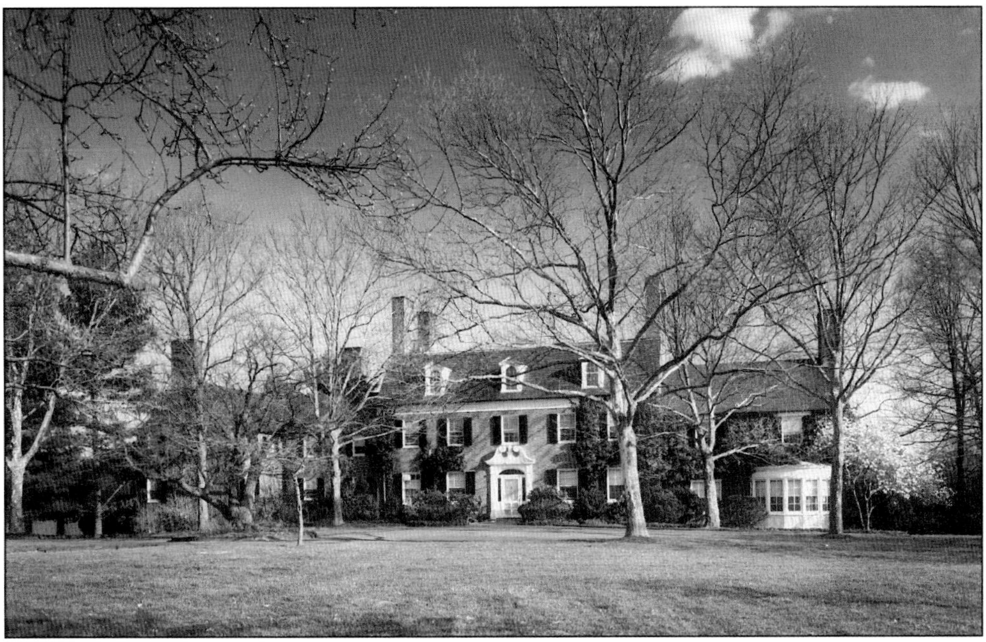

Merry Brook Farm was constructed by Charles and Vera G. Bloodgood Scribner in 1926. Mr. Scribner was the president of the publishing firm of Scribner & Sons. He was a personal friend of Ernest Hemingway, and published all of his works. (Turpin Real Estate.)

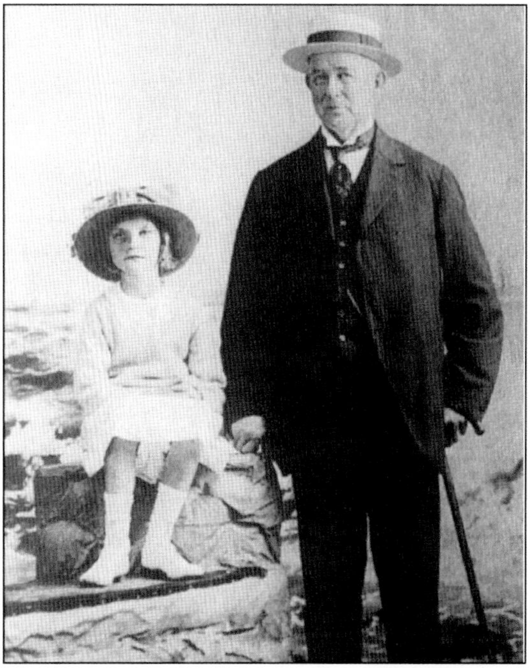

Doris Duke posed for this picture at about the age of seven with her father James Buchannan Duke, the founder of the American Tobacco Company and the Duke Power Company. When he died in 1925 she inherited $70 million. She became known as the "Duchess" and the "Richest Girl in the World." On his death bed he told her never to trust anyone. (Manuscript Department, William R. Perkins Library, Duke University.)

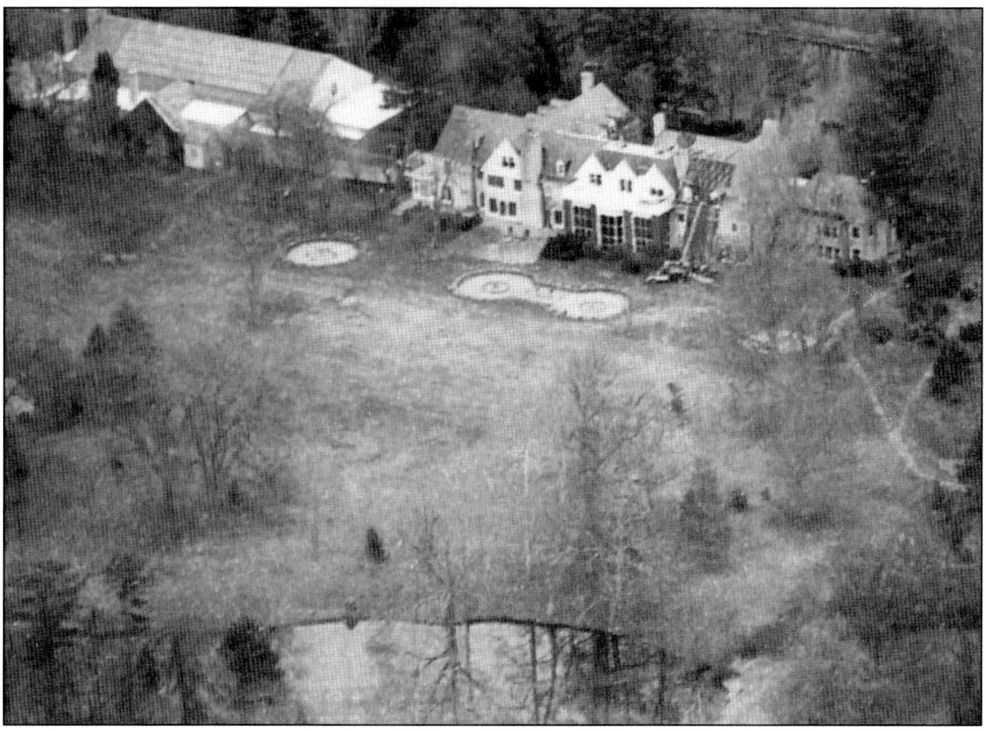

This is Duke estate, as it looked from the air. Mr. Duke planted more than two million trees and shrubs, dug lakes, and built hills, walls, and bridges on his more than 2,000-acre estate in Hillsborough, but he never finished the project. Among Miss Duke's guests have been Cary Grant, Greta Garbo, Marlon Brando, Pearl Bailey, Jacqueline Kennedy, Lady Bird Johnson, Imelda Marcos, and Pee Wee Herman. (The *Courier News*.)

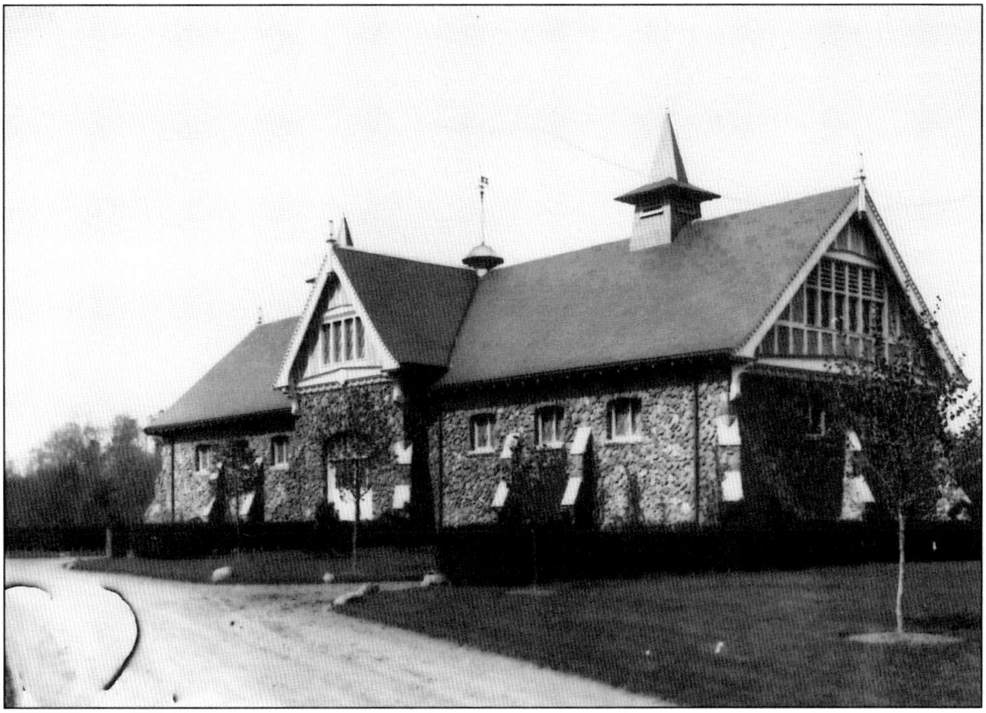

This c. 1920 image shows the stable at Duke Farm. (*The Somerset Messenger Gazette*.)

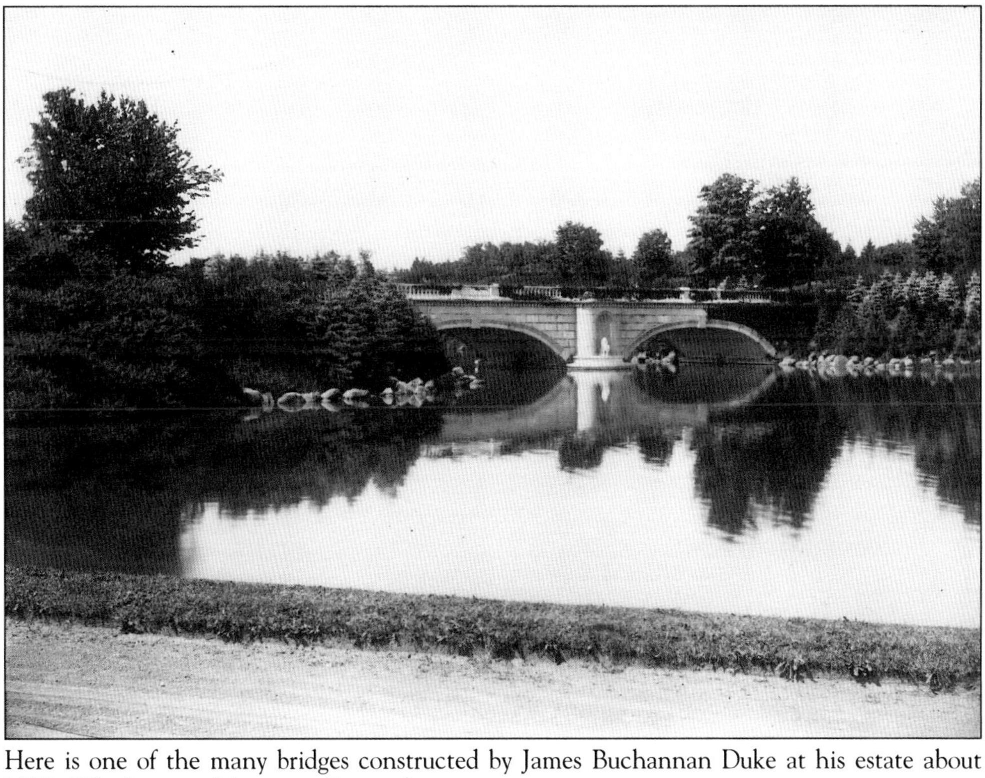

Here is one of the many bridges constructed by James Buchannan Duke at his estate about 1920. (*The Somerset Messenger Gazette*.)

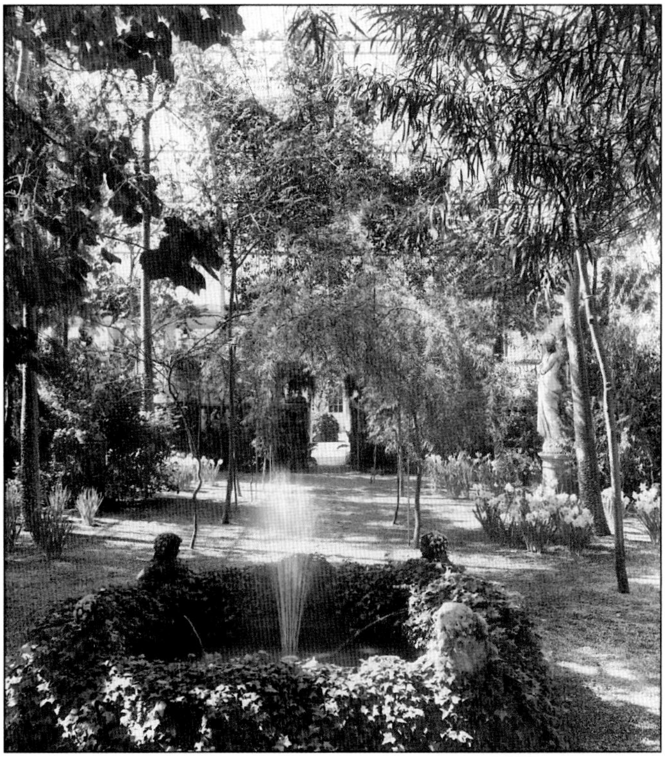

Doris Duke established an indoor botanical garden known as the Duke Gardens. There are many different gardens, each with a national theme. This is the English garden. (Gottscho-Schleisner.)

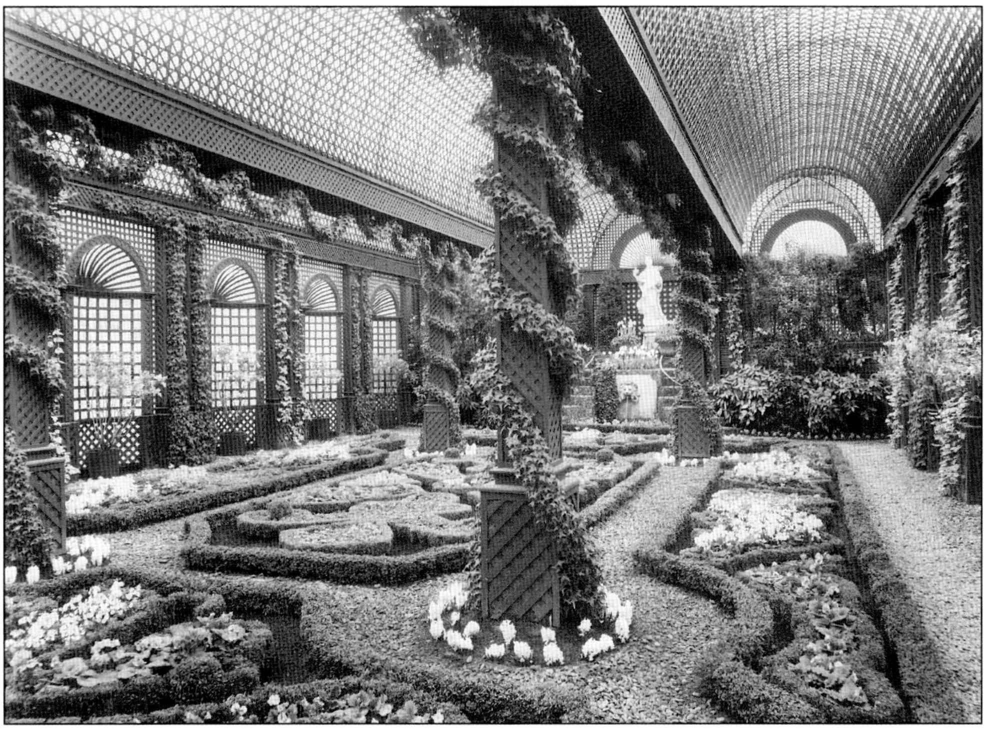

This is the French garden. The Duke Gardens are open to the public by appointment. (Gottscho-Schleisner.)

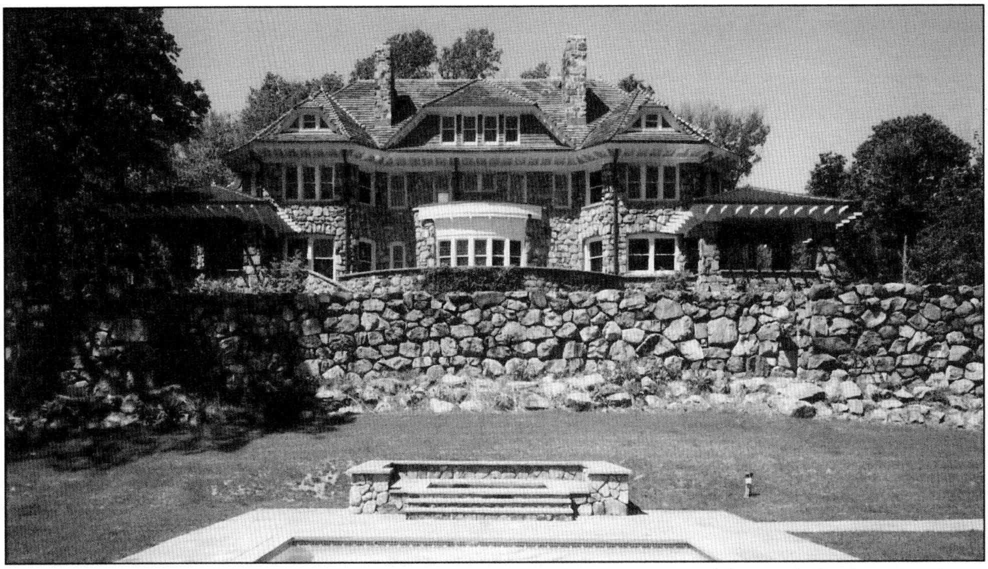

Adolphe de Bary, a wealthy wine importer, built this house as a wedding gift for his daughter, Leonie, and her husband, financier George D. Cross. The thirty-room fieldstone manor, designed by Grosvenor Atterburg of New York, was started in 1901 and finished in 1905. The exterior walls are 3 feet thick. The couple combined their names and called the estate "Baricross." (Turpin Real Estate.)

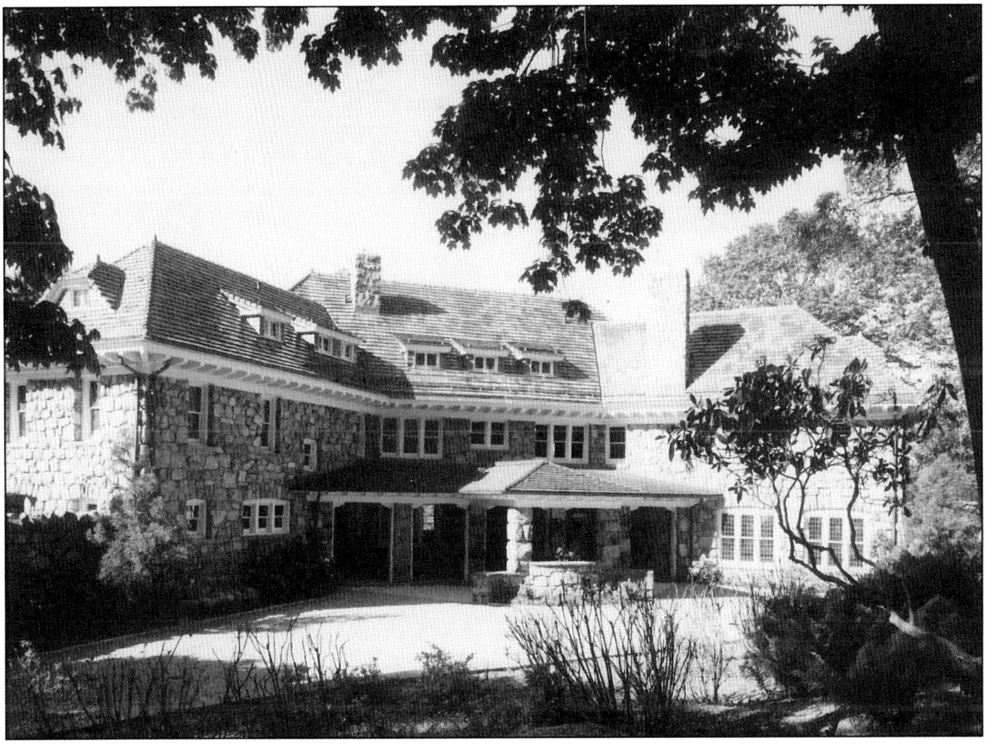

Mr. George D. Cross was elected first mayor of Bernardsville Borough, serving three terms from 1924 to 1930. Later owners of the house renamed it Green Gables because of its green tile roof. (Turpin Real Estate.)

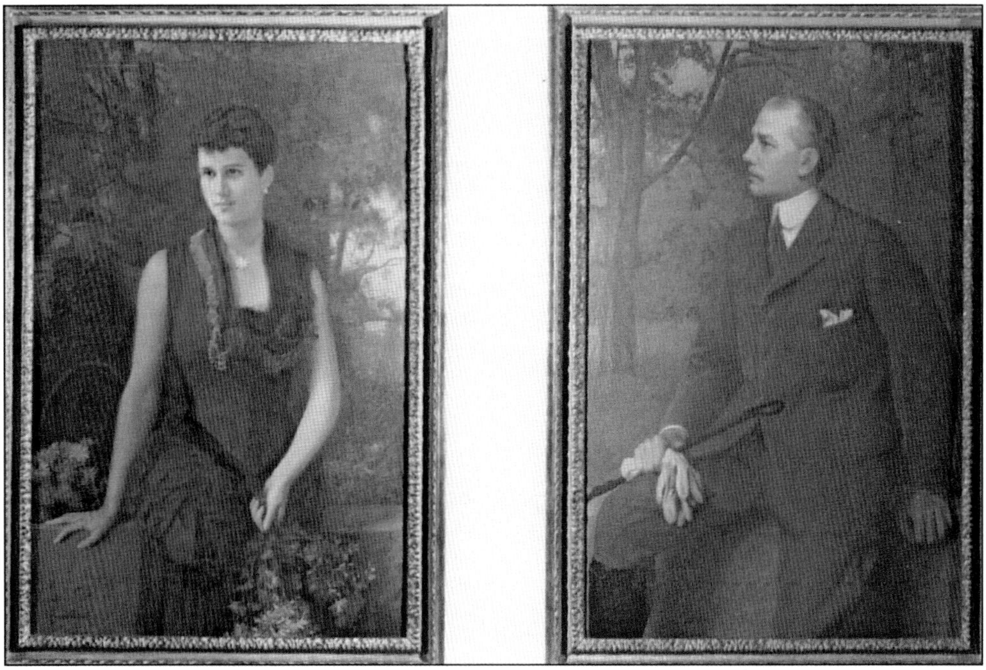

Kate Macy (Mrs. Walter Graeme Ladd) was the daughter of Josiah Macy Jr., a friend and business associate of John D. Rockefeller. Kate Macy was thirteen when her father died, leaving her $21 million in Standard Oil stock. Walter Graeme Ladd was an attorney and principal in the Delaware, Lackawanna & Western Railroad.(Kate Macy Ladd Fund brochure.)

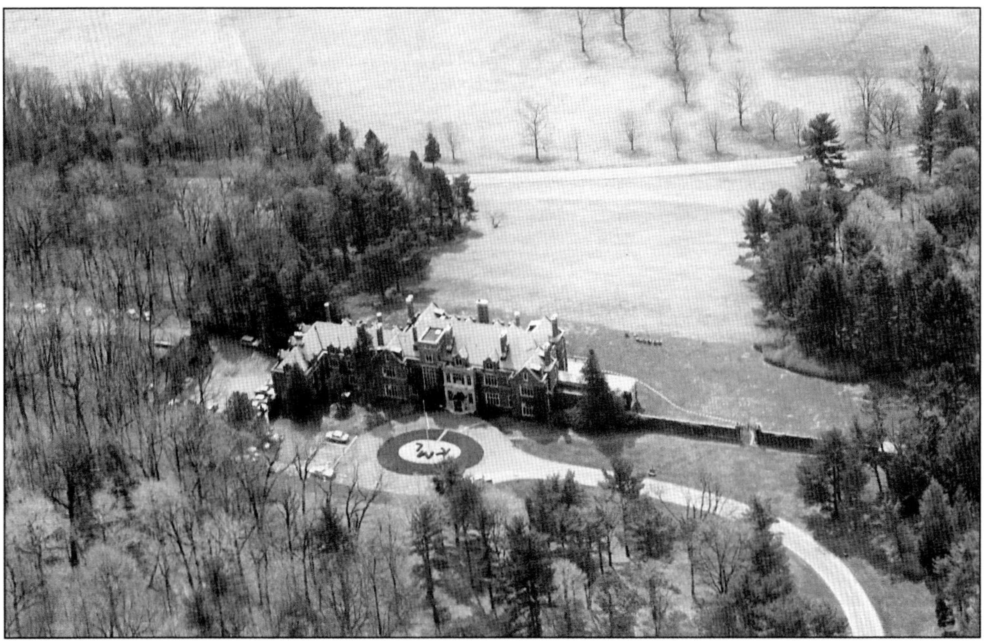

Natirar, the estate of Walter Graeme and Kate Macy Ladd, was built in 1906. It was modeled after Wroxton Abbey in Warwickshire, England, the seat of Lord North, prime minister in 1773 when the Stamp Act was passed. Today the 493-acre estate belongs to King Hassan II of Morocco (see p. 128). (Turpin Real Estate.)

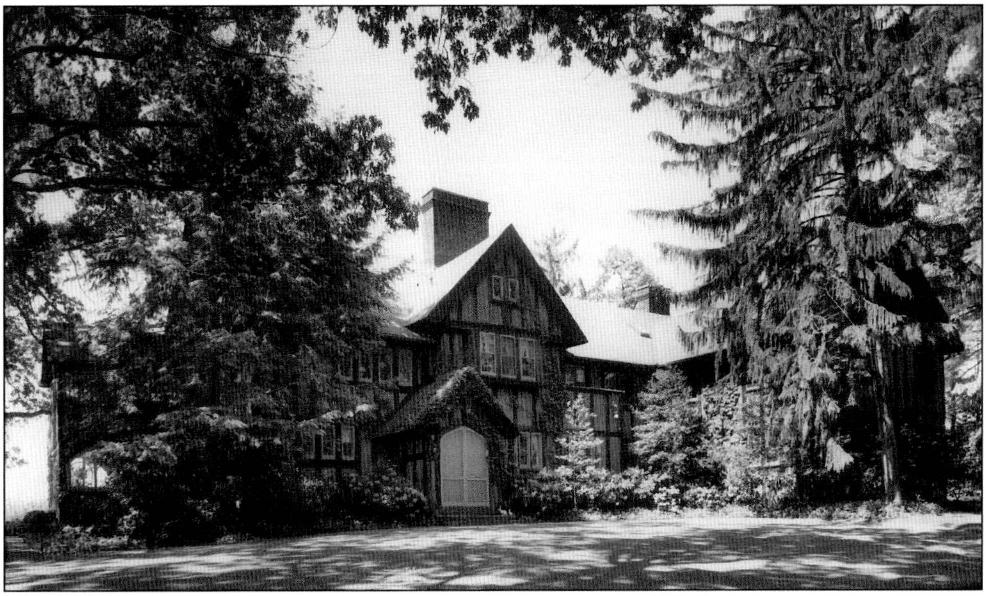

Foxwood was the estate of William Thorn and Frances Dallett Kissel. Mr. Kissel was the son of esteemed banker Gustav Kissel, and the great-grandson of Commodore Cornelius Vanderbilt. When Cornelius Vanderbilt died in 1887, he left an estate of $105 million, which was more money than there was in the United States Treasury at the time. (Turpin Real Estate.)

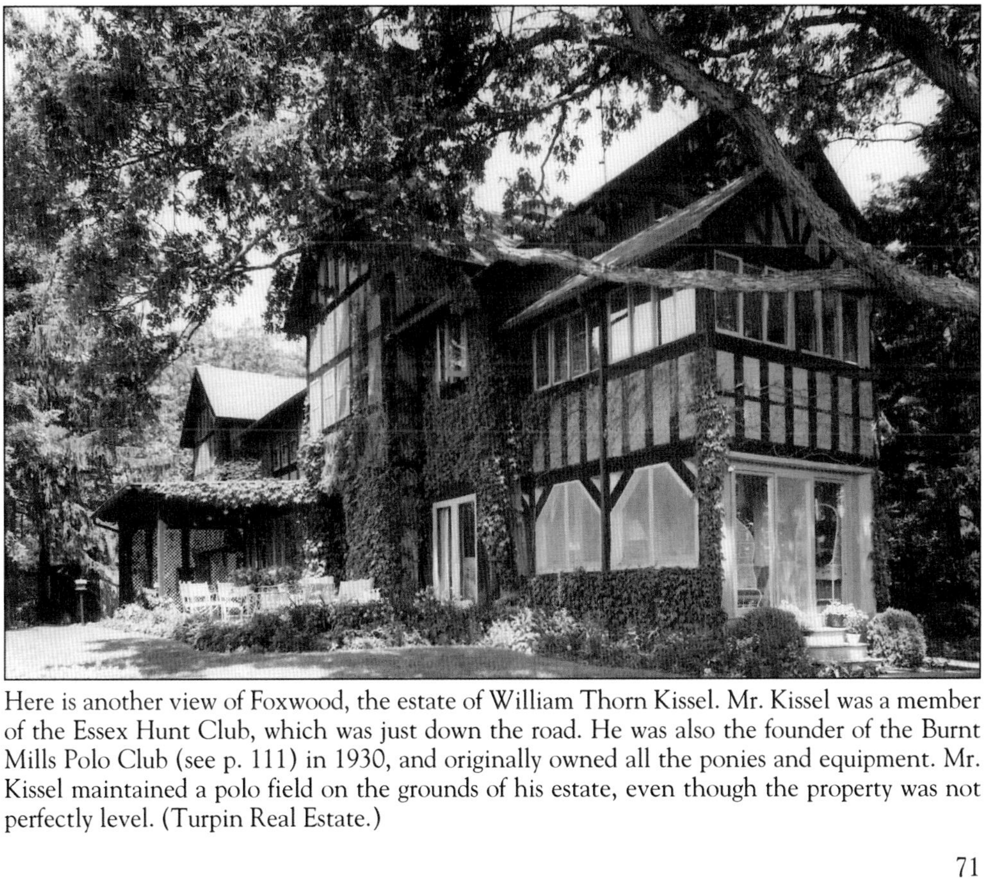

Here is another view of Foxwood, the estate of William Thorn Kissel. Mr. Kissel was a member of the Essex Hunt Club, which was just down the road. He was also the founder of the Burnt Mills Polo Club (see p. 111) in 1930, and originally owned all the ponies and equipment. Mr. Kissel maintained a polo field on the grounds of his estate, even though the property was not perfectly level. (Turpin Real Estate.)

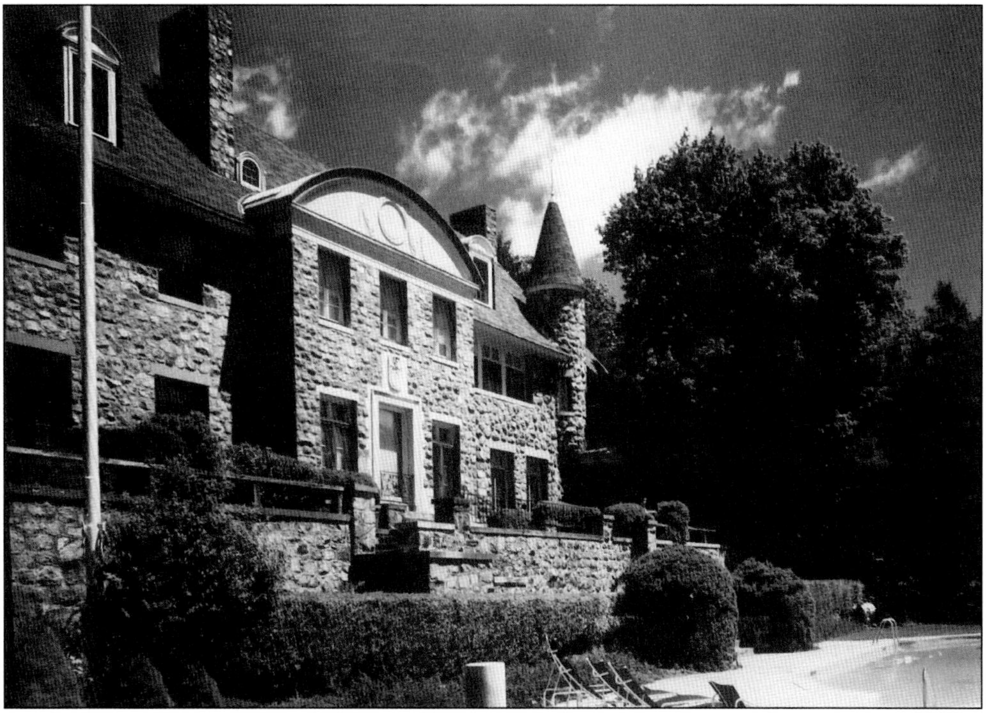

Cragmore, the estate of Charles Engelhard Sr., the founder of both Engelhard Hanovia and the Engelhard Minerals and Chemicals Company. When he died in 1950, he left the company, worth $20 million to his son, Charles Engelhard Jr. (Turpin Real Estate.)

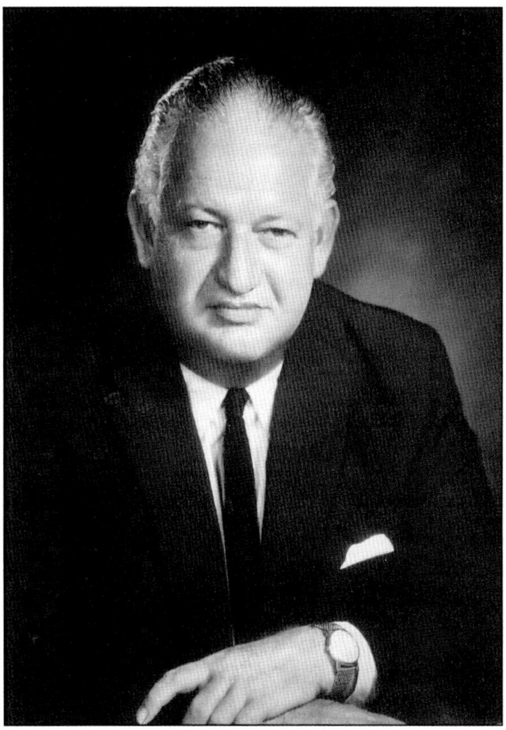

Charles W. Engelhard, Jr. inherited the two companies, Engelhard Hanovia and Engelhard Minerals and Chemicals, from his father. Over the next twenty-one years he ran the value of his holdings up to $300 million, with business enterprises in fifty countries. *James Bond* author Ian Fleming, a friend of Engelhard's, was amazed and enamored by his lavish jet-set lifestyle, his powerful friends, and his precious metals business. Fleming fashioned the character Goldfinger after Engelhard. (The *Bernardsville News*.)

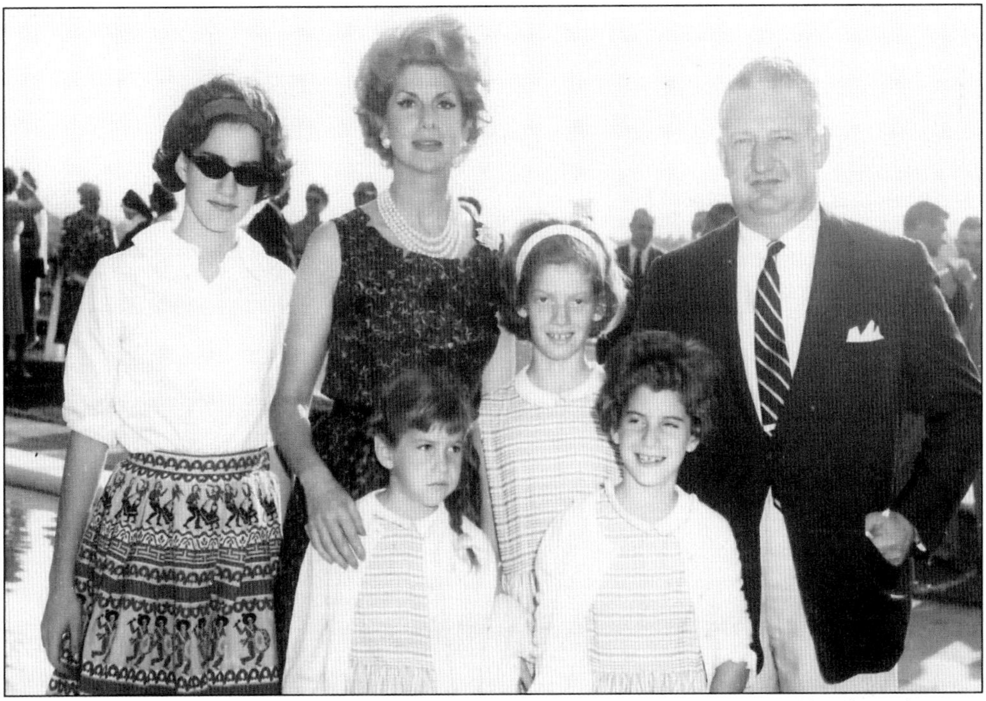

Charles and Jane Engelhard are shown with their four daughters. Mrs. Engelhard was born in China, the daughter of a Brazilian diplomat. She took over the business after her husband's death in 1971. One of their daughters married world-famous fashion designer, Oscar de la Renta. (The *Bernardsville News*.)

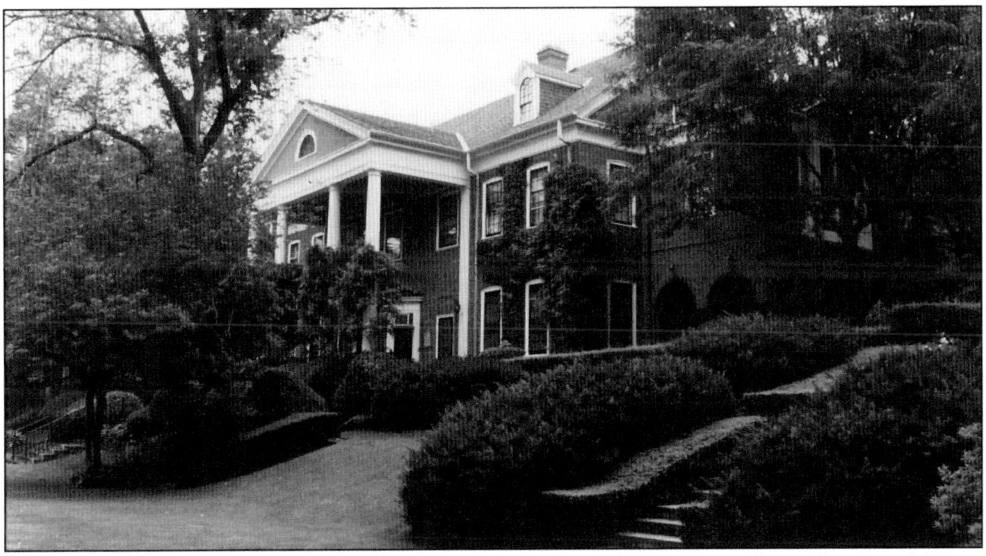

Cragwood, overlooking Ravine Lake, was the main estate of Charles and Jane Engelhard. They also maintained a suite at the Waldorf Towers in New York City; Pamplemousse; an estate on Boca Grande, Florida; another on the Gaspé Peninsula in Quebec, and homes in South Africa and Paris. Guests include Presidents Kennedy and Johnson, the Duke and Duchess of Windsor, Prince and Princess Victor Hohenlohe, and Imelda Marcos. The Engelhards were heavy contributors to the Democratic party. (Collection of the authors.)

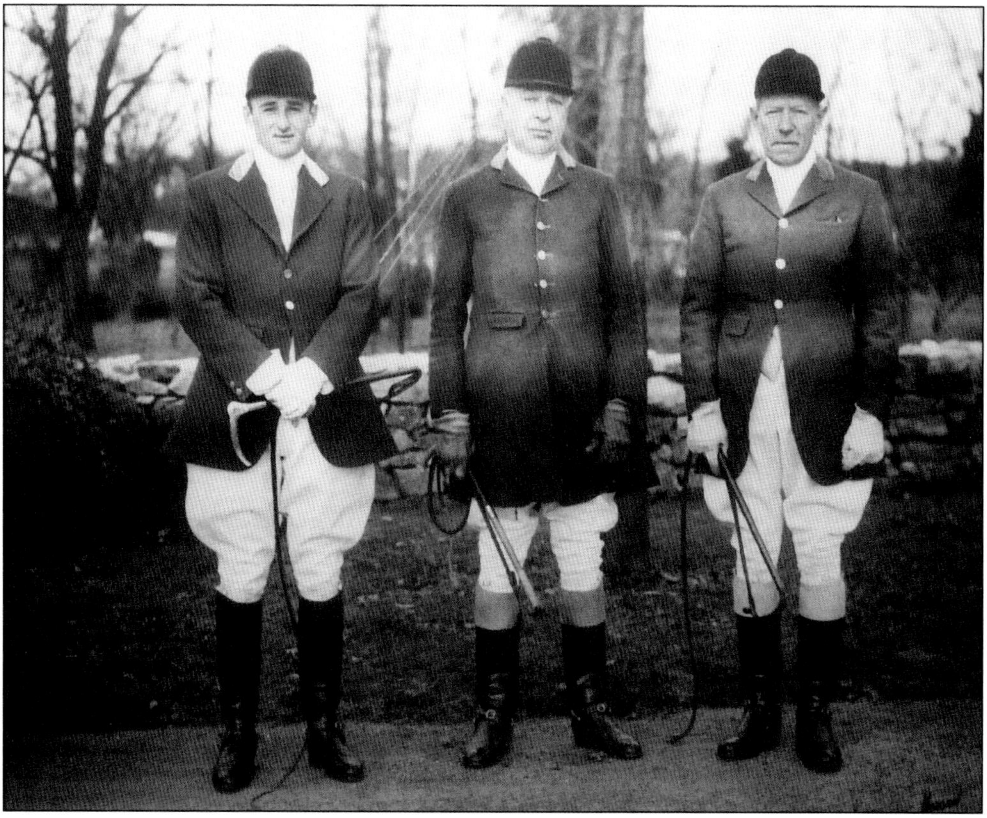

James Cox Brady, Master of the Fox Hounds on the left, George Brice, Huntsman center, and Kenneth B. Schley, Master of the Essex Fox Hounds on the right in 1934 or 1935. Brady was a financier who was attracted to the area by his friendship with Charles Pfizer, and his association with the Essex Fox Hounds. (Kenneth B. Schley Jr.)

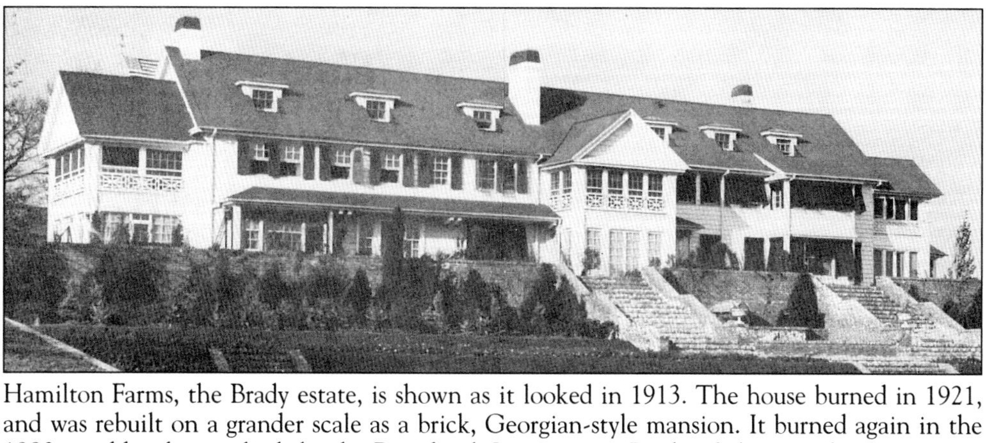

Hamilton Farms, the Brady estate, is shown as it looked in 1913. The house burned in 1921, and was rebuilt on a grander scale as a brick, Georgian-style mansion. It burned again in the 1980s, and has been rebuilt by the Beneficial Corporation. Brady's father, Anthony Nicholas Brady, left Ireland during the potato famine, and became a friend of Thomas Alva Edison. Brady founded several electric utility companies, some of which became Consolidated Edison of New York. (Beneficial Corporation.)

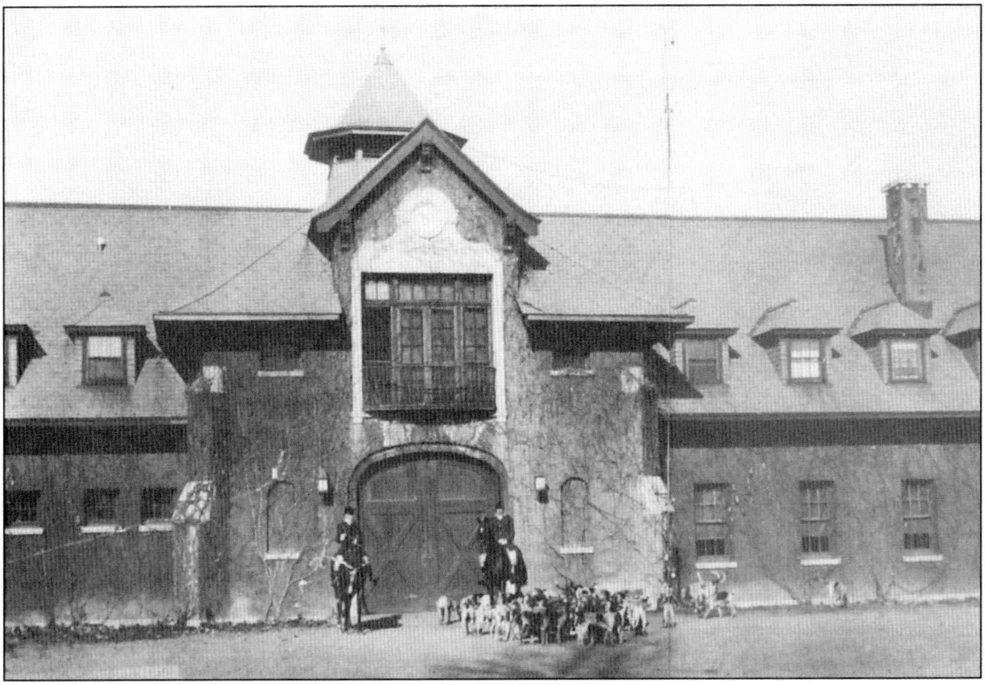

The Essex Fox Hounds in front of the Brady stable in 1923. The stable was considered the most lavish in the United States. The interior has tile walls and terrazzo floors. There are fifty-four box stalls, each 12 feet square. There are forty rooms in the stable including ten sleeping rooms for the staff, and an apartment for the manager, recreation rooms, and a trophy room with a glass floor so that Mr. Brady could inspect his carriage before it left the building. (Beneficial Corporation.)

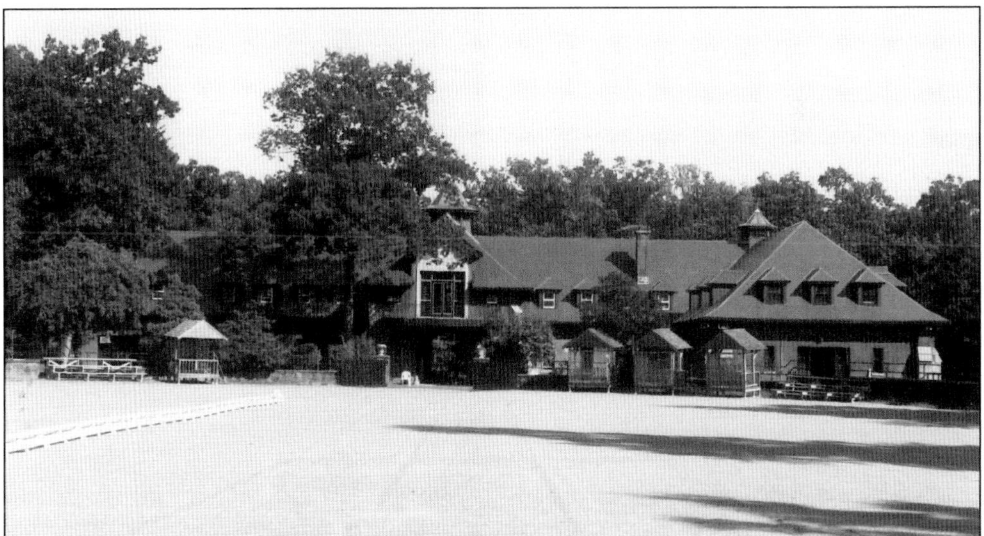

This image presents a look at the Brady stable as viewed from the practice field side. Today it is the home of the United States Equestrian Team. Hamilton Farms was named for Mr. Brady's first wife, Elizabeth J. Hamilton. (Collection of the authors.)

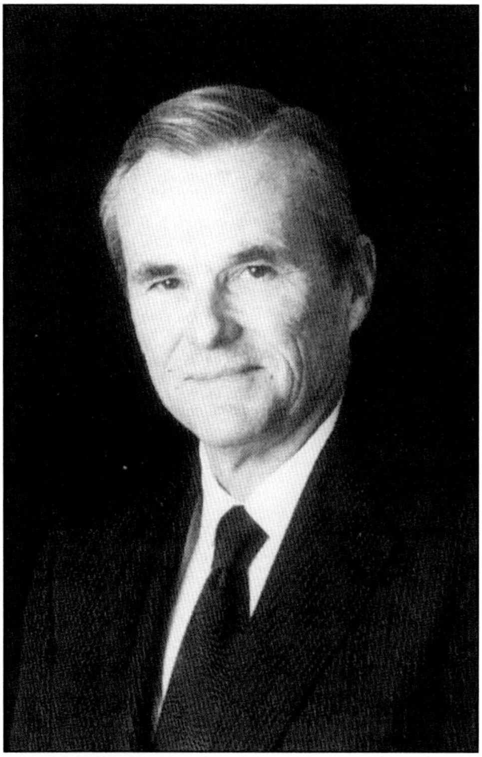

James Cox Brady's son, Nicholas Brady, became president and CEO of Dillon Read & Co. in 1971. In 1982, Governor Kean appointed him to the United States Senate to finish the term of Harrison Williams, who had resigned. In 1988 President Reagan named him secretary of the treasury, and President Bush retained him in that position. Bush and Brady were close friends. (Somerset County Library.)

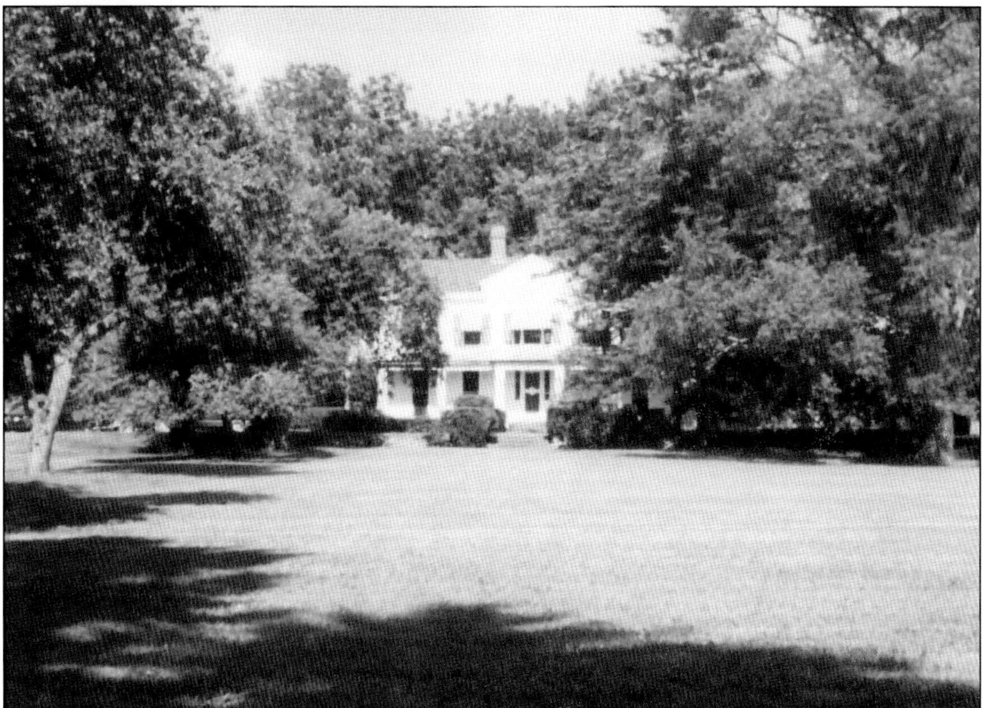

Nicholas Brady calls his estate Dogpatch. His son now lives in the house. (Collection of the authors.)

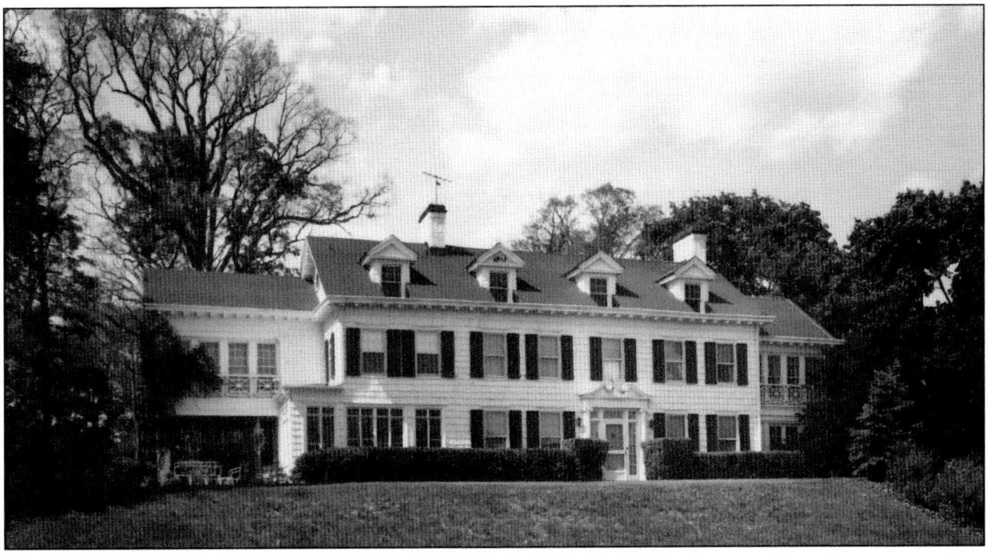

In 1915 a house that had been a colonial stagecoach stop on Lamington Road was moved to this site and enlarged to become White Oaks Farm, the seat of the master and hounds of the White Oaks Foot Beagles. The owner of the estate, Mr. Frederick W. Clucas, was the owner of the stock brokerage firm of F.W. Clucas. He was James Cox Brady's personal stock broker. He was also the grandfather of the world-renowned mezzo-soprano opera star, Frederica von Stade ("Flicka") who grew up in Oldwick. (Turpin Real Estate.)

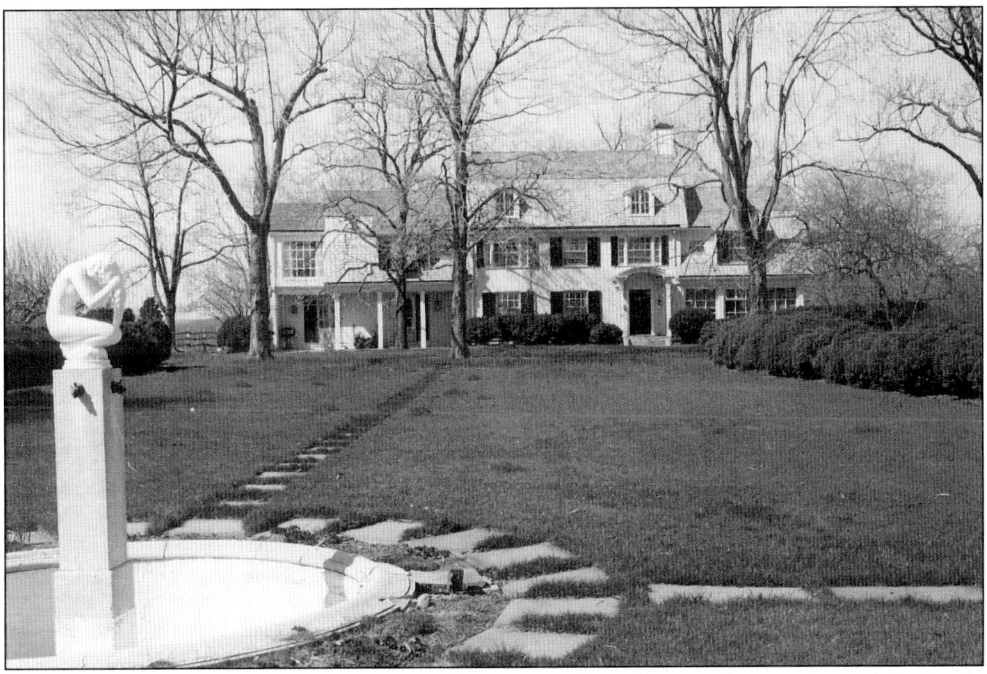

Spook Hollow Farm is the estate of Mr. William V. Griffin, who was the president of the Brady Security and Realty Company. He was also the head of the English Speaking Union, a group dedicated to the improvement of relations between the United States and Great Britain, before and during World War II. After the war, Spook Hollow played host to such notables as Field Marshal Viscount Bernard Montgomery. (Turpin Real Estate.)

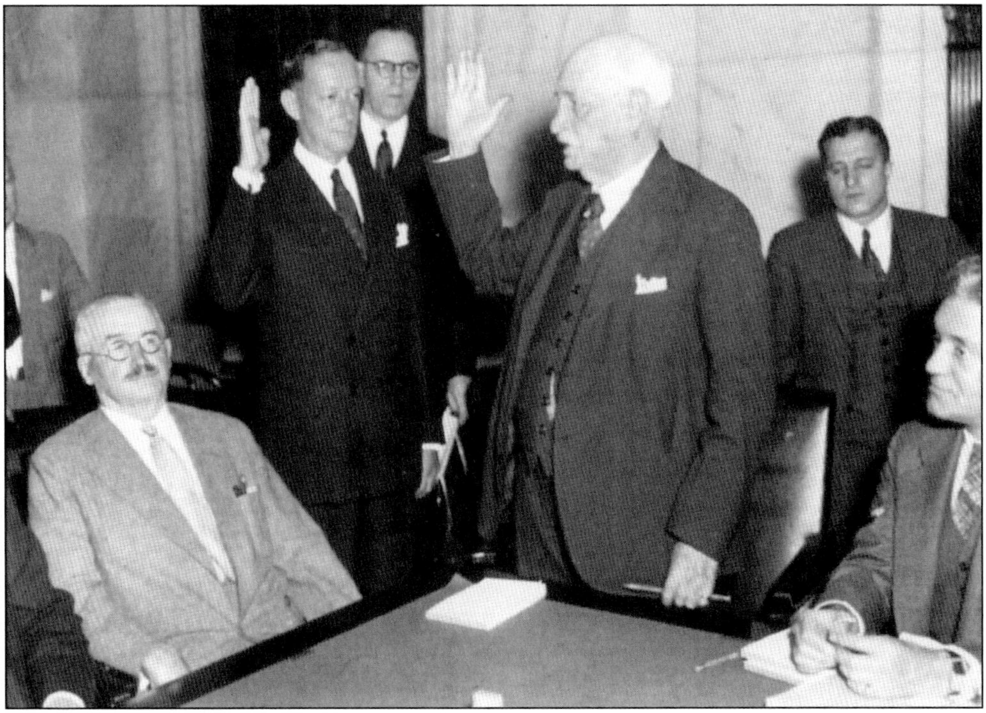

Clarence Dillon (left) and John Pierpont Morgan Jr. are sworn in before testifying to congress in 1933. Dillon's Polish immigrant father scrimped and saved so that his son could get a good education and a start in life. Clarence Dillon graduated from Harvard and joined William A. Read & Co. Soon he took over the company, renaming it Dillon Read & Co. (*Forbes*, July 13, 1987.)

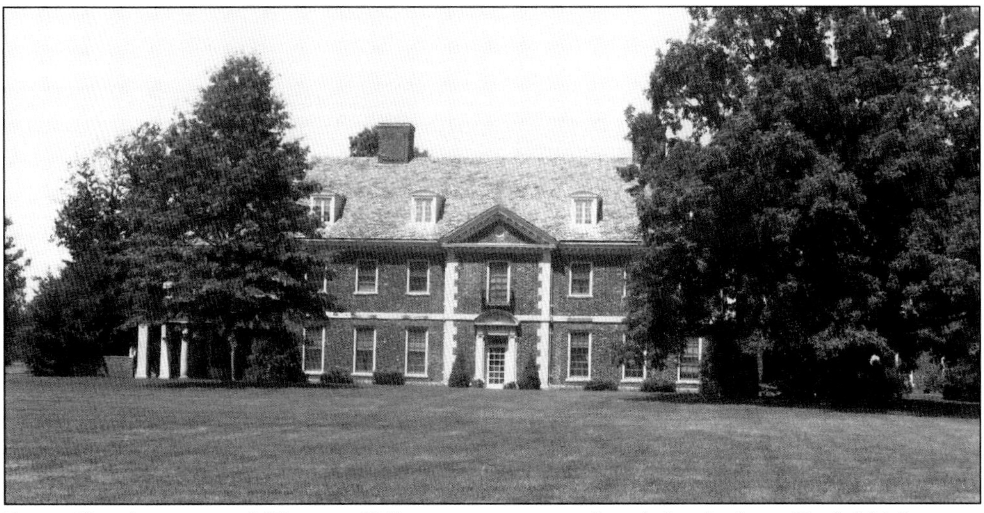

Dunwalke, the estate of Clarence Dillon,was constructed with bricks from Hatfield Manor in Virginia. In 1921 Dillon saved the Goodyear Tire & Rubber Co. from bankruptcy by issuing high-yield bonds. In 1925 he purchased Dodge for $146 million in cash, outbidding J.P. Morgan & Co. He also created National Cash Register (NCR). After his death in 1979, the estate and 126 acres were given to Princeton University for a conference center and retreat. (Princeton University.)

C. Douglas Dillon, son of Clarence Dillon, served as Chairman of Dillon Read & Co. from 1945 to 1953 when he turned the reins over to his neighbor, Nicholas Brady. He became the under secretary of state and ambassador to France under President Eisenhower, and treasury secretary under Presidents Kennedy and Johnson. (*The Somerset Messenger Gazette.*)

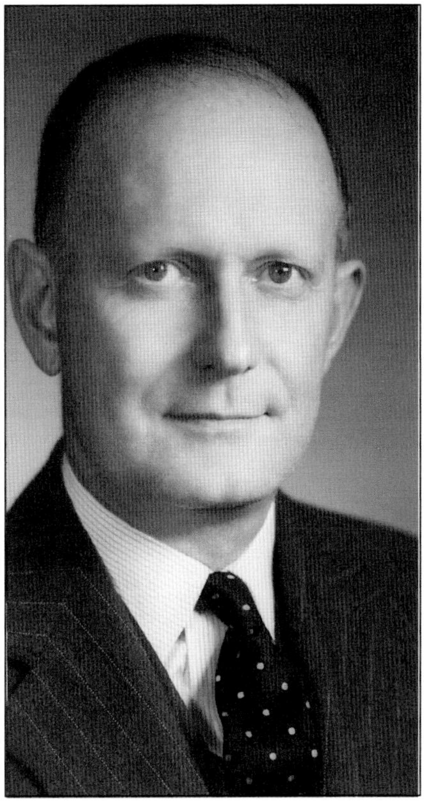

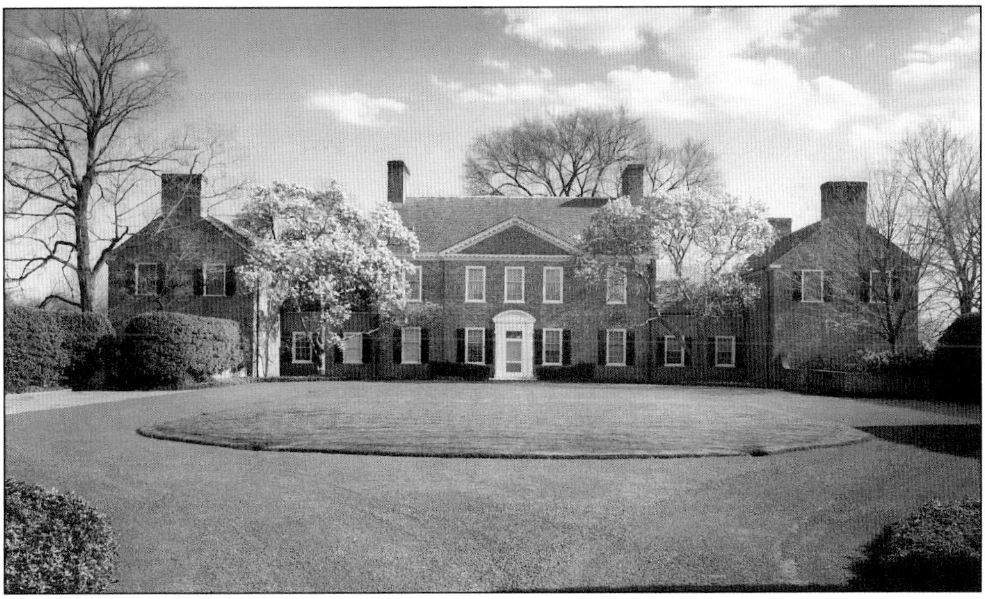

Dunwalke East, was the estate of C. Douglas Dillon. After his retirement from public service, Mr. Dillon became the chairman of the New York Metropolitan Museum of Art. He also owned the famous Haut Brion vineyards in France. His daughter, Joan, became a duchess by marrying Prince Philippe de Mouchy. Their children are Prince Robert and Princess Charlotte de Luxembourg. (Turpin Real Estate.)

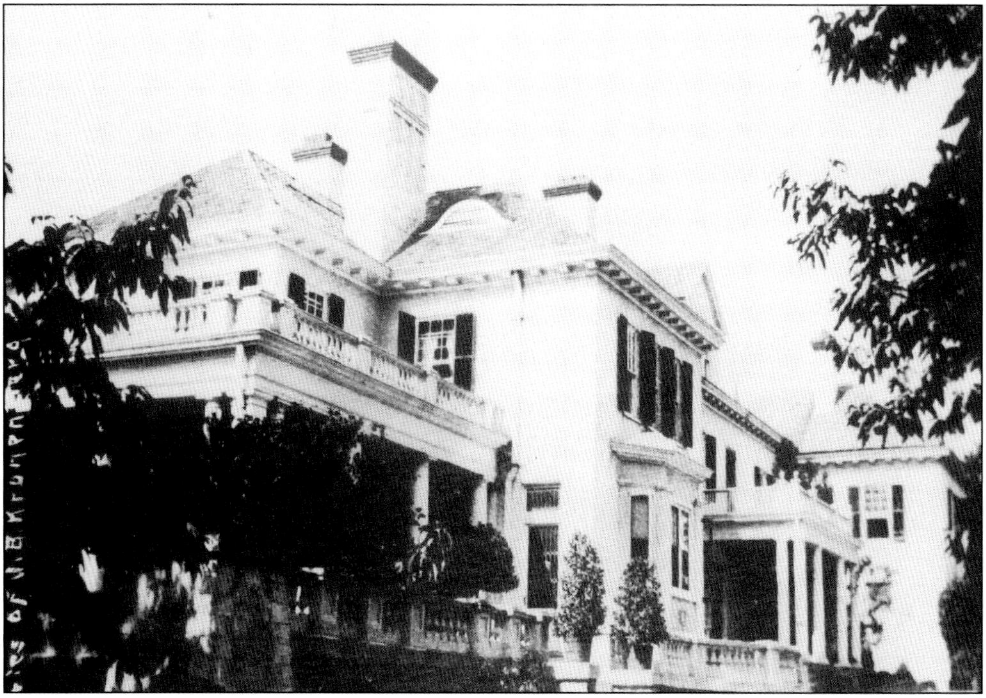

The estate of Ramsey Turnbull was designed by the famous architect, George B. Post. Mr. Ramsey Turnbull's brother, Arthur, was married to Mr. Post's daughter, Alice. (Chatfield's.)

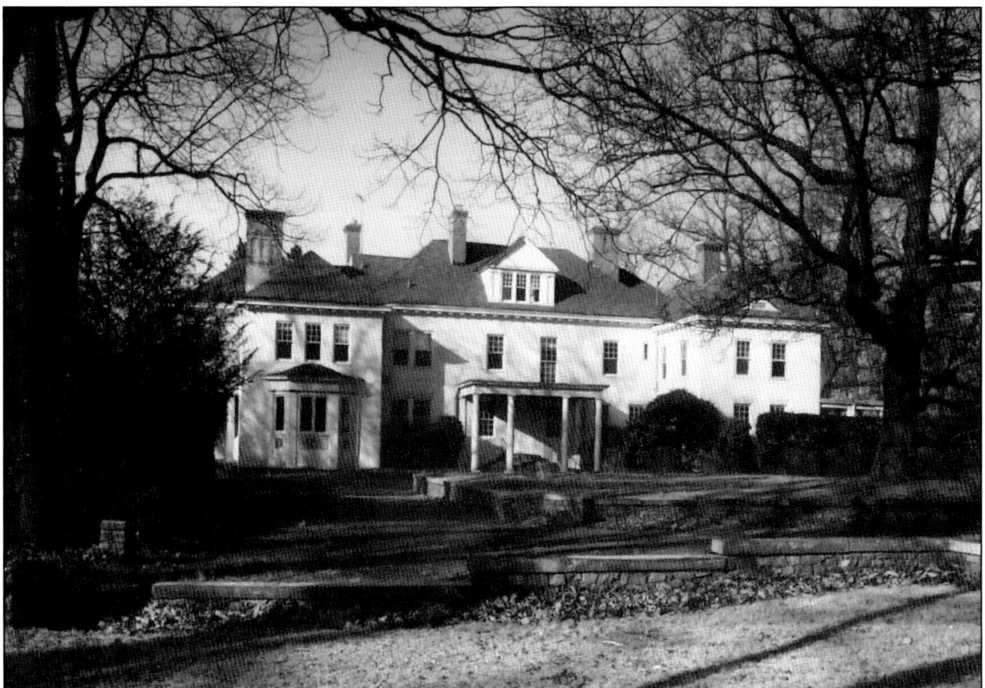

Another view of the Turnbull estate. In later years, the estate belonged to Mr. Turnbull's daughter, Helen Gardiner. She called it Appletrees. (Turpin Real Estate.)

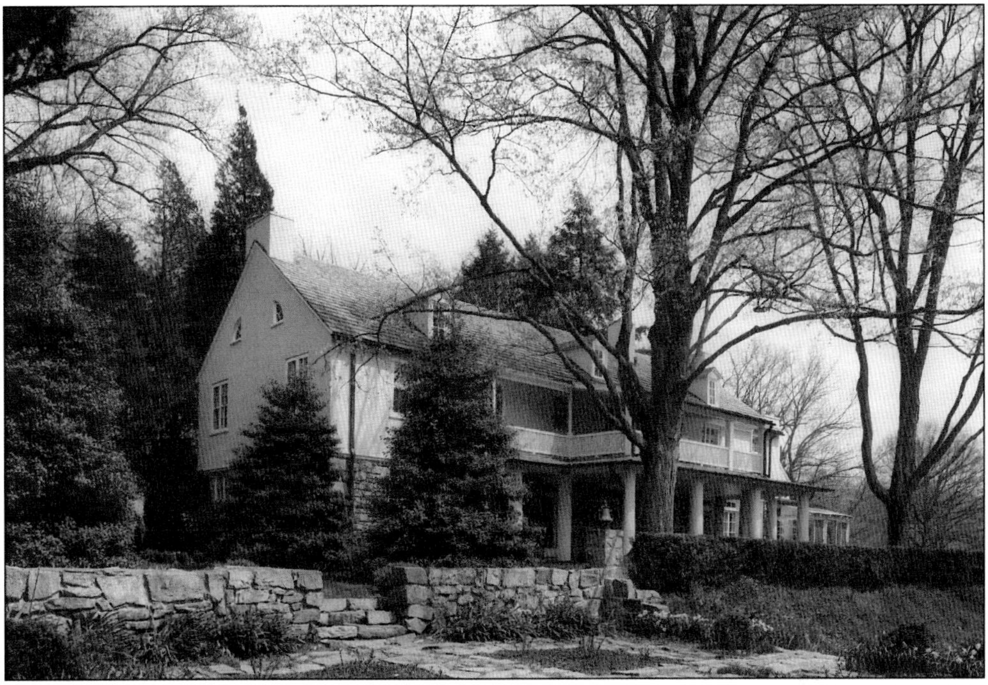

Teviot Farm is the home of Mr. William Turnbull. Through his mother, Alice Post, Mr. Turnbull is the grandson of George B. Post, the famous architect. This house was designed by the sons of George B. Post, William and Otis, who were also of the same architectural firm. (Turpin Real Estate.)

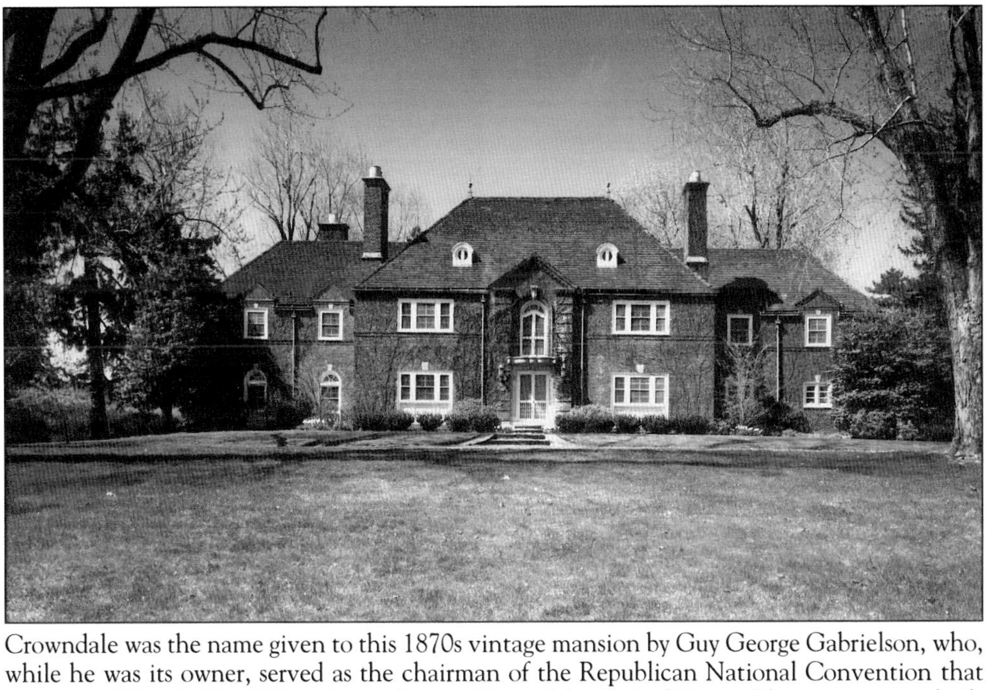

Crowndale was the name given to this 1870s vintage mansion by Guy George Gabrielson, who, while he was its owner, served as the chairman of the Republican National Convention that nominated Dwight David Eisenhower for president of the United States. The mansion was built by A.V. Stout, and later belonged to J.H. Ballantine. (Turpin Real Estate.)

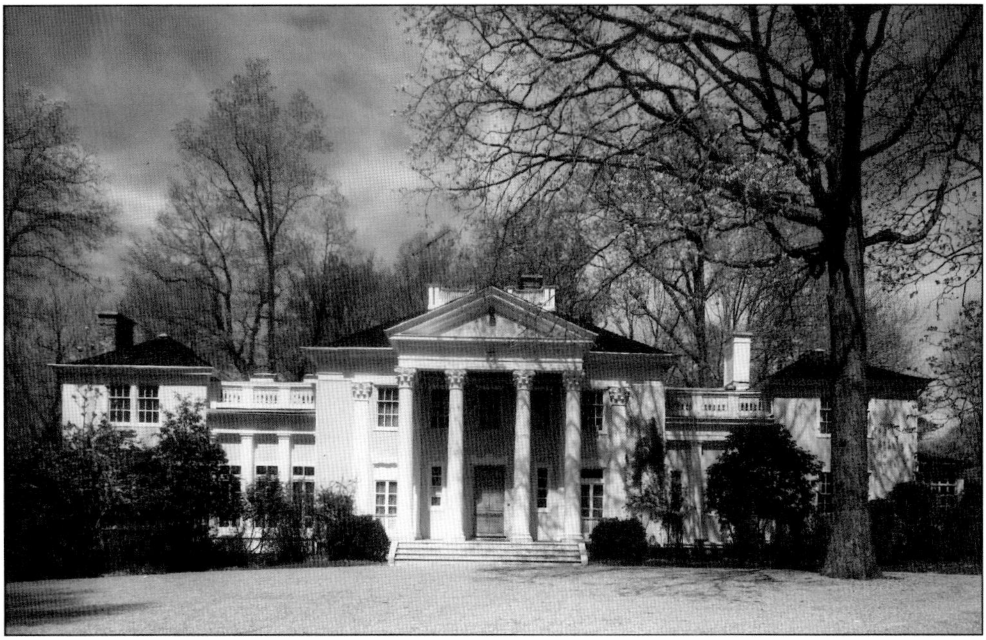

Woodedge was designed by renowned architect George B. Post, and his son, William, as a home for George B. Post Jr. It is designed in the Classical Revival style, and was completed in 1898. (Turpin Real Estate.)

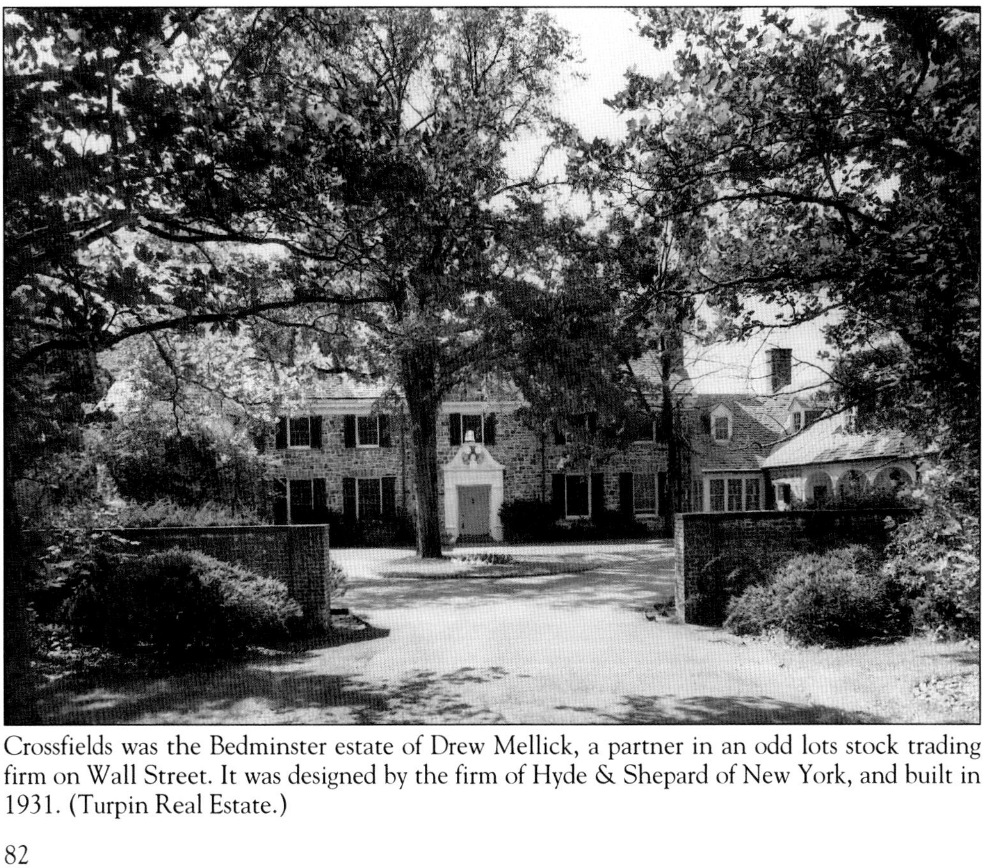

Crossfields was the Bedminster estate of Drew Mellick, a partner in an odd lots stock trading firm on Wall Street. It was designed by the firm of Hyde & Shepard of New York, and built in 1931. (Turpin Real Estate.)

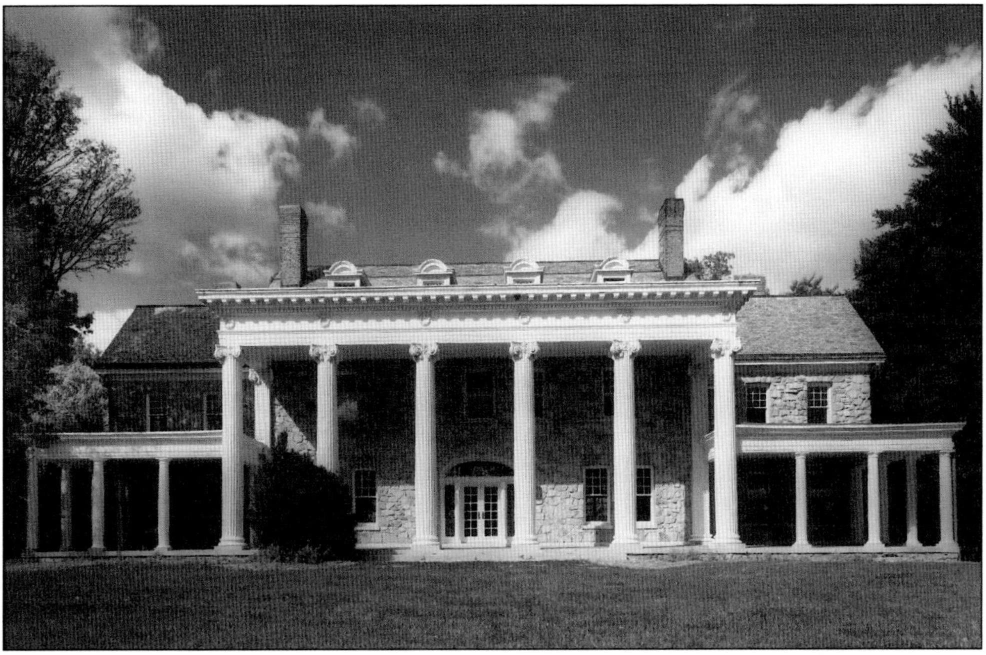

Brushwood was the estate of Louis Warren, a partner in the prestigious New York law firm of Kelly, Drye & Warren. (Turpin Real Estate.)

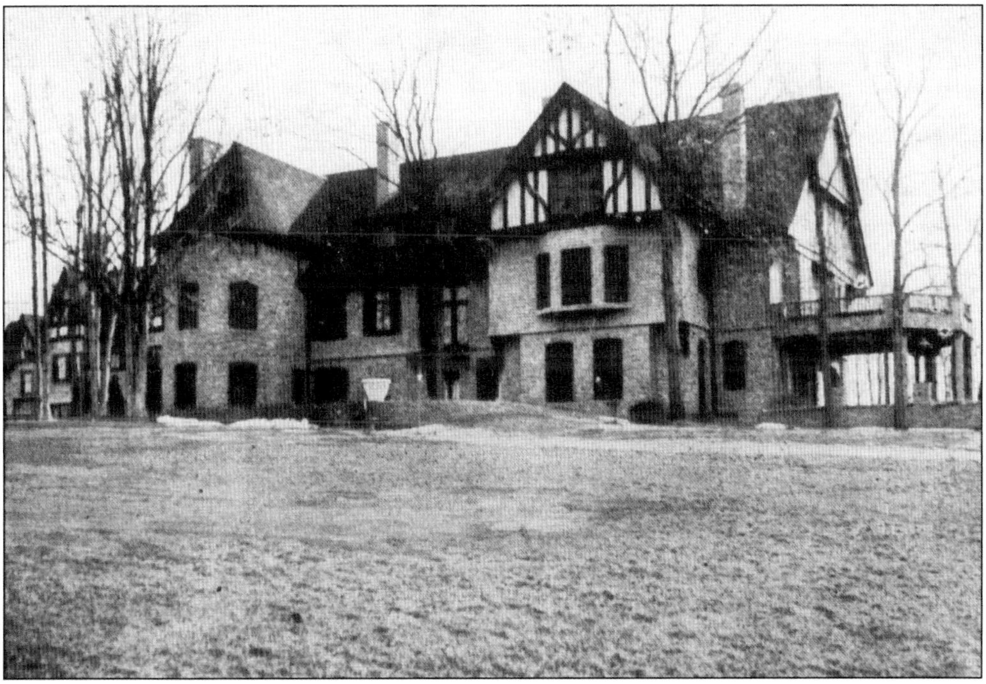

Oakdene, in Mendham, was built before the turn of the century by Brooklyn lawyer Charles W. Ide. It was later acquired and enlarged by William S. Pyle of New York. His daughter, Mary, married the famous violinist, Albert Spalding, in 1919. Deep in the forest behind the house stands the Little Church in the Wildwood, a private stone chapel built by Edward Balbach in 1908. (Bernardsville Public Library Local History Collection.)

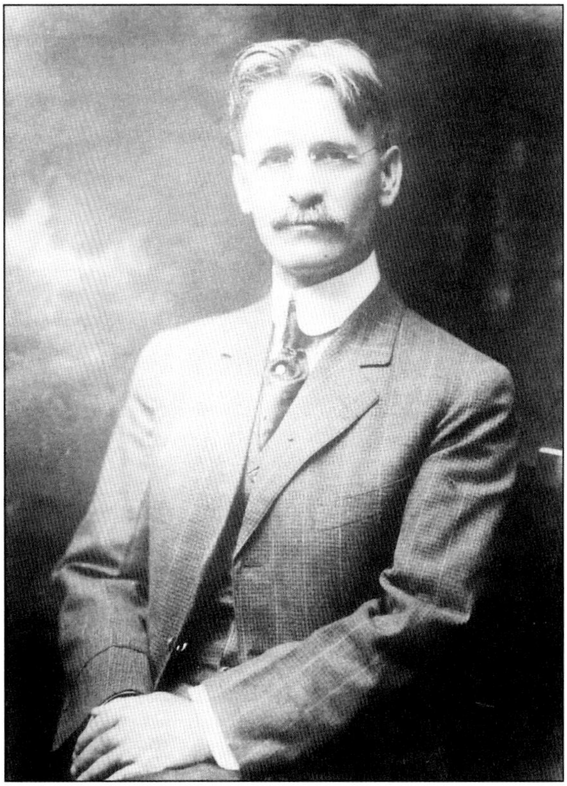

Samuel S. Childs was the founder of the Childs Restaurant chain. Locally, he turned a 1767 colonial grain barn into The Old Mill Inn, opened in 1930, and now called the Grain House Restaurant. He was elected to the New Jersey State Senate as a Democrat in 1902. (Bernardsville High School Library.)

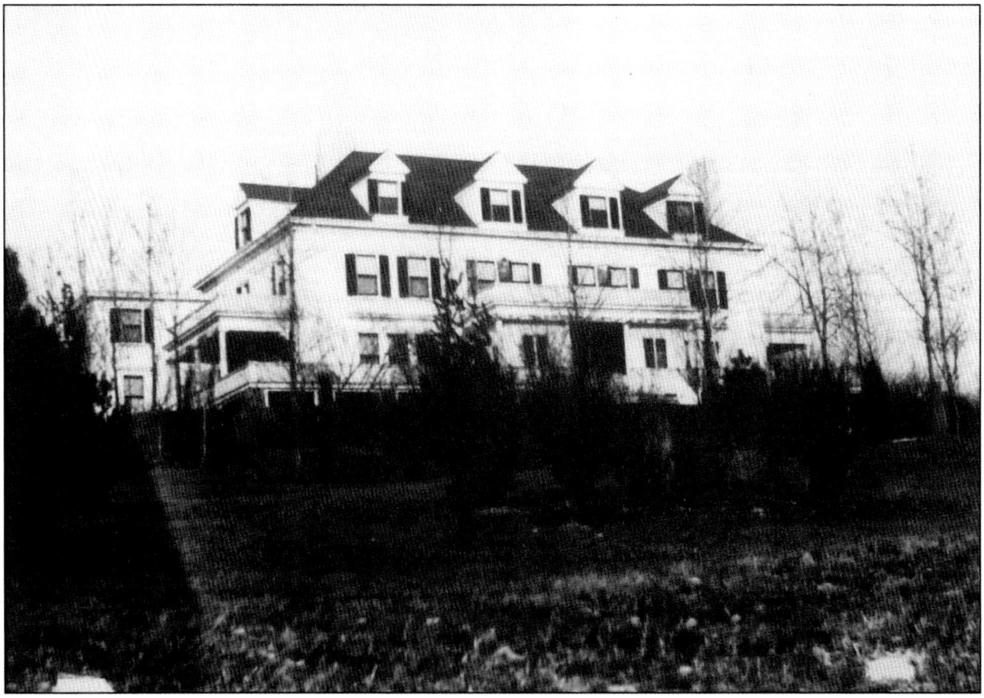

Shannon Lodge, the estate built by restaurateur Samuel S. Childs. Today the home belongs to the Fellowship Deaconry. (Bernardsville Public Library Local History Collection.)

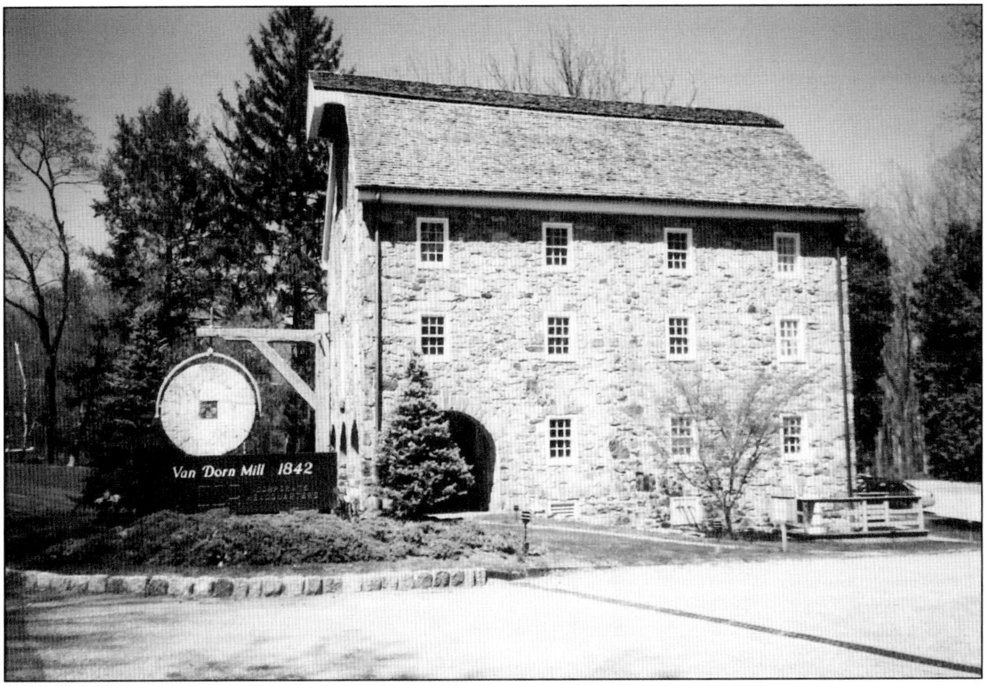

Samuel S. Childs also restored the stone Ferdinand Van Dorn mill which was built in 1842 on the site of the original colonial grist mill. The mill was more recently remodeled to become the offices of the Haines, Lundberg and Waehler architectural firm. (Turpin Real Estate.)

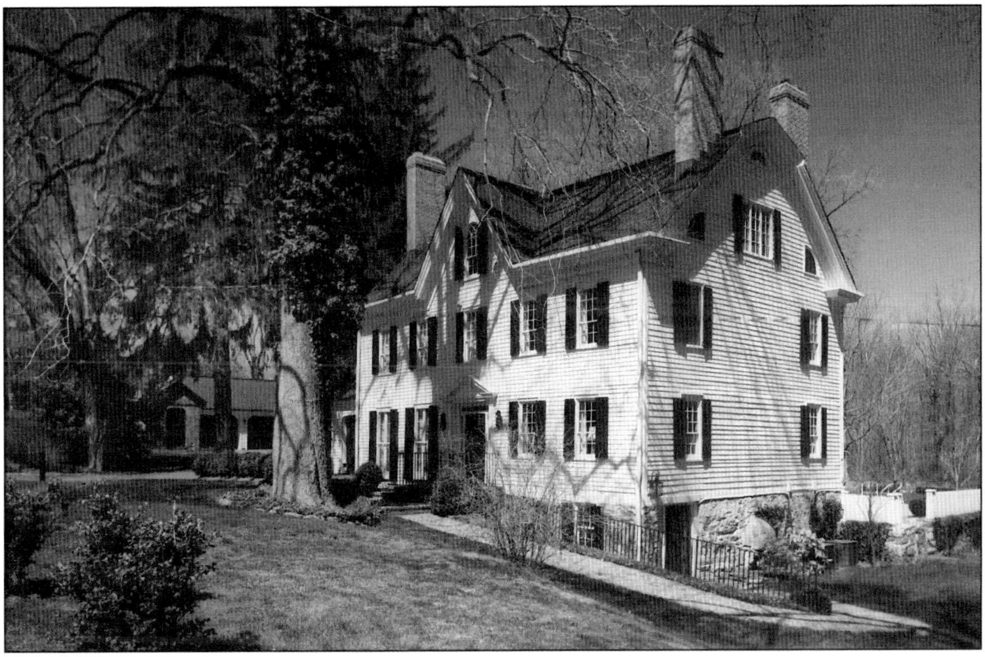

Parts of the Van Dorn homestead date from 1762. Van Dorn, who operated the mill next door, supplied flour for the Continental Army during the 1779–80 winter encampment. Ten thousand of General Washington's soldiers spent the coldest winter of the Revolution at nearby Jockey Hollow. (Turpin Real Estate.)

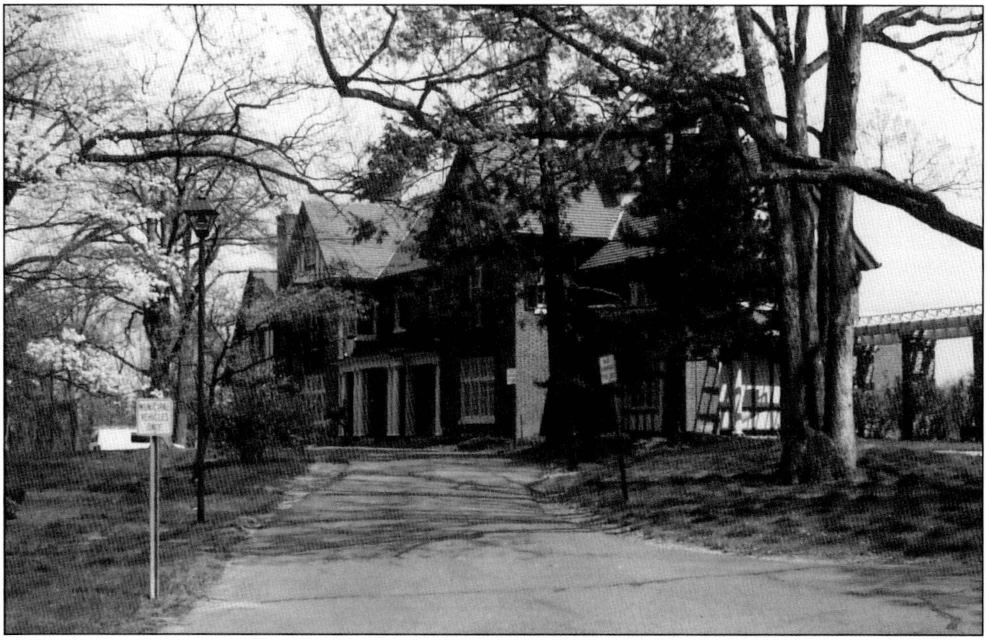

Cedar Hill, the John Jacob Astor Jr. estate, was built by Samuel Owen, a pharmaceutical manufacturer in 1913. The twenty-room estate was purchased by Mr. Astor in 1950. Today it serves as the Bernards Township Municipal Building. The house and grounds are open to the public. (Collection of the authors.)

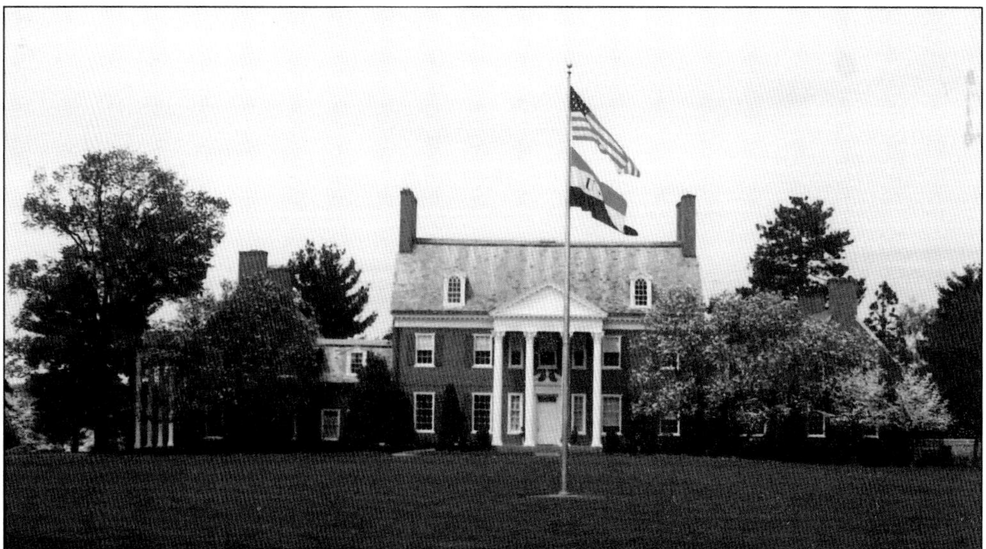

This mansion was designed by John Russell Pope, who also designed the Jefferson Memorial and the National Gallery in Washington, D.C. It was built by Thomas Frothingham in 1919, and later sold to John Sloane. Mr. Sloane's daughter, Grace, married Cyrus Vance who served as secretary of the Army, and later as secretary of state under President Jimmy Carter. The mansion now belongs to the U.S. Golf Association, and is open to the public. Mr. and Mrs. Vance live next door in the carriage house of the estate, which has now been converted into a home. (Collection of the authors.)

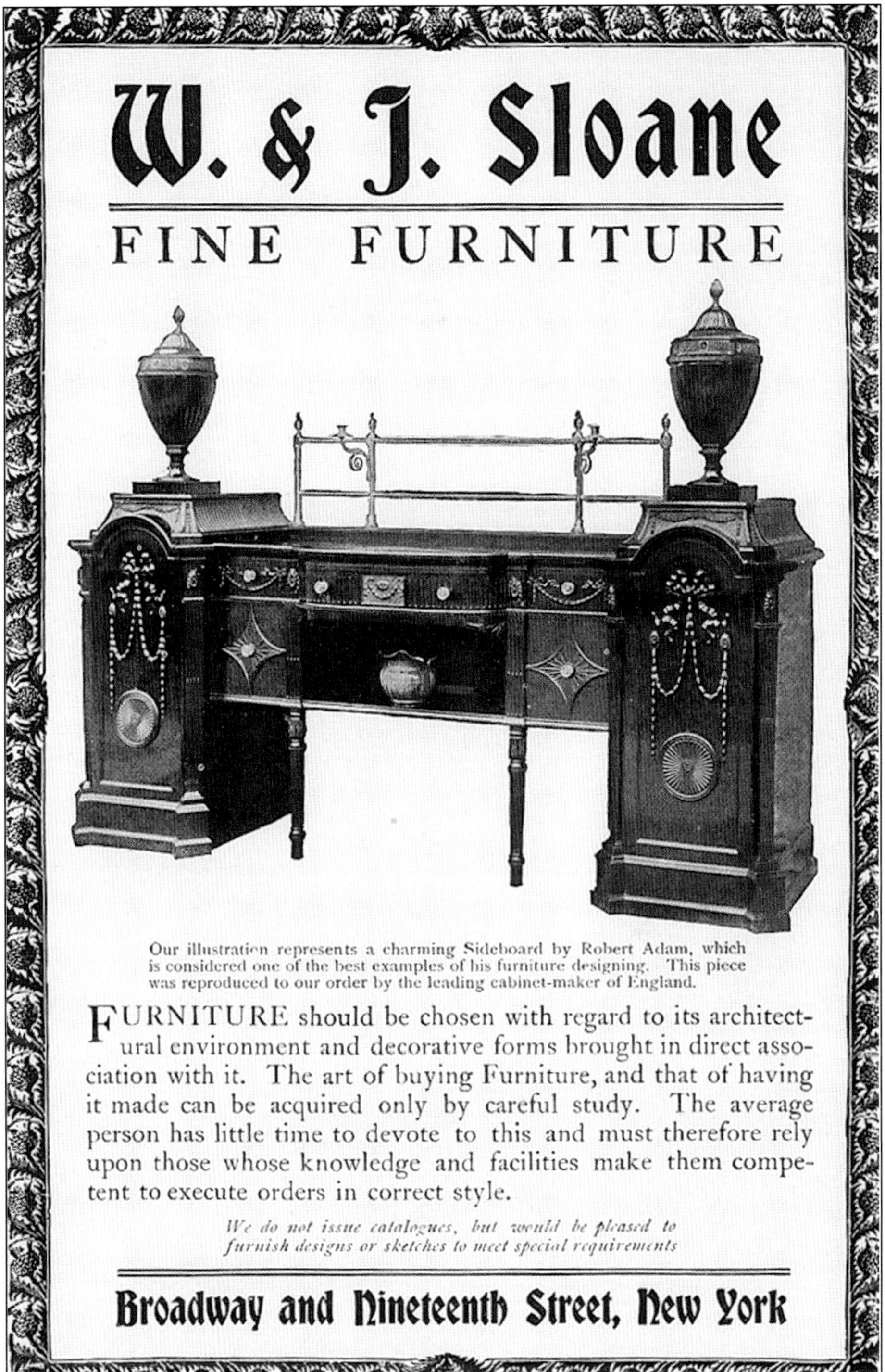

John Sloane was the founder of the W. & J. Sloane furniture store on 5th Avenue in New York City. This advertisement for the store dates from 1902. (*Country Life in America* magazine, 1902.)

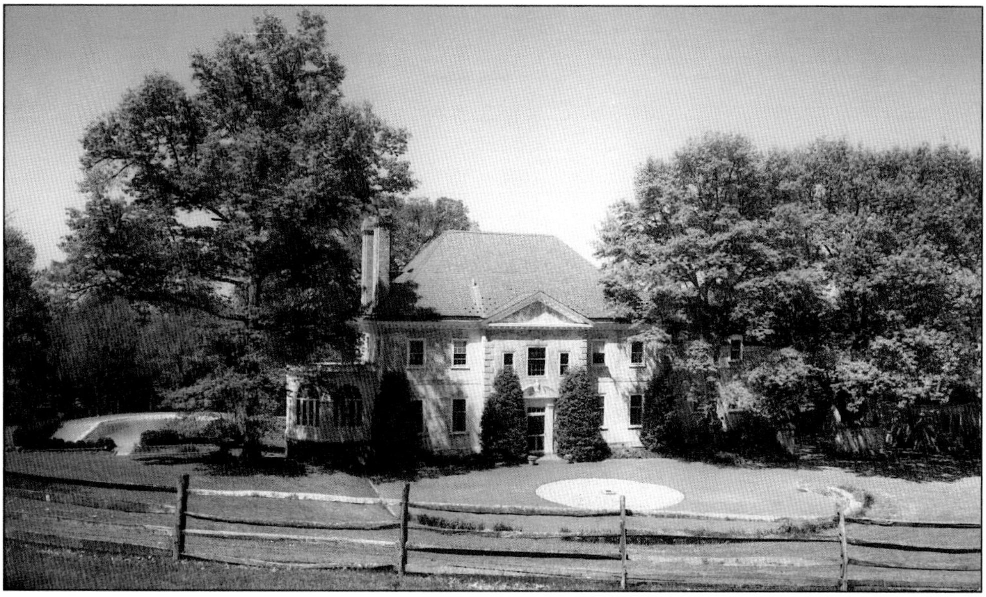

This classic Georgian manor house, known as Winton, was designed by the architect John Sanford Shanley and built about 1936 for the Bernard Shanley family. Mr. Bernard M. Shanley III was a key figure in securing the Republican presidential nomination for Dwight Eisenhower in 1952. Thereafter Mr. Shanley served as special counsel and deputy chief of staff in the Eisenhower administration. Mr. Shanley also became the northeast regional chairman of the Republican National Committee. (Turpin Real Estate.)

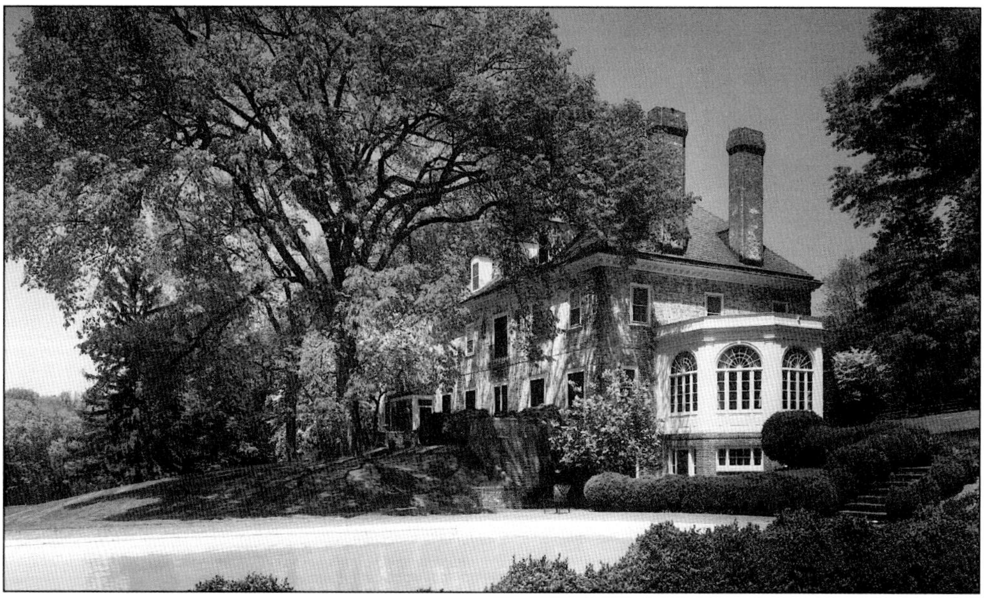

Mr. Shanley's grandfather helped to build the Public Service Electric and Gas Company. His great-great-great-aunt was Saint Elizabeth Seton. Mr. Shanley himself was honored by the Pope, and became a Knight of St. Gregory. While attending Columbia University, his roommate was Lou Gehrig. Mr. Shanley was the founder of the Shanley and Fisher law firm. For fifteen years he was the owner of the Roxiticus Golf Club, which adjoins the rear of his Winton estate. (Turpin Real Estate.)

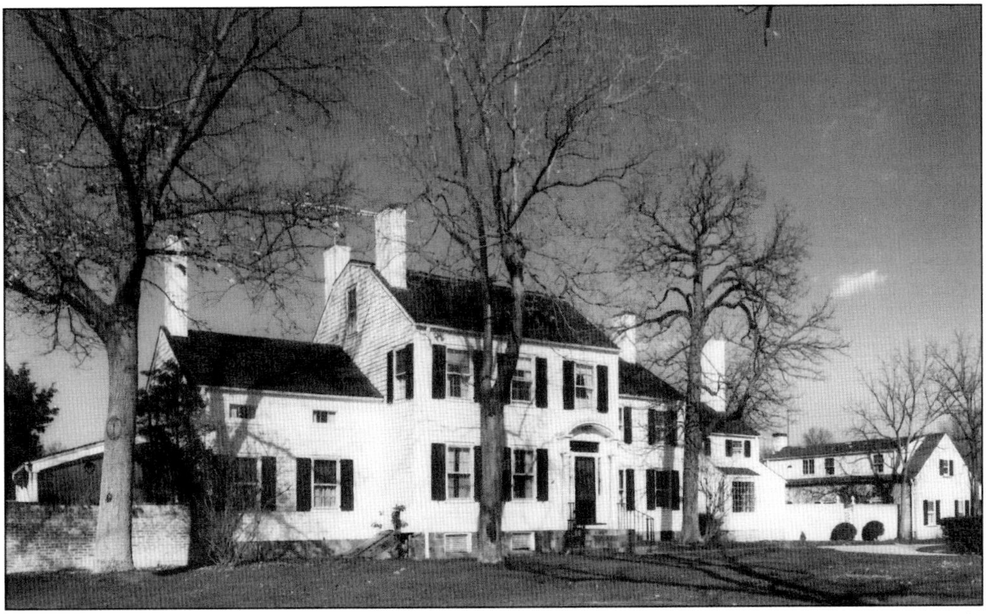

Hickory Corner, is the estate of Jacqueline Mars, heiress to one-fourth of the Mars candy fortune. The company was founded in 1911 by her grandparents, Frank and Ethel Mars. The first big success was the Milky Way bar, suggested by Jacqueline's father because of his fondness for malted milk. He also is credited with developing M&Ms after seeing candy-coated chocolate drops during the Spanish Civil War. (Turpin Real Estate.)

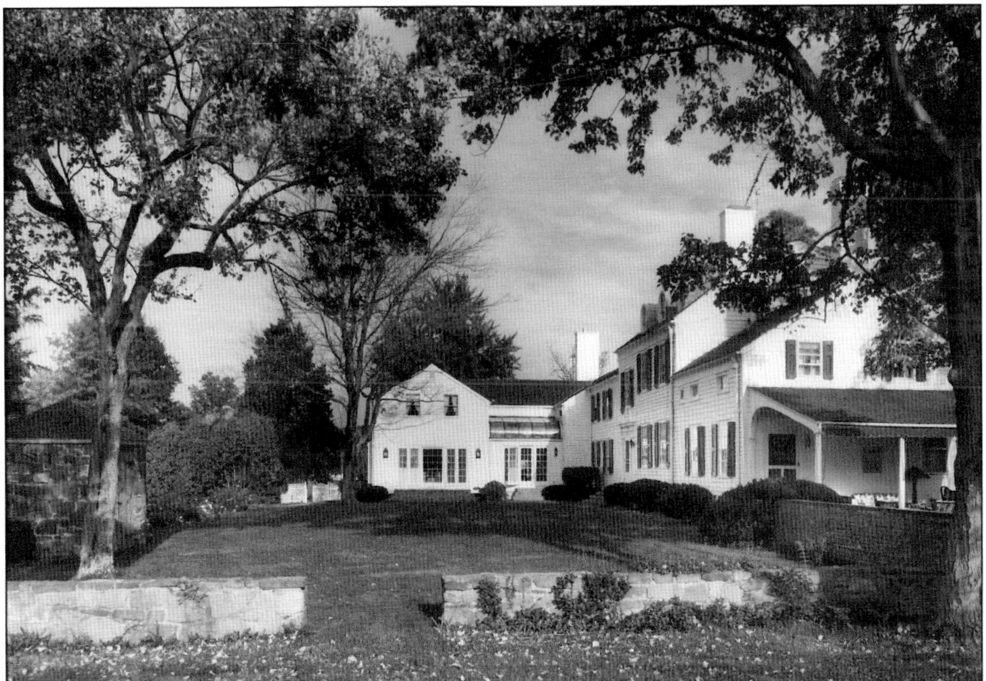

Built in 1815 as a country retreat, Hickory Corner is seen here from the rear. Jacqueline Mars' interest in Mars, Inc. has been estimated to be worth \$3 billion, which could make her the richest woman in the world. (Turpin Real Estate.)

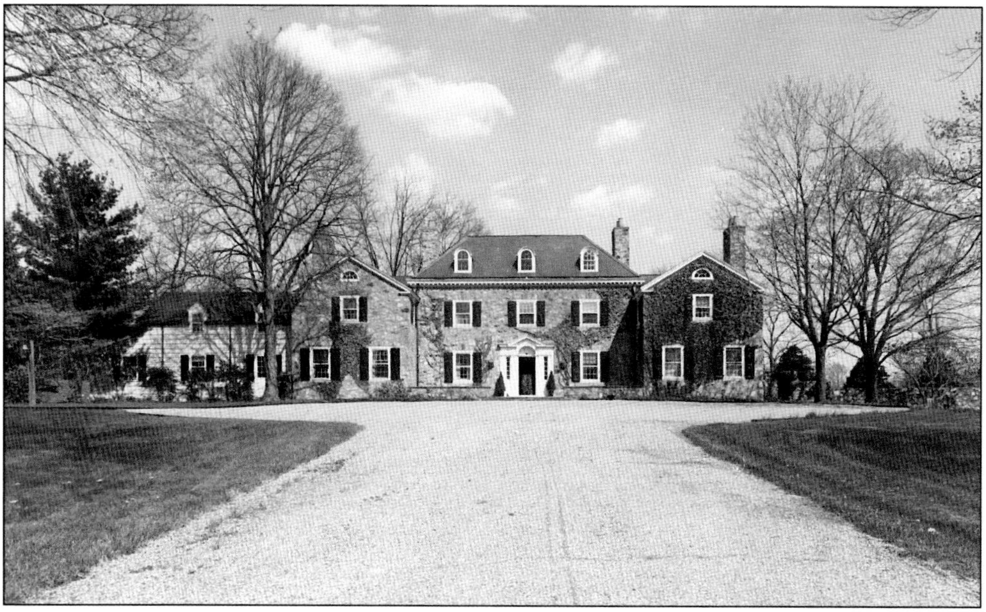

Designed by Henry R. Sedgewick, and built between 1928 and 1932, this estate on Cowperthwaite Road was called Middlebrook by its owner, Mr. Harold Fowler. A member of the Essex Hunt Club, Mr. Fowler hosted the hunts of the Essex Fox Hounds on many occasions, including Thanksgiving day 1932. Today the property is called Stone Bridge Farm. (Turpin Real Estate.)

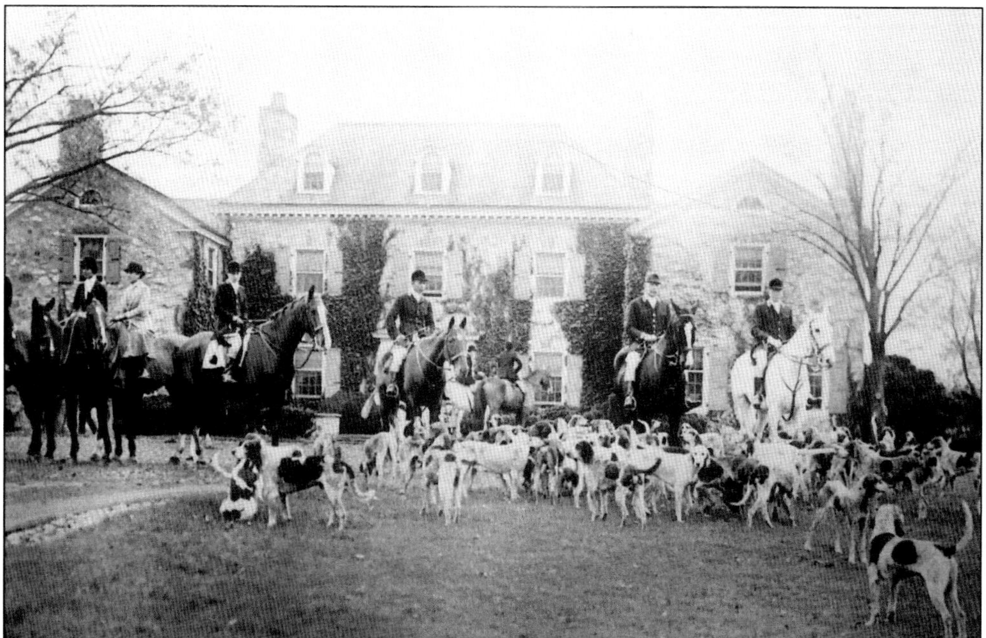

The Essex Fox Hounds were captured on film at the Fowler's Middlebrook Farm in November 1932. From the left, the people are: Betty Thompson, Vera (Mrs. Charles) Scribner, Virginia Brice, Miles Valentine, George Brice (the huntsman), and Ken Schley (Master of the Essex Fox Hounds). (Kenneth B. Schley Jr.)

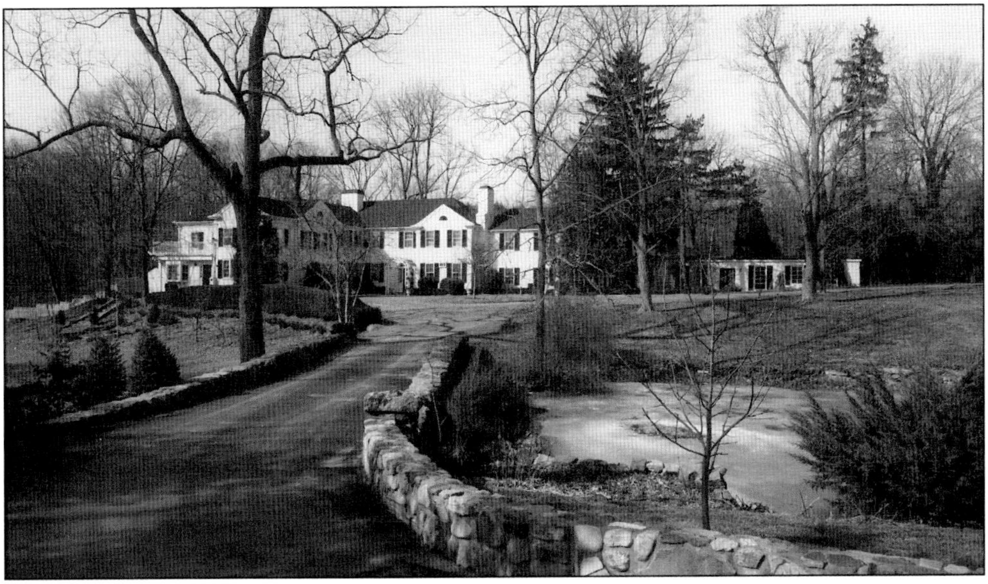

Merriewold West was the name given to this estate by its former owner, Mary Lea Johnson D'Arc. Mary Lea Johnson is the daughter of Seward Johnson, and the granddaughter of Robert Wood Johnson, the founder of Johnson & Johnson. She lived in this house during her marriage to psychiatrist Victor D'Arc. She named the estate after Merriewold, the house she grew up in, across the river from Johnson & Johnson headquarters in New Brunswick. Today it is called Rheinland Farm. (Turpin Real Estate.)

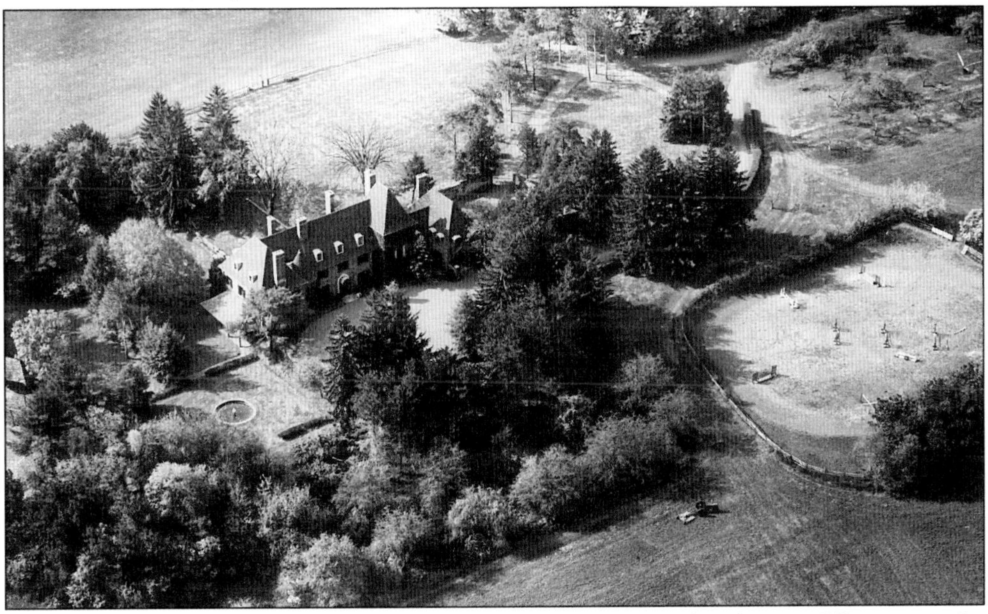

Designed by Musgrove Hyde and constructed in 1930 of topaz-colored stone, Ellistan was the residence of Frank Johnson, partner of M.W. Kellogg, who hired Percival "Dobie" Keith to design the Oak Ridge Project. The property is now owned by Henry Slack, the grandson of Drew Mellick. Mr. Slack married the daughter of Harry Oppenheimer, chairman of De Beers Consolidated Mines, Ltd., and head of the London Central Selling Organization of the diamond cartel. (Turpin Real Estate.)

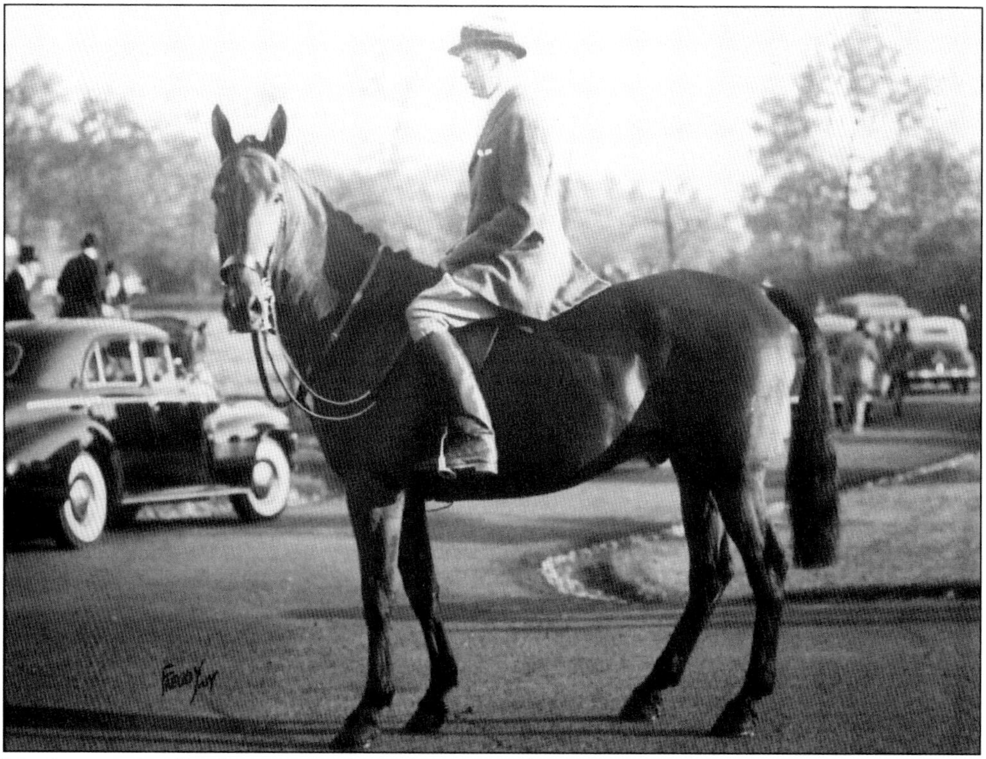

Mr. Screven Lorillard, great-grandson of Pierre Lorillard, the founder of the P. Lorillard Tobacco Company, is seen here at an event of the Essex Hunt Club in the early 1940s. Mr. Screven Lorillard served in the Army Air Corps during World War II. and later, on the Bedminster Township Committee and Planning Board. (Masters of the Essex Fox Hounds.)

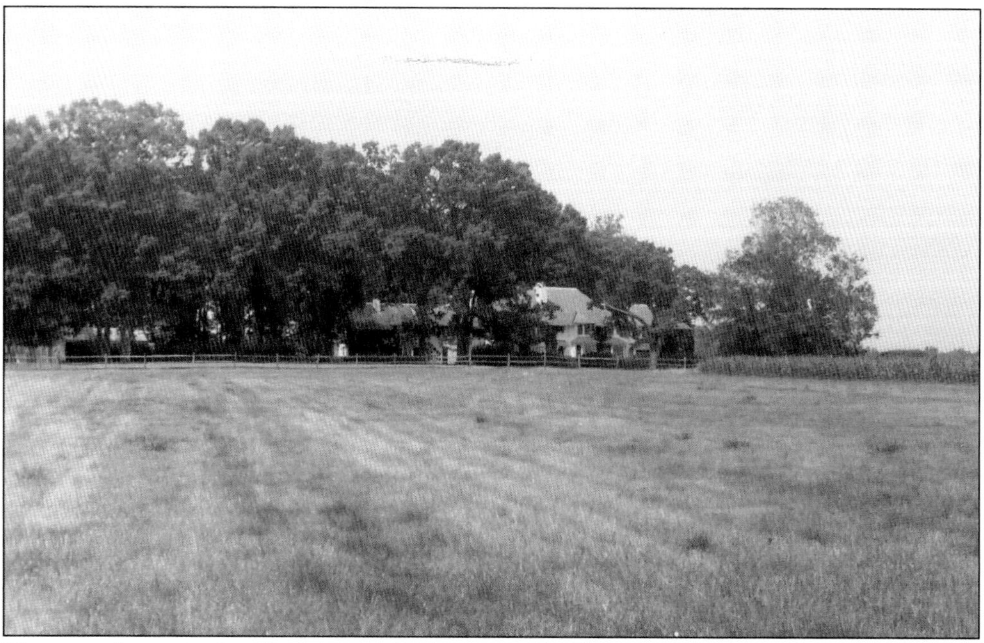

This view shows the Lorillard farm in Bedminster. The farm is called Bindon Farm.

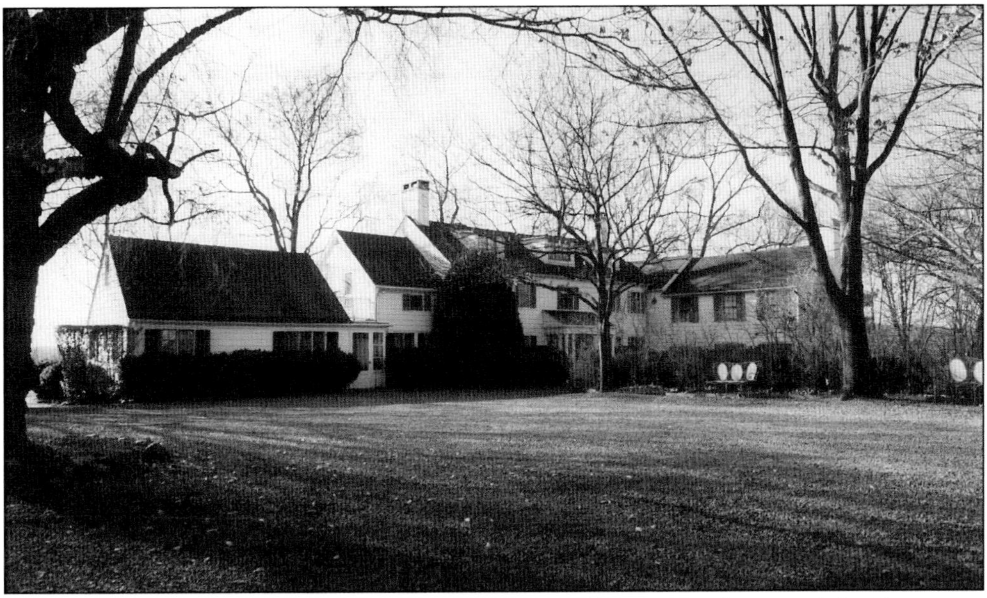

Adjacent to the Lorillard's Bindon Farm, is Peapacton Farm, once the seat of the Pierrepont family. Mr. John Pierrepont was a direct descendant of Sir Robert de Pierrepont, who was a companion-in-arms of William the Conqueror in 1066; the Reverend James Pierrepont, one of the founders of Yale University; and John Jay, the first chief justice of the U.S. Supreme Court. He is also related to J. Pierpont Morgan, and the Earl of Manvers. (Turpin Real Estate.)

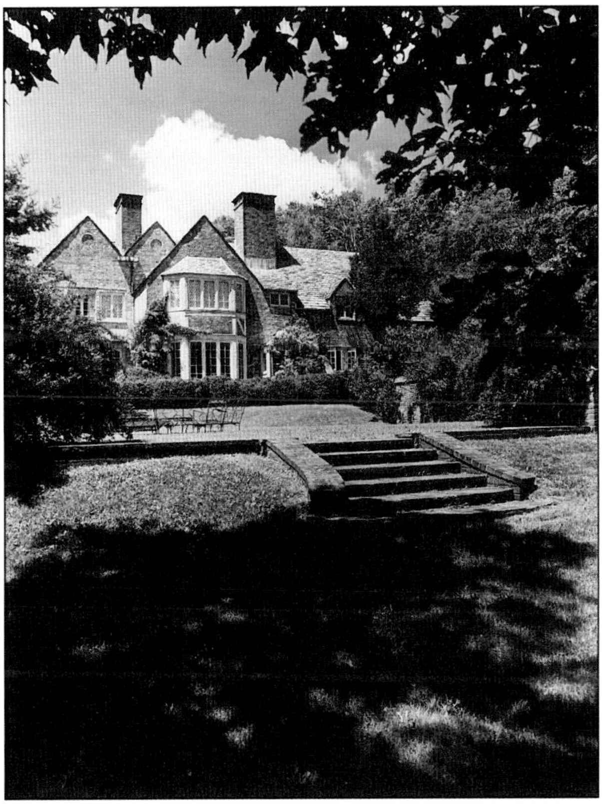

Balcarres, on the Bernardsville mountain, was the estate of Mrs. R. Burnham Moffat, the sister of Rutherford Stuyvesant Pierrepont, and aunt of John Pierrepont, formerly of Bedminster. She is related to J. Pierpont Morgan, and the Earl of Manvers. Designed as a Scottish manor house, by the firm of Godwin-Thompson & Patterson, the mansion was built in 1929. (Turpin Real Estate.)

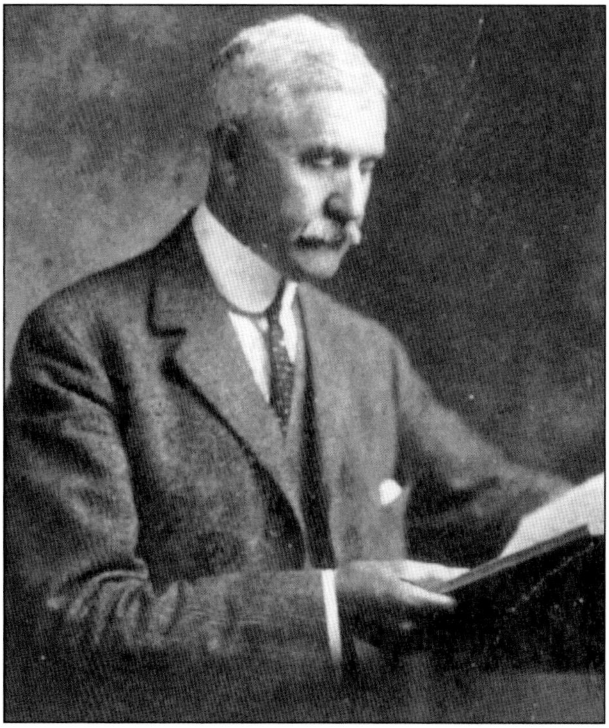

Richard Vliet Lindabury, esq., nationally known corporate lawyer and head of the Newark law firm of Lindabury, Depue & Faulks, was an associate of John D. Rockefeller and J. Pierpont Morgan. He was a local boy who made good. He was born and raised in Peapack and studied law under Alvah Clark in Somerville. He represented and counseled Metropolitan & Prudential Life Insurance Co., U.S. Steel, J.P. Morgan, Standard Oil Co. of N.J., Central Railroad of N.J., International Harvester Co., Bethlehem Steel, American Sugar Refining Co., and the Pennsylvania Railroad. (Branchburg Historical Society.)

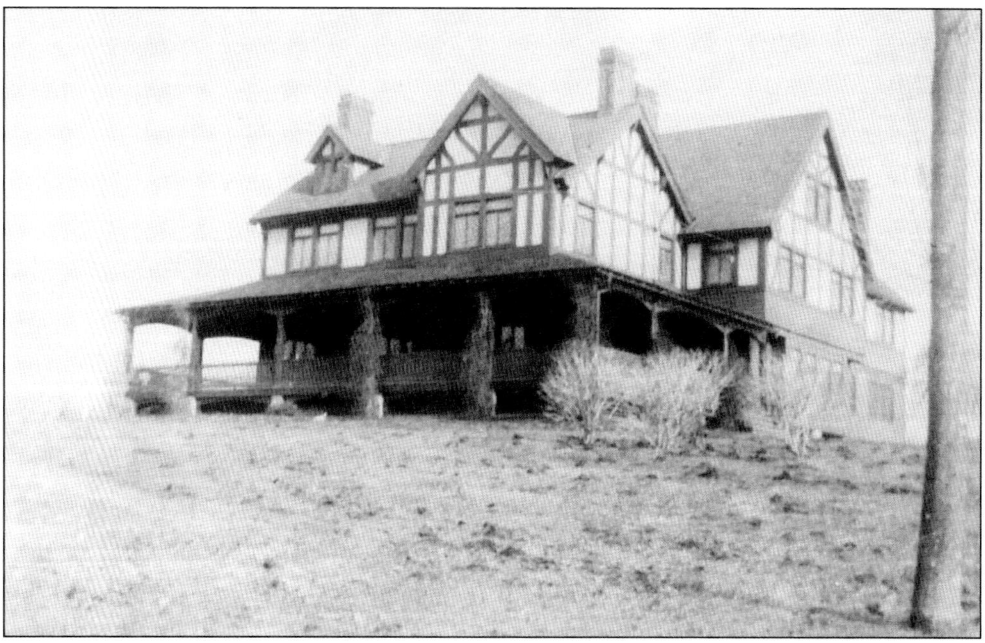

Mr. Lindabury's estate was called Meadowbrook Farm, a name by which it is still known. He bought the property about 1892, and at its height it encompassed a thousand acres. There he raised Guernsey cattle, Hampshiredown sheep, Berkshire pigs, and Plymouth Rock chickens. Having grown up on a farm, he was always able to keep his operation profitable. It was his custom to oversee his farm on horseback before breakfast. He died in 1925 at the age of seventy-four as the result of falling from his horse. (The *Bernardsville News*.)

Two

Leisure Activities

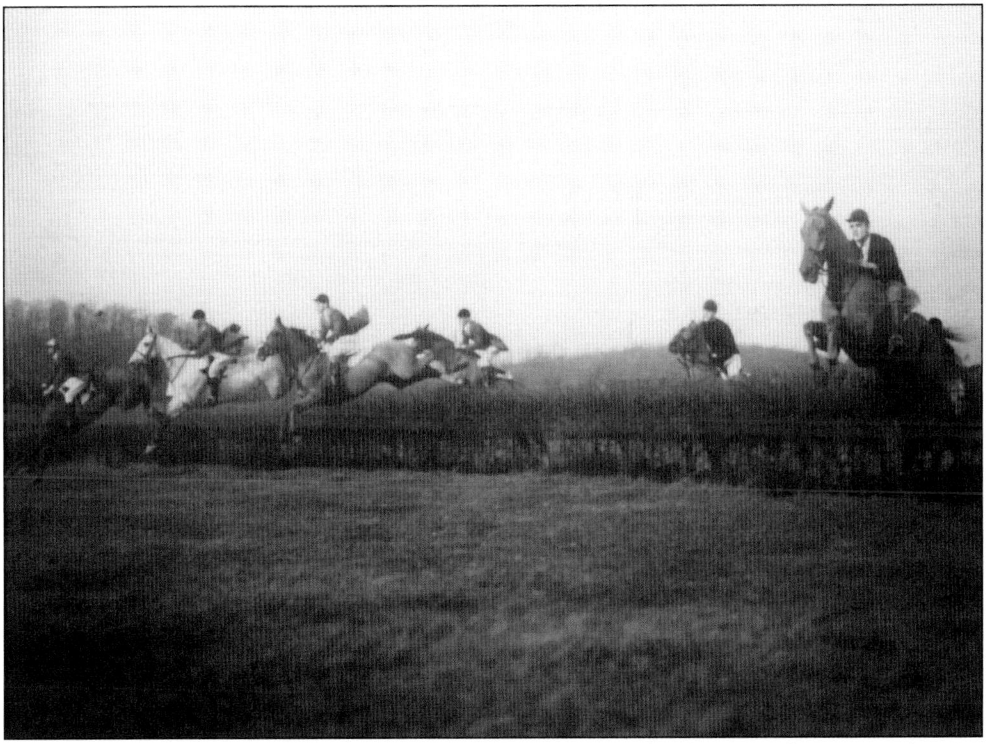

The first running of the Charles Pfizer Cup took place on Thanksgiving day, November 30, 1933. The riders are as follows, from the left: Mr. J.L. Winston on Dromore, Mr. F.L.Winston on Mr. G.M.Carnochan's Mischief, Mr. James Cox Brady on Lady's Brougham, Mr. F.S. Mosley Jr. on Red Amber, Mr. O.L.Winston on Mr. J.L.Winston's Happy, and Mr. R. Schley Jr. on Mr. James Cox Brady's Speed Limit. (Masters of the Essex Fox Hounds.)

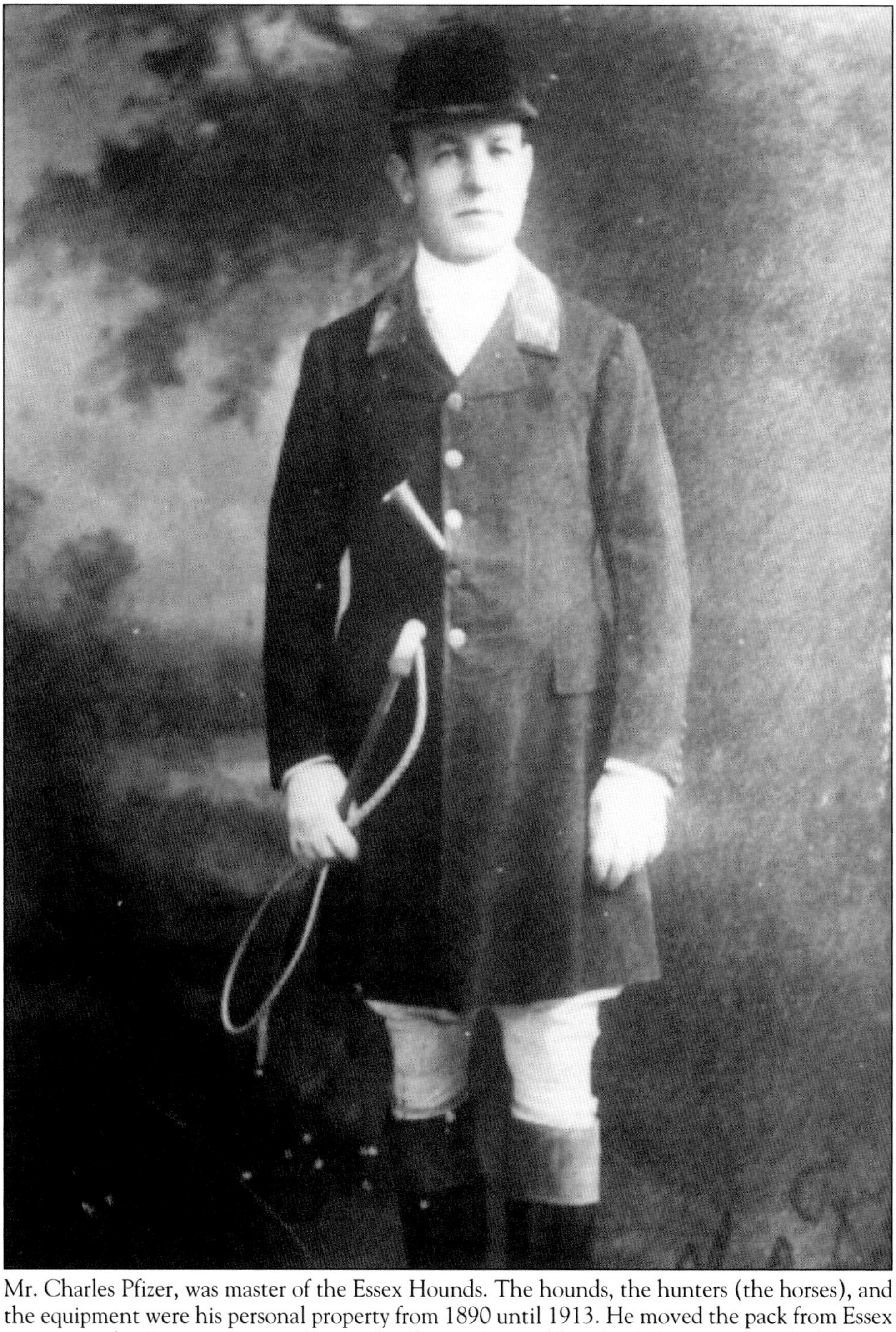

Mr. Charles Pfizer, was master of the Essex Hounds. The hounds, the hunters (the horses), and the equipment were his personal property from 1890 until 1913. He moved the pack from Essex County to the Seney cottage in Bernardsville in 1892 and bought 200 acres west of Gladstone the following summer. All those who hunted with the Essex Hounds during this period, were the guests of Mr. Pfizer. (Masters of the Essex Fox Hounds.)

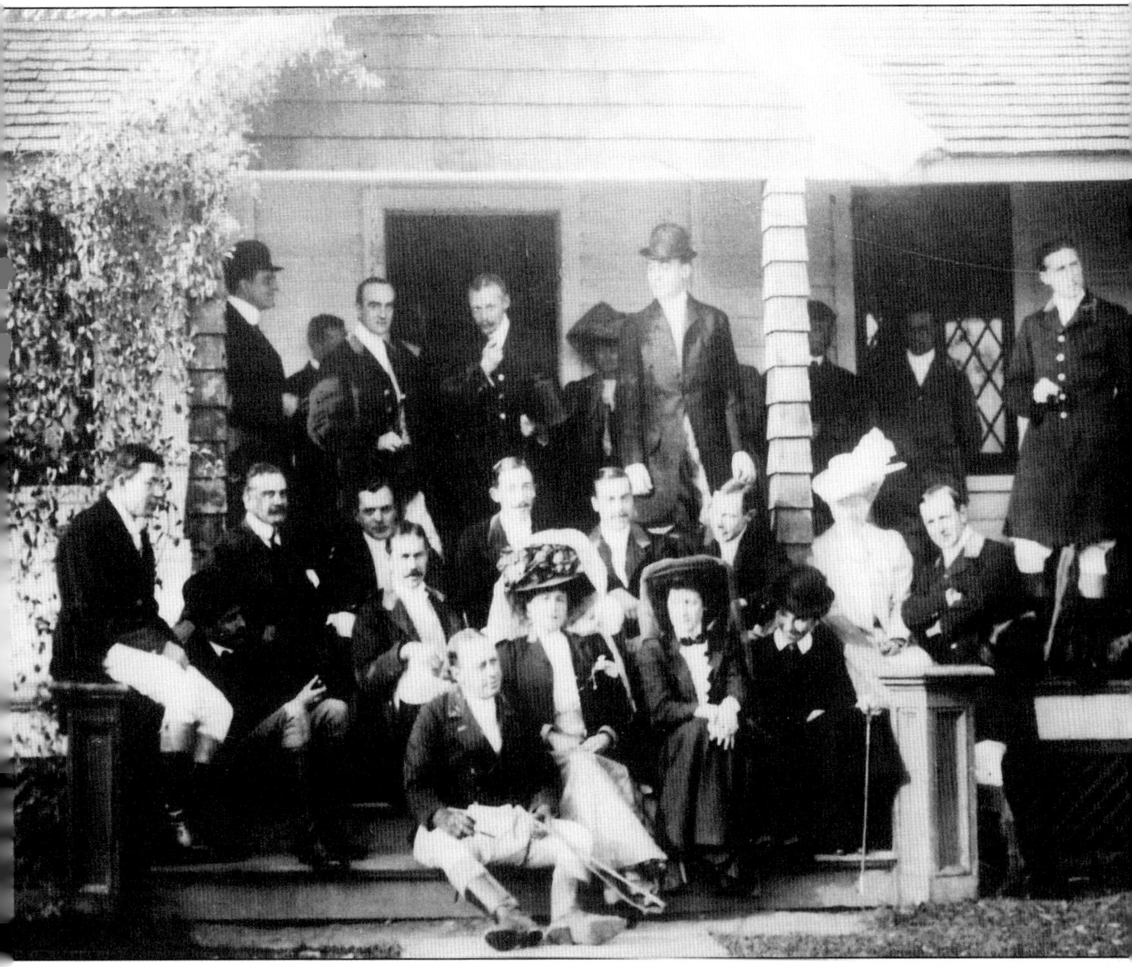

A gathering of those associated with the Essex Hunt took place on the porch of the Lower Kennels, c. 1895. Seymour Cromwell is standing on the porch (far left) and Guerdon Maynard on the far right. Mrs. Pfizer is seated in the center of the steps with her daughter, Lulu (on her left), and Jack Wilmerding (on her right). Florence Jones (in white) is seated by the post and Charles Pfizer, master of the Essex Hunt, is standing beside her. (James S. Jones.)

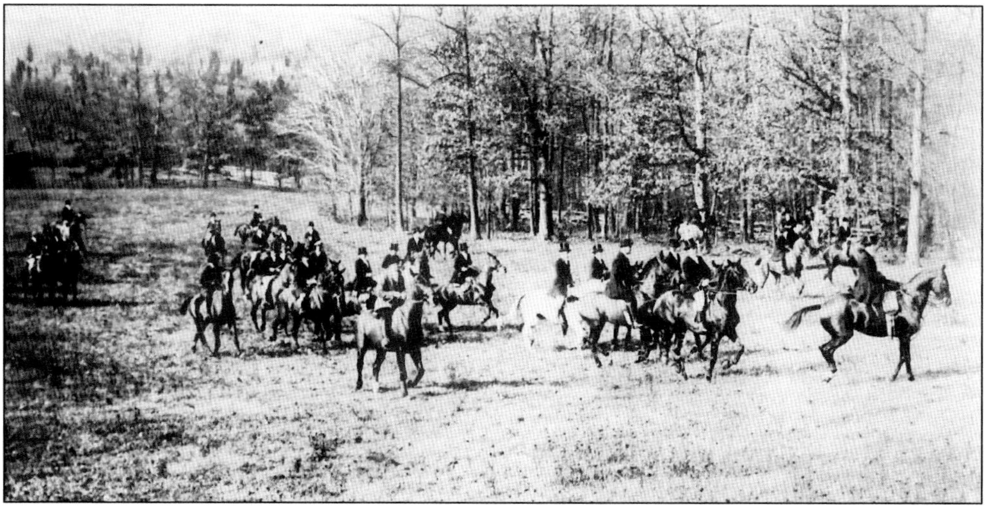

The field was comprised of about thirty guests of Mr. Pfizer. Some were wealthy New York financiers and industrialists who lived in the area on the weekend, or who took the train for a weekend adventure. A few, like Frederick W. Jones, Jr. were members of Squadron A of the 7th New York National Guard who wanted to get some real riding experience instead of just training in a ring in New York City. Mr. Pfizer would meet the train at Whitehouse with a string of horses and a wagonload of top hats in boxes. (James S. Jones.)

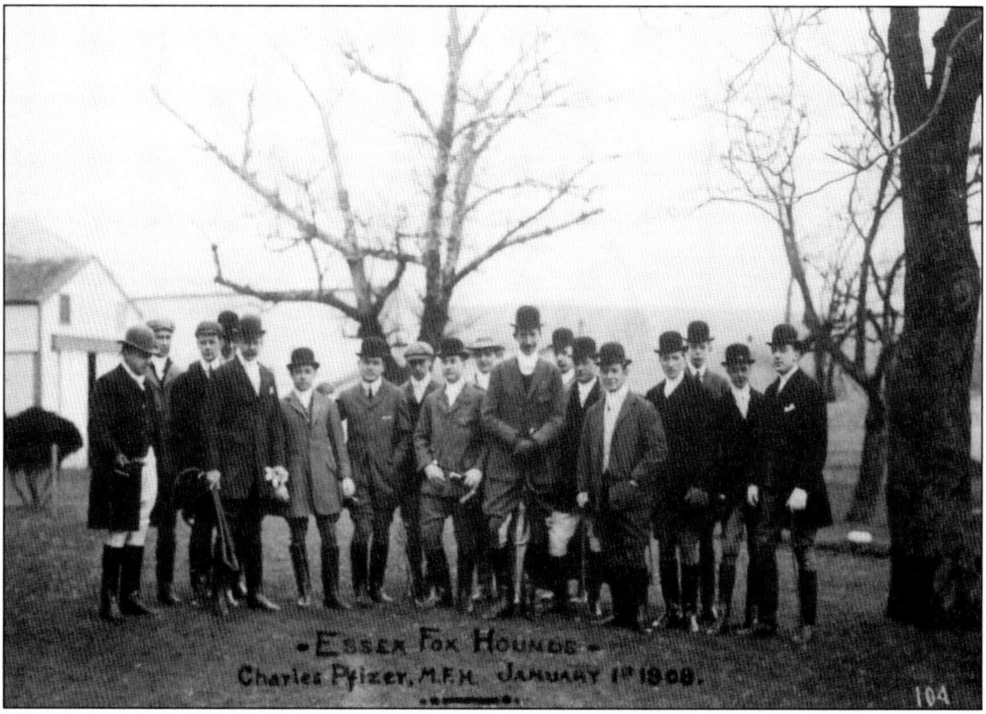

A gathering at the hunt club on January 1, 1908, including, from left to right: Mr. Jack Wilmerding, Mr. William Larned, Mr. Nick Tilney, Mr. Walker, Mr. A. Fillmore Hyde, Mr. Alexander Phillips, Mr. Arthur Fowler, Mr. Leonce Fuller, Mr. Francis Stevens, Mrs. Florence Jones, Mr. Adams, Mr. Thomas Holland, two unknowns, Mr. Charle Pfizer, Mr. Guerdon Maynard, two more unknowns, and Mr. Harry Hoy. (Masters of the Essex Fox Hounds.)

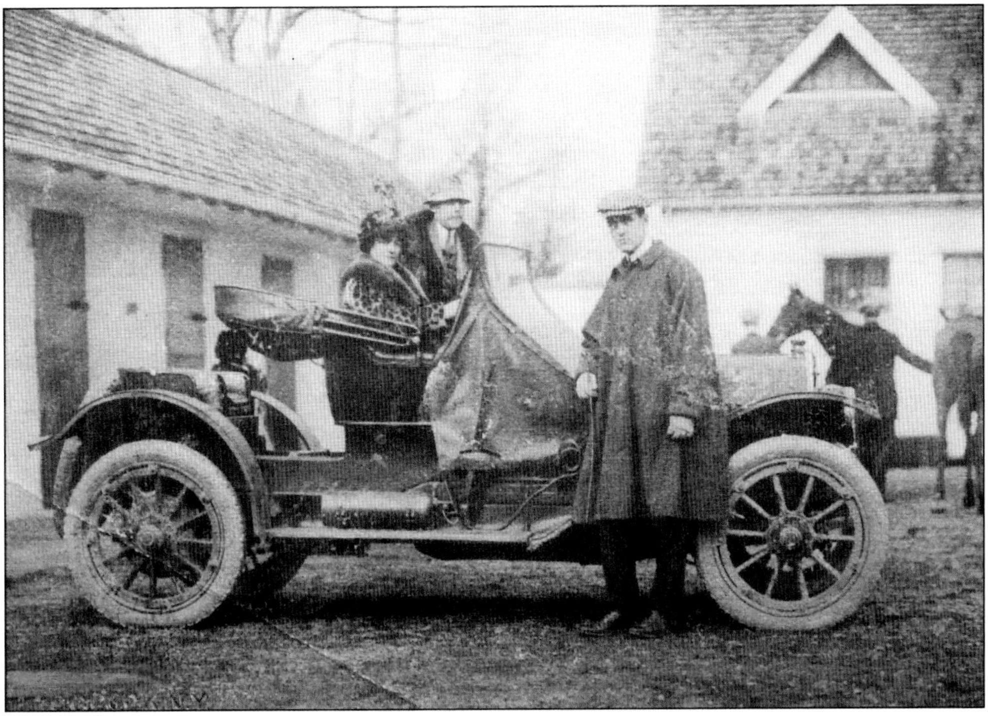

Winnie Hagen, Frederick W. Jones, and Arthur Hagen were photographed in the Fowler stable courtyard about 1912. (James S. Jones.)

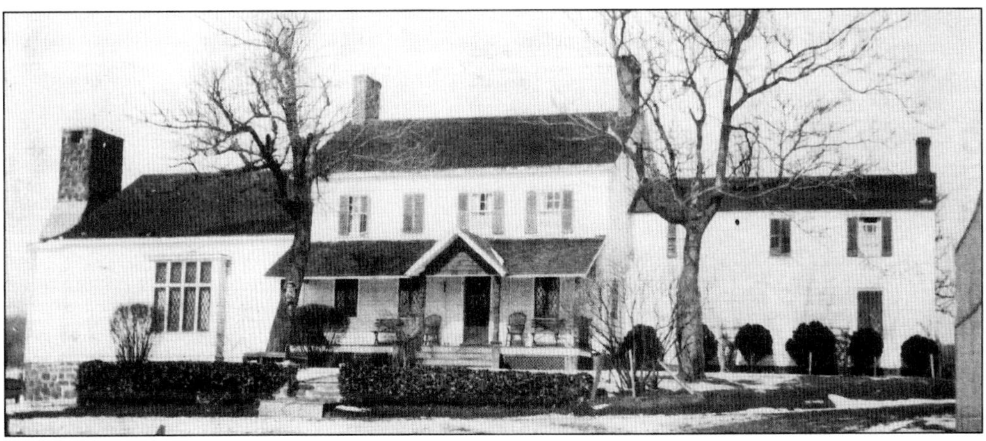

This is the house at the lower kennels in Gladstone. The room on the left was added for dinners and parties. There were guest rooms for people who came from New York. This building burned down prior to 1912. (James S. Jones.)

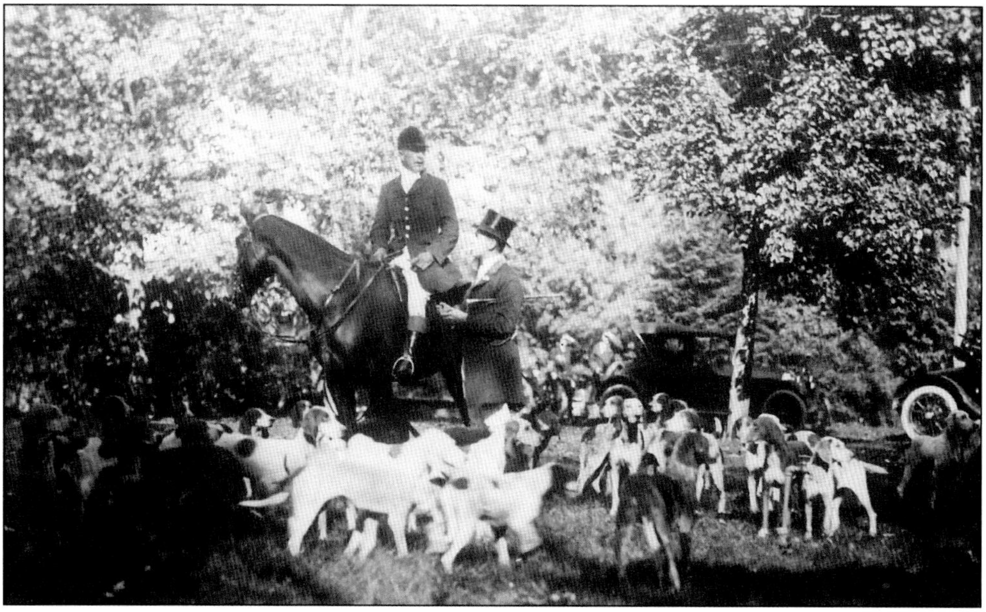

In 1913 the Essex Hunt was incorporated as the Essex Fox Hounds and (Grant) Barney Schley and William Larned became joint masters. They persuaded George Brice, who maintained a private pack of hounds in Chestertown on Maryland's Eastern Shore, to relocate to New Jersey to take charge of the pack. Here is George Brice with the Hounds in November of 1916. Mr. Richard Whitney is standing beside him. (James S. Jones.)

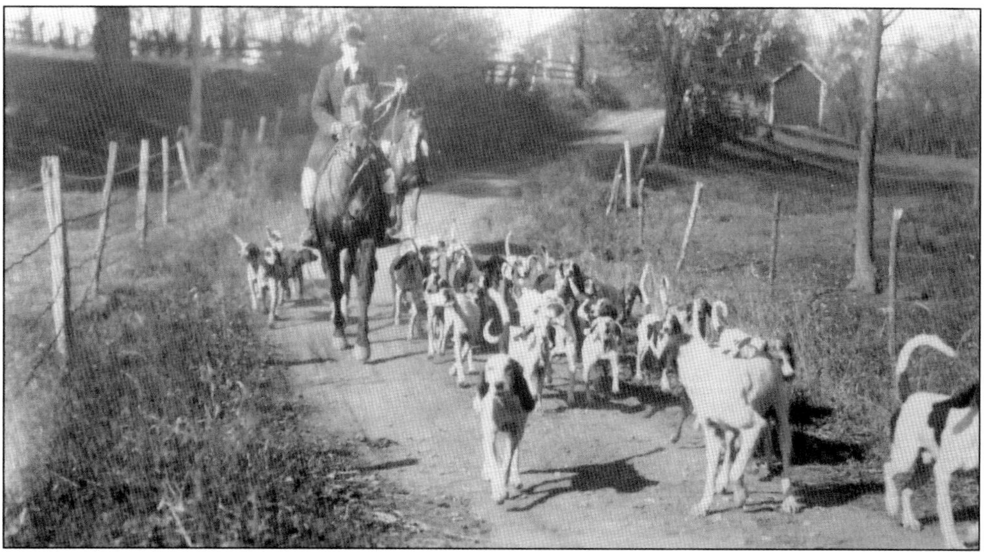

George Brice is seen here with the Essex Fox Hounds near Burnt Mills. George Brice brought his pack of blue ticked Eastern Shore hounds with him from Maryland. His pack became the core of the Essex Fox Hounds. A blue ticked hound is reputed to have a better nose than his English counterpart, giving rise to the following verse: "Oh your 'Belvoir Tan' is gallant and bold, on a scent you can cut with a knife, breast high; But to sing on the fallow when the scent lies cold, you must trust to the old blue pie." (James S. Jones.)

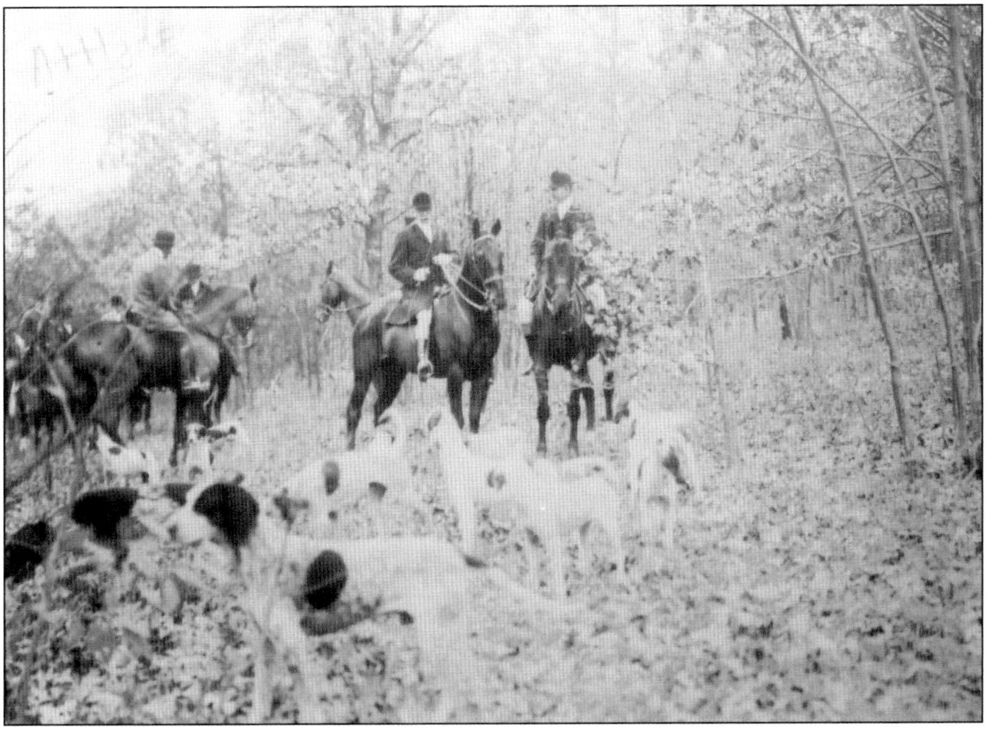

Following Messrs. Schley and Larned, A. Fillmore Hyde became master of the Essex Fox Hounds in late 1913, serving for fifteen years. Here is A. Fillmore Hyde (center) with George Brice (right). (James S. Jones.)

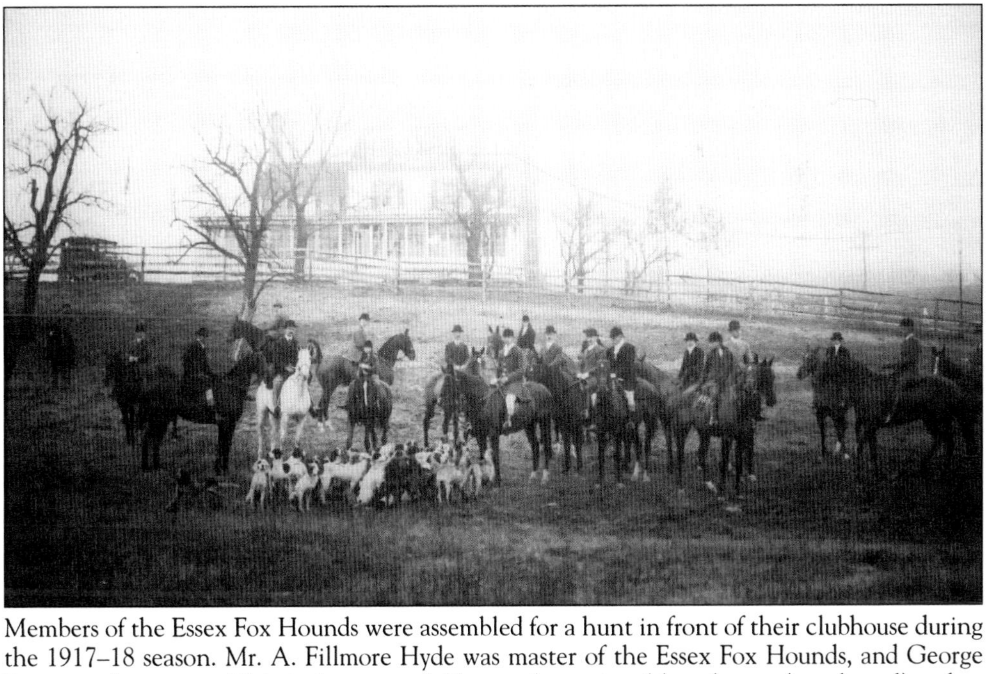

Members of the Essex Fox Hounds were assembled for a hunt in front of their clubhouse during the 1917–18 season. Mr. A. Fillmore Hyde was master of the Essex Fox Hounds, and George Brice was huntsman. This is the same clubhouse that exists (though greatly enlarged) today. (Masters of the Essex Fox Hounds.)

THE FIFTH ANNUAL

HUNTER-TRIALS

UNDER THE AUSPICES OF THE ESSEX FOX HOUNDS

will be held at

The Fields' Farm, Rattlesnake Bridge

by kind permission of

KENNETH B. SCHLEY, ESQ., M. F. H.

on

SATURDAY, SEPTEMBER 10, 1932

at 2:30 P. M.

E F H

JUDGES

Mrs. Lawrence C. Smith, Ex-M. F. H.
Dr. Howard D. Collins, M. F. H.
M. Roy Jackson, Esq., M. F. H.

STEWARDS

Kenneth B. Schley, Esq., M. F. H.
A. Fillmore Hyde, Esq., Ex-M. F. H.
Shelton E. Martin, Esq.
Arthur R. Jones, Esq.
Richard Whitney, Esq.
Charles Scribner, Esq.

COMMITTEE

Anderson Fowler
Frank Johnson
David Pyle
Ben Johnson
Tolman Pyle
J. S. Jones

This is how the cover of the program for the Fifth Annual Hunter-Trials looked. The Hunter Trials were races designed to test the skills of hunters (horses). Charles Pfizer, and later the Essex Fox Hounds, were always interested in the breeding of good hunting horses. To this end, the service of good-quality stud horses was offered free to local farmers to encourage them to raise hunters which the members of the Essex Fox Hounds would buy. (James S. Jones.)

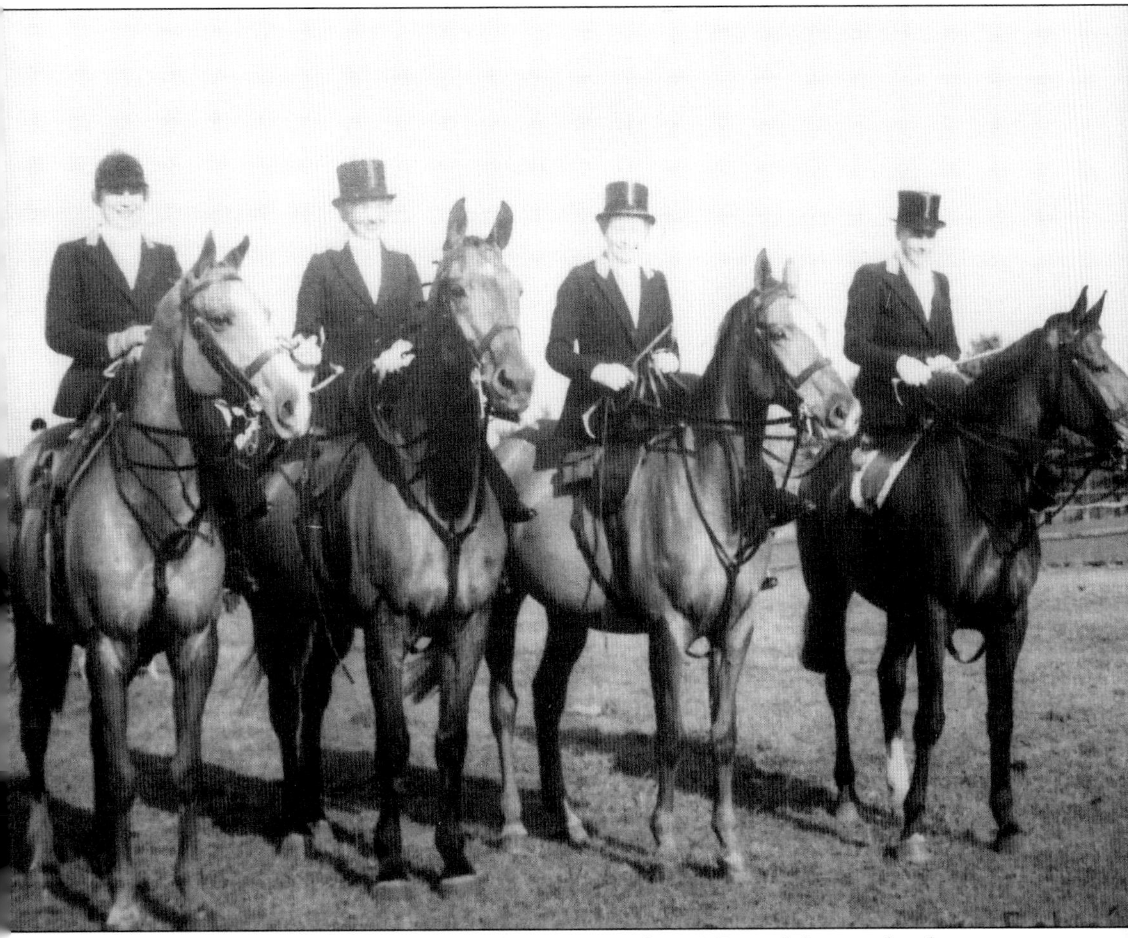

In 1949 they called themselves "The Galloping Grandmas." From left to right they are as follows: Mrs. Charles (Vera) Scribner on Nearsight, Mrs. David (Dorothy) Pyle on Bull Run, Mrs. Lester Perrin on Notable, and Mrs. DeCoursey (Dorothy) Fales on Red Ember. Note that they are all riding side-saddle. (Masters of the Essex Fox Hounds.)

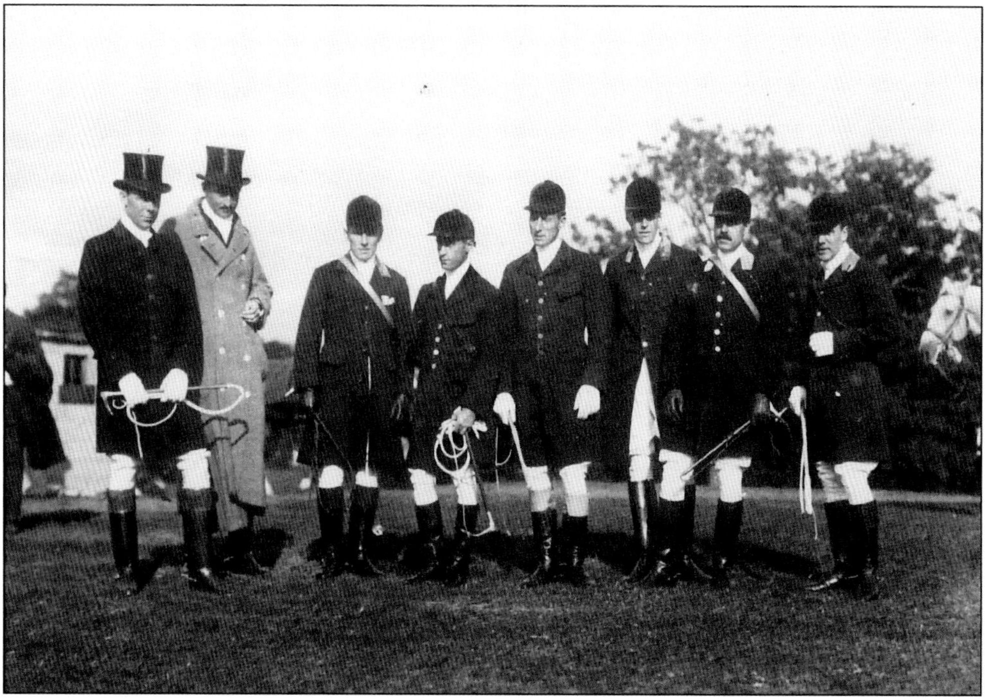

This is the Somerset Hills contingent at the 1912 Morristown Horse Show, held at the Whippeny River Club, from left to right: Joseph Willis; Richard Williams; Kenneth B. Schley; Leonce Fuller; Guerdon Maynard; Barney (Grant) Schley; Bill Camman; and Arthur Fowler. (James S. Jones.)

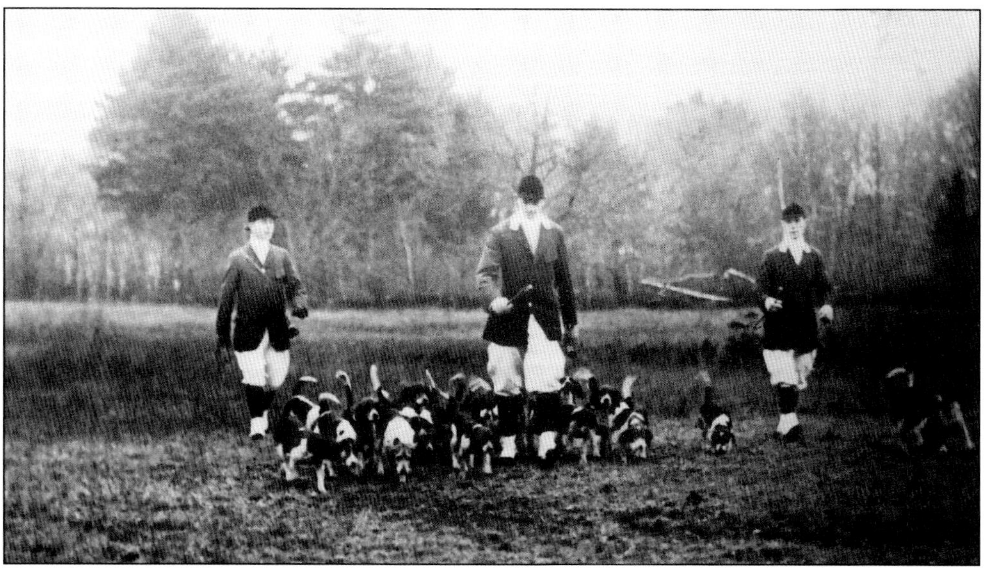

Here are the Vernon Beagles in 1915, with Mr. Richard Gambrill, master. Mr. Gambrill maintained the pack for hunting hare. The pack was named after his estate, Vernon Manor. Mr. Gambrill also had an estate in Newport, RI, named Vernon Court. (Anthony Villa.)

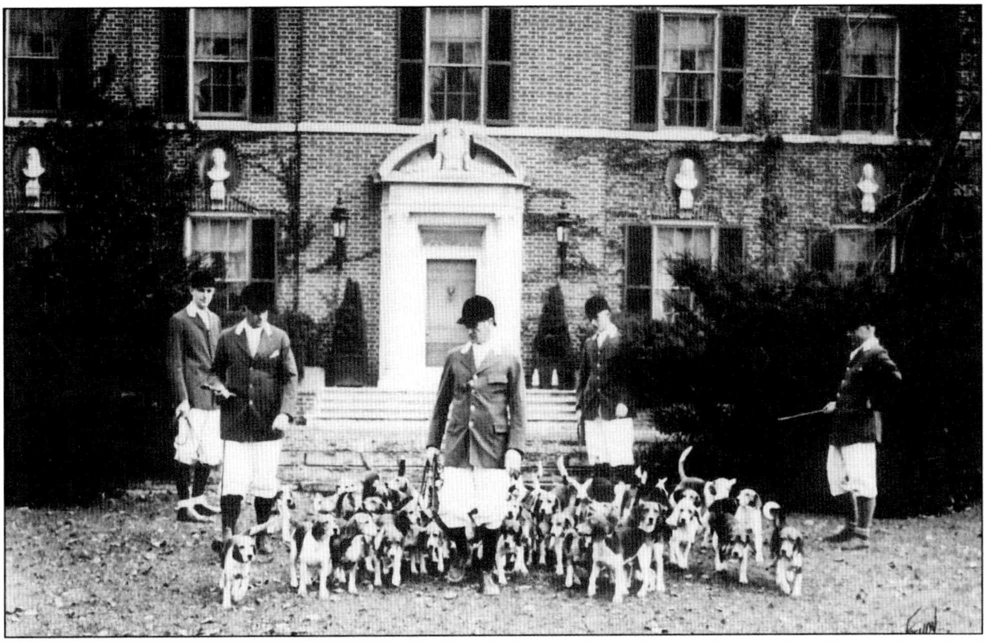

After the death of Mr. George B. Post, Richard Gambrill took over his pack of hounds, called the Somerset Beagles, which had been founded in 1888. Thereafter Mr. Gambrill called his pack the Vernon Somerset Beagles. Here is Mr. Richard Gambrill (second from the left) with his Vernon Somerset Beagles on the lawn of his estate, Vernon Manor. (Anthony Villa.)

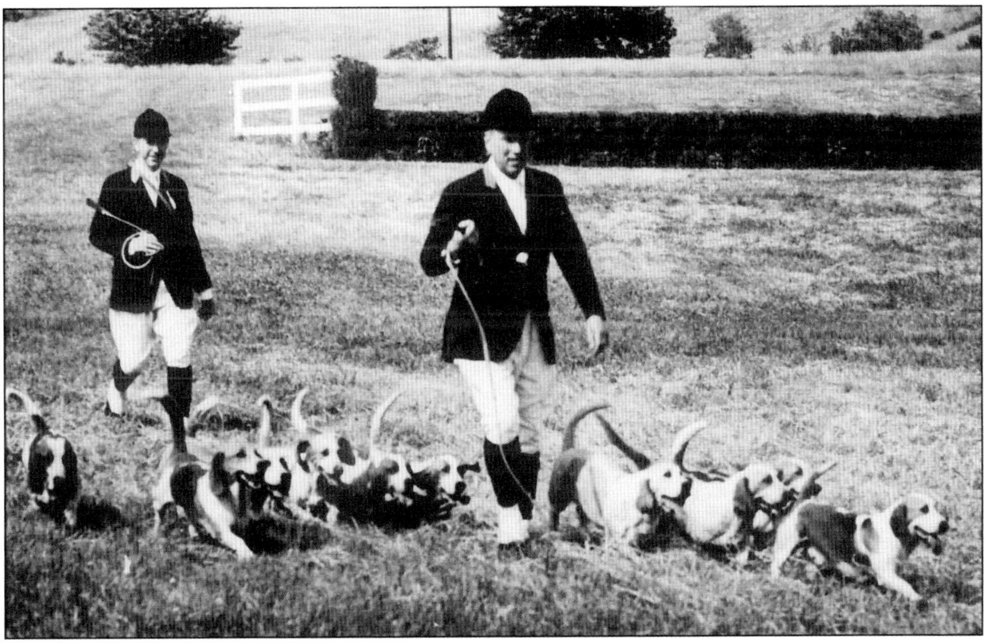

The Tewksbury Foot Bassets were founded in 1950 by Mr. Haliburton Fales II, and James S. Jones. In 1953, following the death of Richard Gambrill, it was reorganized on a subscription basis as a successor group to the Vernon Somerset Beagles. The hounds go out for early morning hunting on Saturdays and Sundays during the season. Here are the Tewksbury Foot Bassets with James S. Jones (master, center) and Joe Wiley (whipper-in, left). (James S. Jones.)

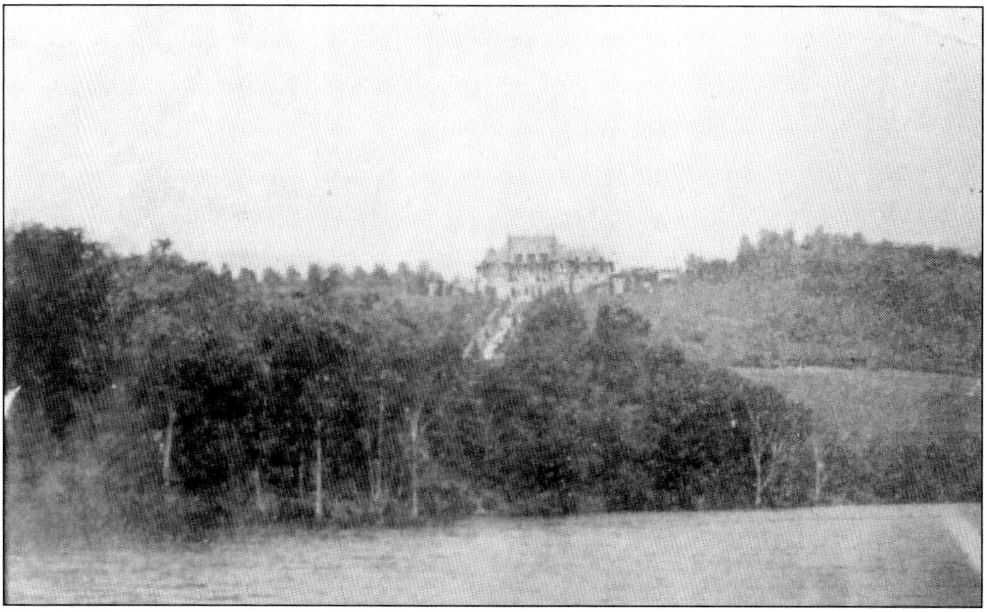

This view of Blairsden above rising Ravine Lake was taken in 1905. It was C. Ledyard Blair who first conceived of building a dam and creating Ravine Lake. The stone for the dam came from quarries at Waterloo and in the German Valley of Morris County. The first stone was laid on October 1, 1898, with the eldest Blair daughter, Marjory, officiating. Mr. Blair had terraces cut into the hillside leading down to the lake. (Bernardsville Public Library Local History Collection.)

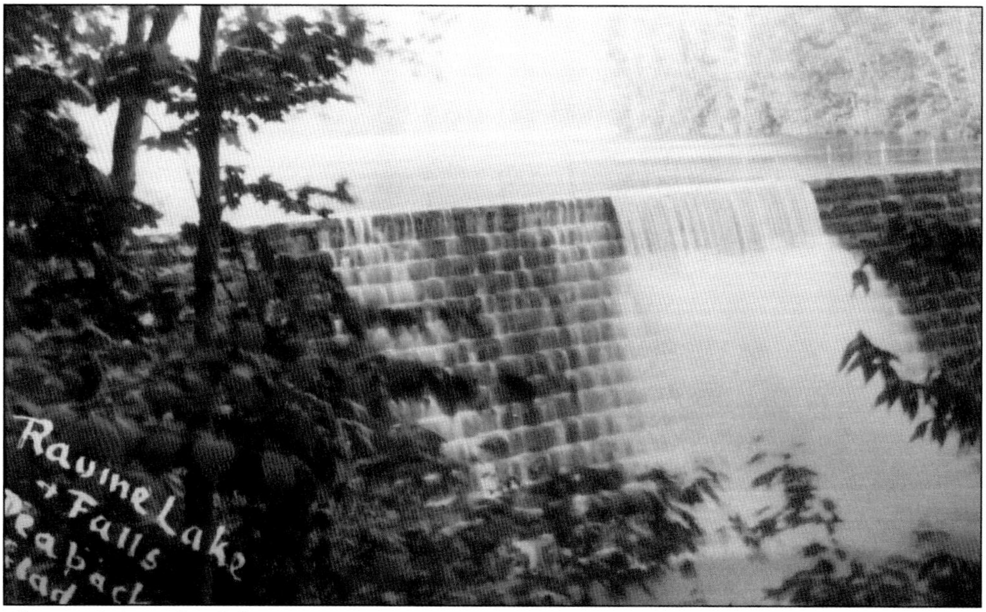

The north branch of the Raritan River was dammed in the ravine below Blairsden, creating what was called Blair's Lake, but is today called Ravine Lake. Mr. Blair's youngest daughter was born on the day in 1899 when the final stone was laid in the dam. Thereafter she was known as that "dam baby." The lake was actually completed almost three years before Blairsden. (Chatfield's.)

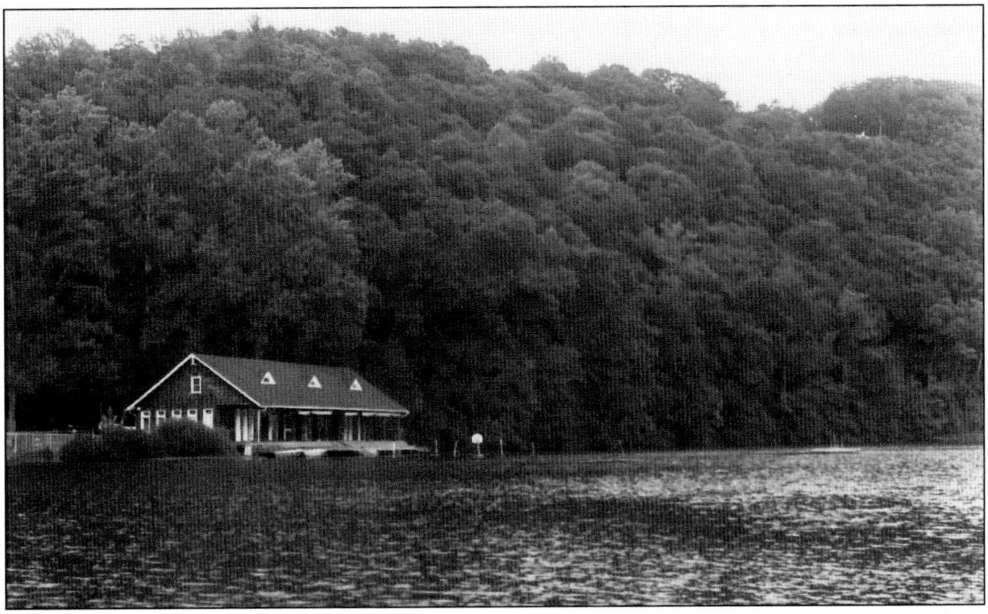

As early as 1894 a group of men formed an association to establish a country club. J. Herbert Ballantine, George B. Post, Robert L. Stevens, and Edward T.H. Talmage each pledged $8,000 to buy the land. Ravine Lake became an integral part of their plan. The list of 31 shareholders of the Ravine Association in 1900 reads like a who's who of the Bernardsville Mountain Colony. (Collection of the authors.)

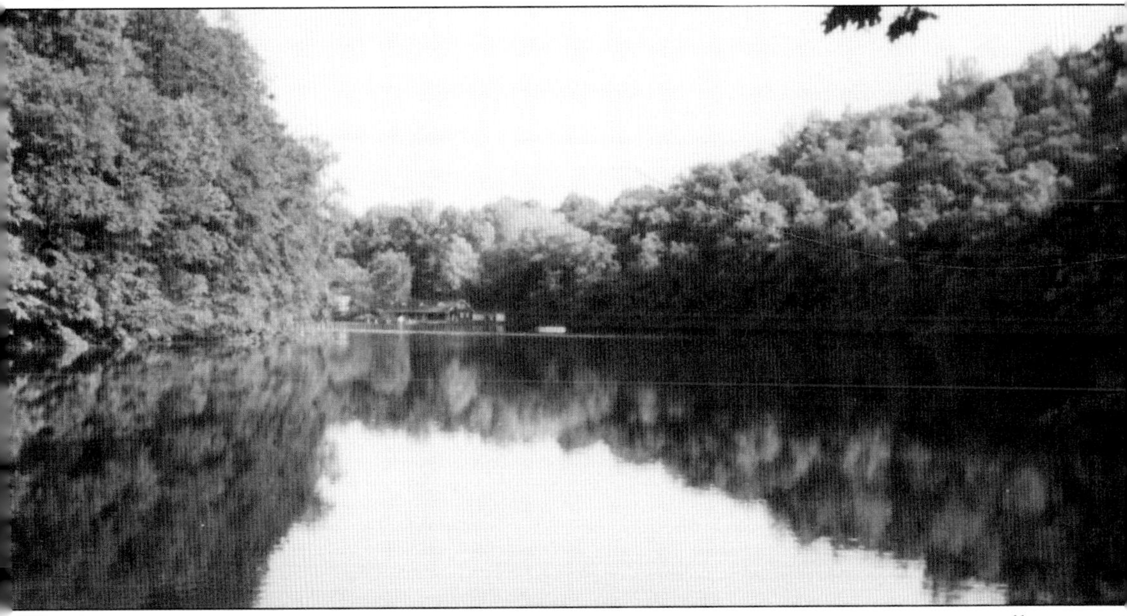

The Ravine Lake Club looks today just as it did in 1903, when it was part of the Somerset Hills Country Club. A nine-hole golf course and three grass tennis courts were laid out on the hill overlooking the lake. This continued to be the site of the Somerset Hills Country Club until 1917, when it was re-established in its present location. The Ravine Lake and Game Club was set up in December 1917 to operate the lake facility as a separate entity from the country club. (Collection of the authors.)

The Hosts

John A. Bensel
Frank Bergen
Walter P. Bliss
William P. Bonbright
James C. Brady

Palmer Campbell
Charles M. Chapin
J. William Clark
William Clark, Jr.
Seymour L. Cromwell
George D. Cross

Clarence Dillon
Forrest F. Dryden

Charles Engelhard

De Coursey Fales
Haley Fiske
Arthur A. Fowler

Richard V. N. Gambrill
George H. Gaston
Michael Gavin
Robert M. Grant
William V. Griffin

Ogden H. Hammond
William P. Hardenbergh
John R. Hardin
G. Beekman Hoppin

Fred W. Jones, Jr.

J. Frederic Kernochan
Dr. Augustus S. Knight
Anthony R. Kuser
Dryden Kuser

Walter G. Ladd
Joseph Larocque
Edward A. LeRoy
Francis G. Lloyd

Shelton E. Martin
Clarence Blair Mitchell
Charles A. Moran

Benjamin Nicoll

Edwin Packard
William H. Page
R. Stuyvesant Pierrepont
A. Wright Post
George B. Post
Percy R. Pyne

W. Willis Reese
John A. Roebling

Dean Sage
John Sloane
Julius A. Stursberg
Frederick C. Sutro

Frank S. Tainter
Edward T. H. Talmage
John F. Talmage
Arthur Turnbull
Ramsay Turnbull

Schuyler S. Wheeler
Arthur Whitney
Richard Whitney
H. Otto Wittpen
Chalmers Wood, Jr.

Henry Young

Invited Guests

Reverend Thomas A. Conover
Reverend James Hollyday Stone Fair
Reverend John Mitchell Harper
Reverend William I. McKean

A list of the members of the Somerset Hills Country Club from a program for a "neighborhood dinner" to honor Richard Vliet Lindabury on his seventieth birthday in 1920. (Bernardsville Public Library Local History Collection.)

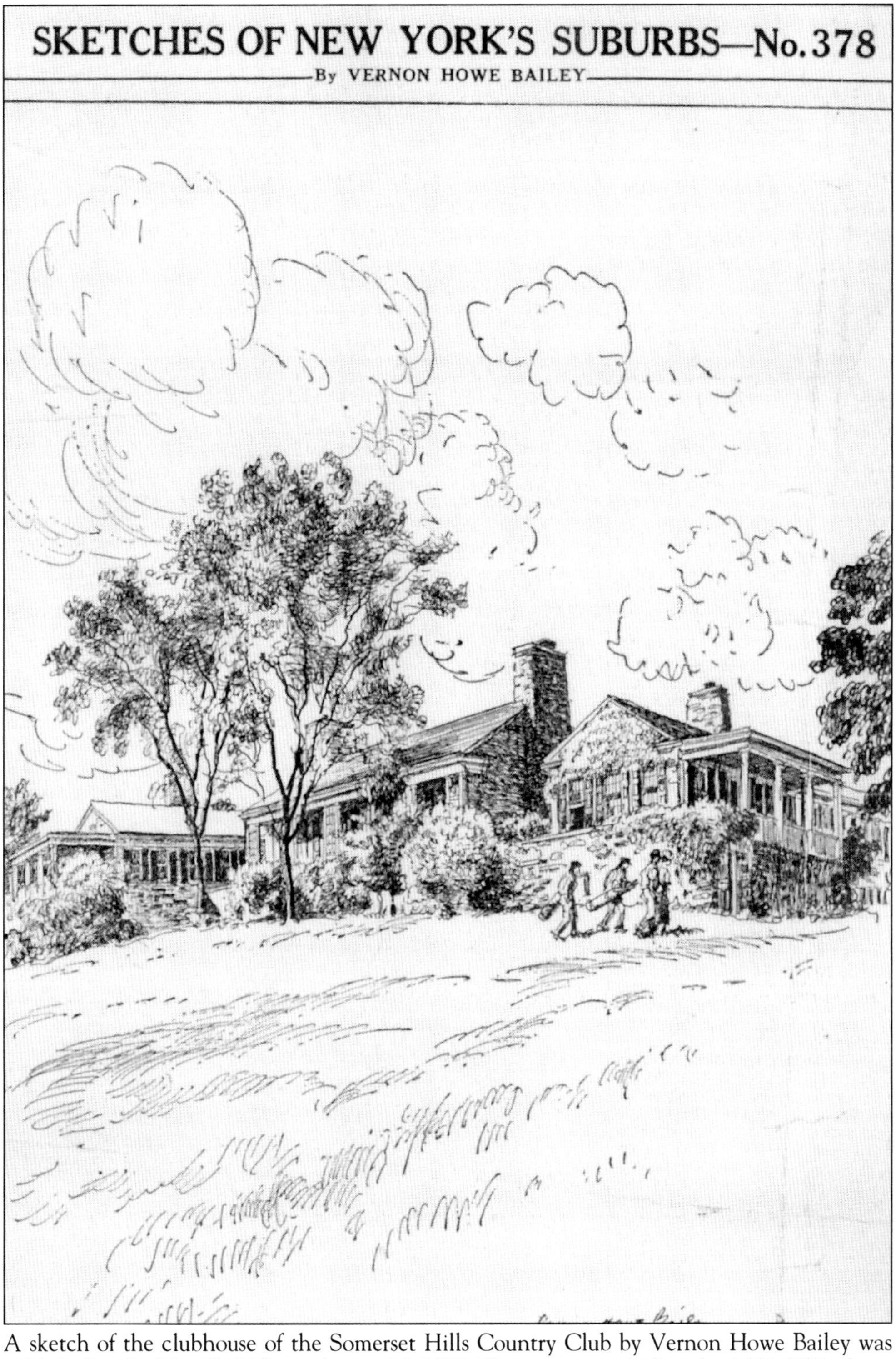

A sketch of the clubhouse of the Somerset Hills Country Club by Vernon Howe Bailey was published in the *New York Times*, August 15, 1936. The course was laid out by A.W. Tillinghast. (Bernardsville Public Library Local History Collection.)

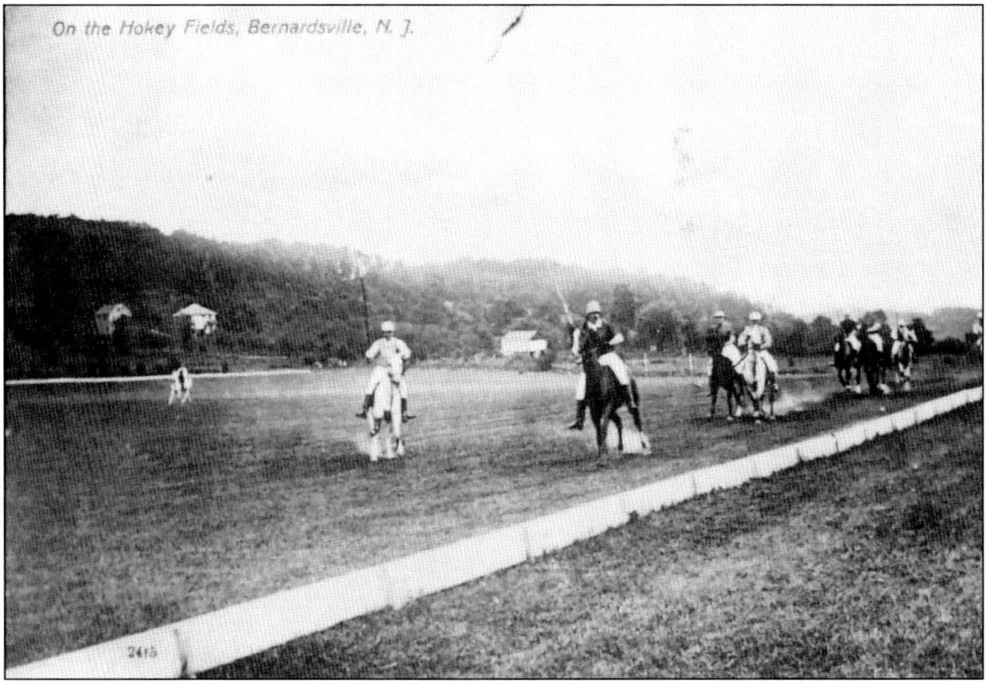

Apparently the creator of this postcard had no idea what polo was, and did not know how to spell hockey. (Bernardsville Public Library Local History Collection.)

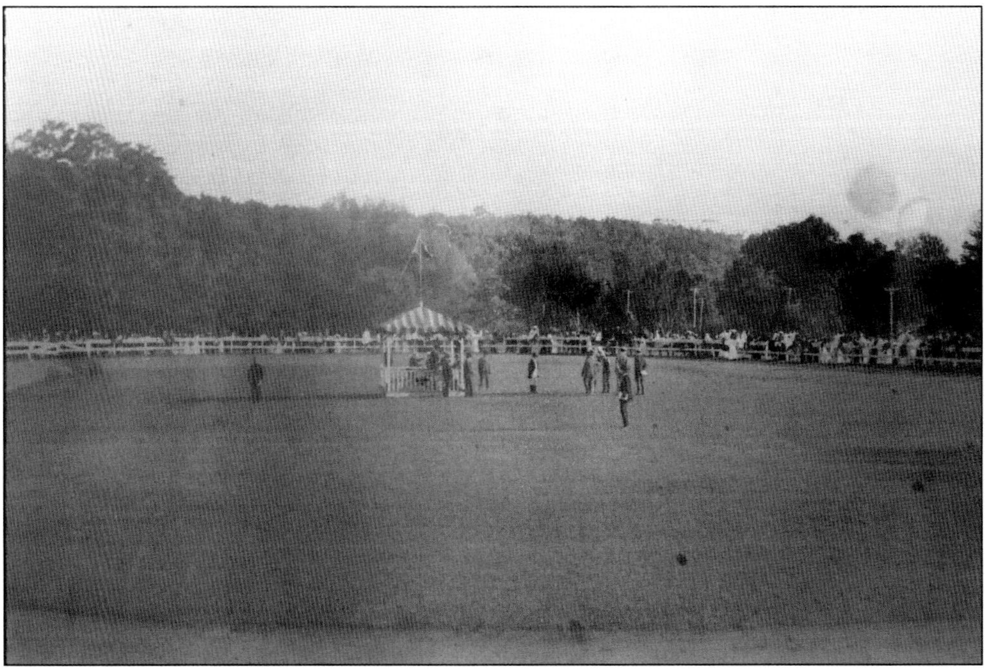
The judges' stand at the polo grounds in 1906. (Chatfield's.)

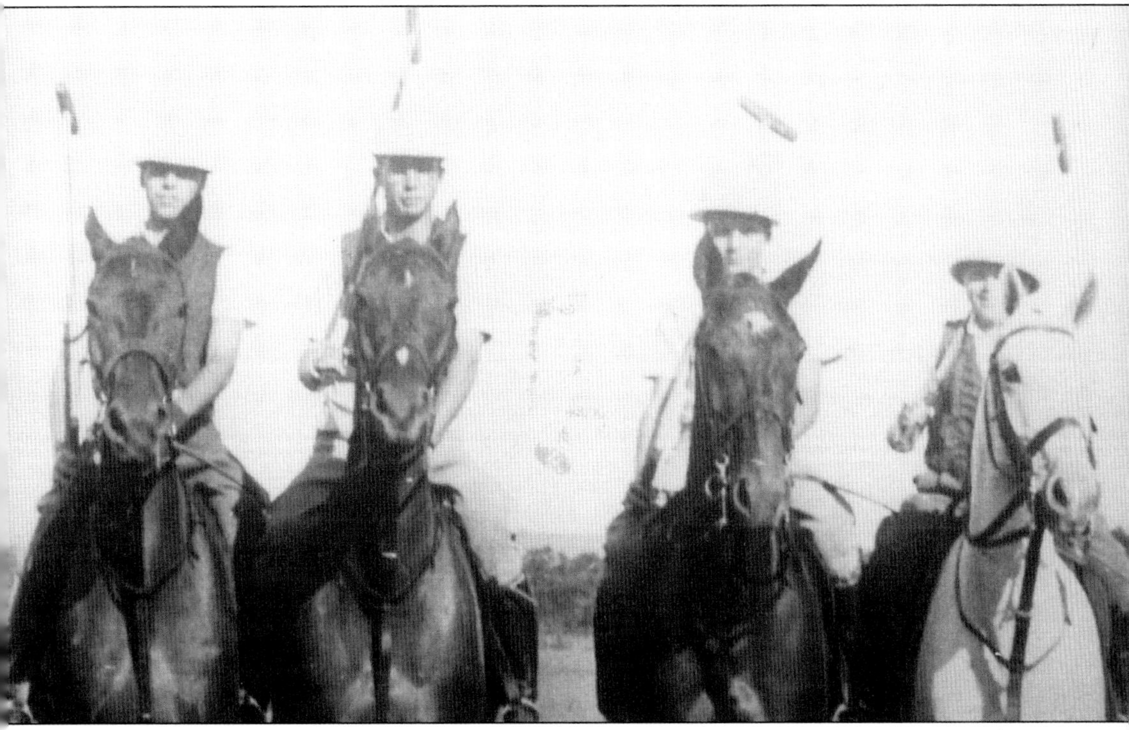

The Mine Mountain Hurricanes polo team were at a match on September 18, 1931 when someone took this picture. From left to right are Percy Pyne, Andy Fowler, Eben Pyne, and John Pyne. (Masters of the Essex Fox Hounds.)

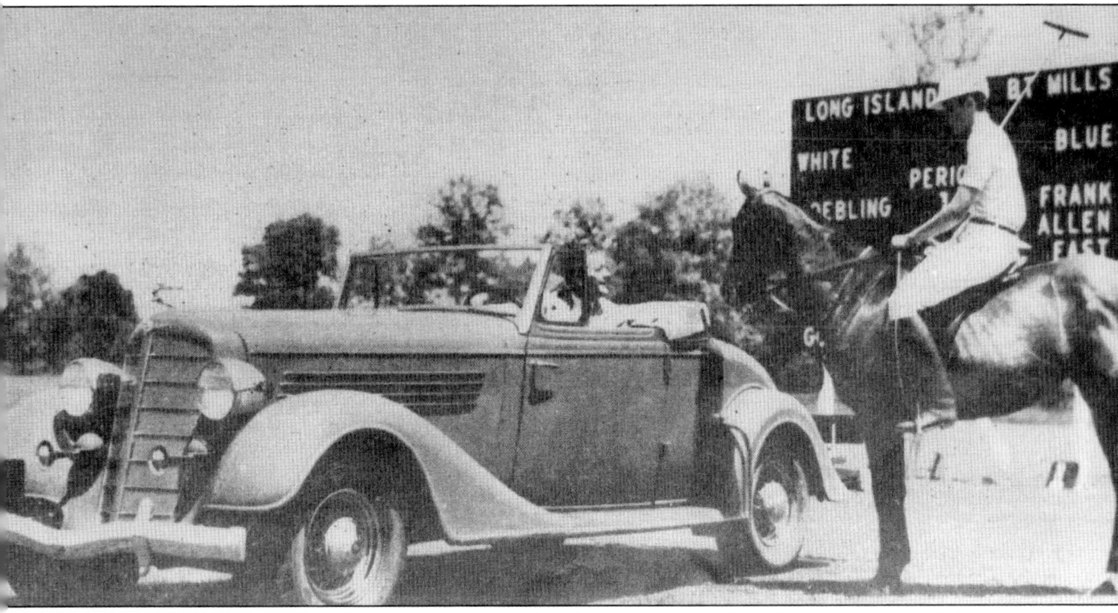

In 1929, Mr. William Thorn Kissel instituted a kind of polo revival in the area. He established a small and somewhat sloped polo field at his estate (see p. 71) and later founded the Burnt Mills Polo Club. This photograph was taken from one of the club's 1935 brochures. Note Burnt Mills on the scoreboard. (Bernardsville Public Library Local History Collection.)

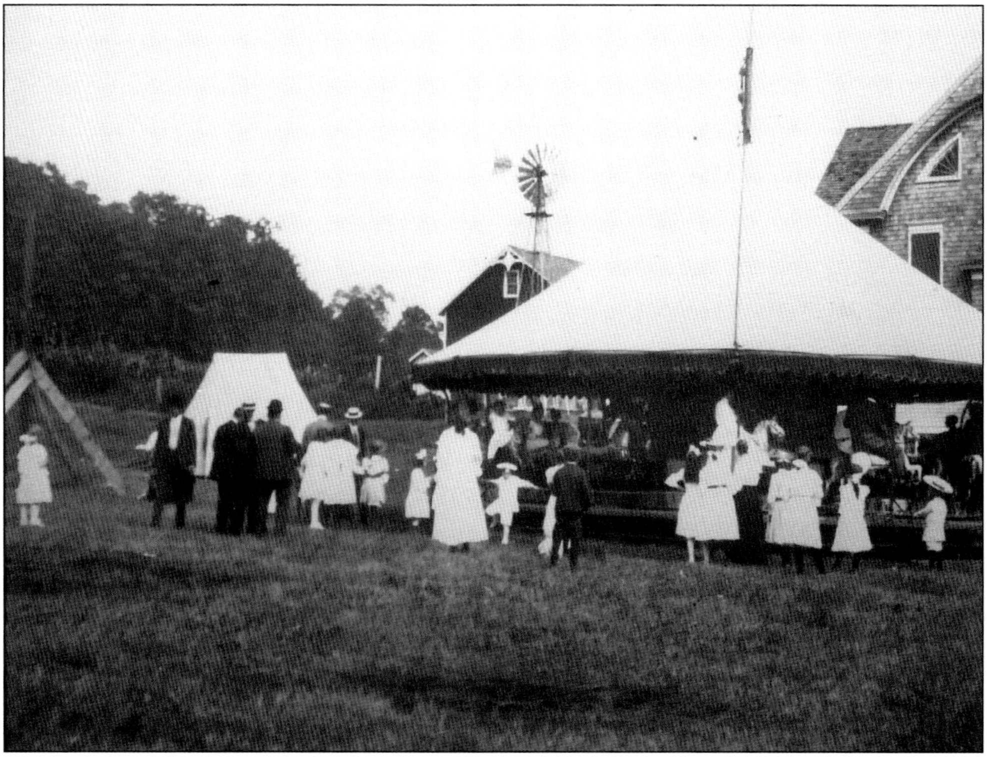

This carousel was at the annual Peapack Valley Fire Department carnival, *c.* 1905. (Chatfield's.)

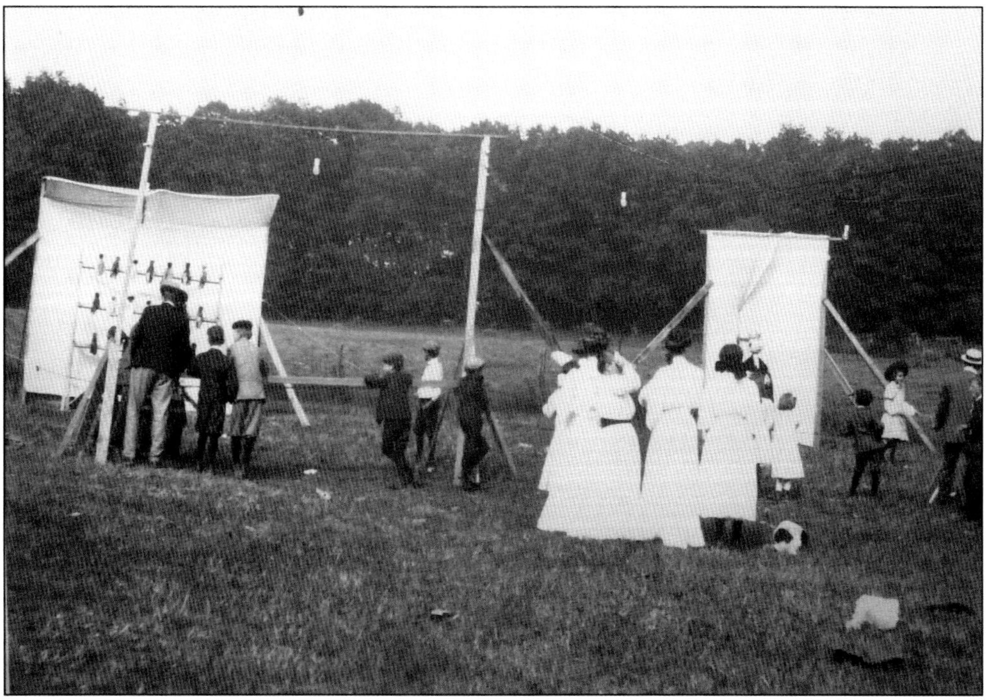

Games of skill were featured at the firemen's carnival in Peapack, *c.* 1905. (Chatfield's.)

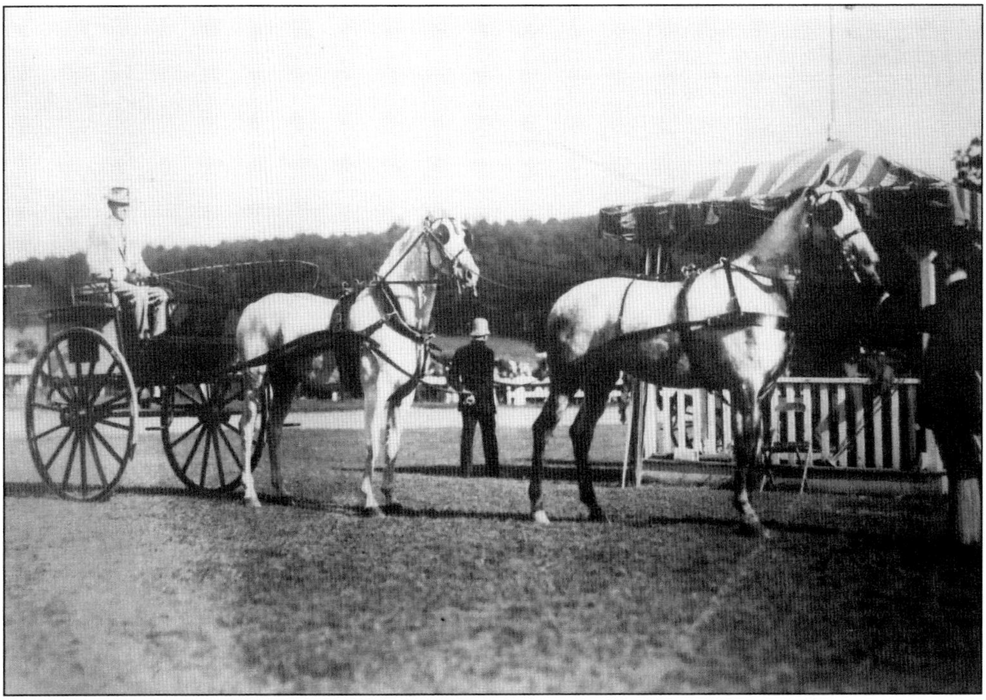

Mr. C. Ledyard Blair traveled to a horse show at the polo grounds in a tandem. A tandem was a small cart pulled by two horses, one in front of the other. A gentleman would drive such a vehicle to a hunt, or an event such as this, and then would unhitch the lead horse, and ride him in the hunt or event. The horses are Smoke and Jack Frost. (Chatfield's.)

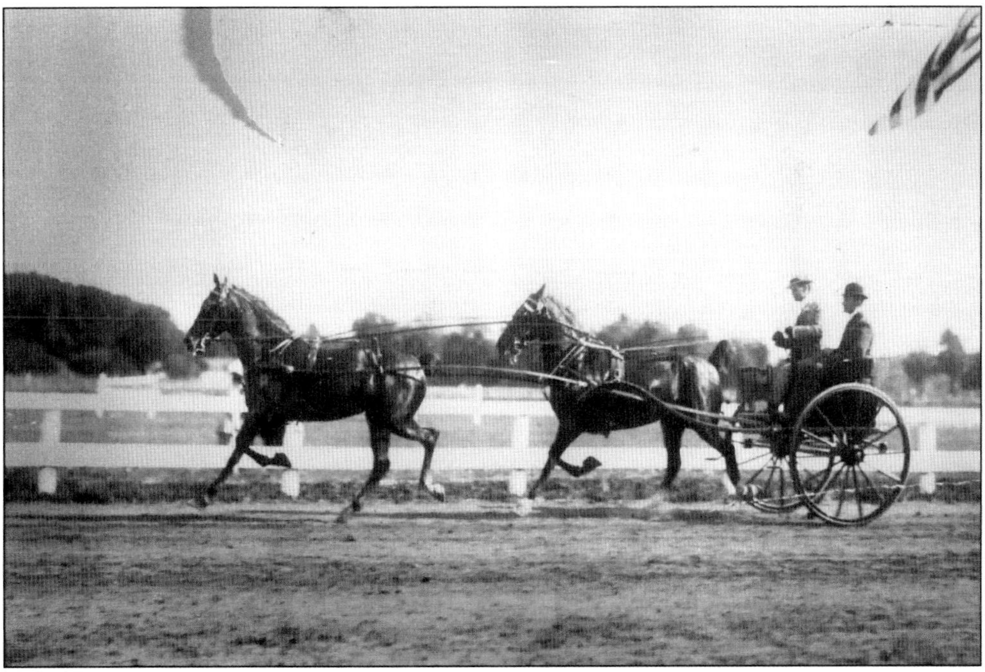

Here, Miss Evelyn Schley is with Pride and Prejudice, her two horses, this time driving a tandem. Notice the hard rubber tires on the tandem, a prized attribute of the day. (Chatfield's.)

Second Annual

Farmers' Day Race Meeting

BY INVITATION OF

THE ESSEX FOX HOUNDS

UNDER SANCTION FROM THE HUNTS COMMITTEE OF THE NATIONAL STEEPLECHASE AND HUNT ASSOCIATION

To be held at the Club House, Peapack, N. J.

Saturday, October 23rd, 1915

RACES BEGIN PROMPTLY AT 2 O'CLOCK

CONDITIONS.

As it is the aim of the Race Committee to provide a course to test the qualities of a hunter, the steeplechases will be laid over a fair hunting country (post and rail).

Any horse schooling over the course after the flags are up will be disqualified.

Unless otherwise stated racing colors are required.

Riders must weigh out at least twenty minutes before the start of their race.

All horses must be saddled in the Paddock and must parade before the Judges' Stand.

Scratches must be made to the Clerk of Scales.

Any owner wishing stable accommodation should apply to the Race Committee not later than Wednesday, October 20th.

The Race Committee reserves the right to pass on the eligibility of all entries and riders.

Entries must be made in writing to the Race Committee, Essex Fox Hounds, Peapack, N. J., on or before Monday, October 18th, at 6 P. M.

Overweight allowed if declared.

Race Committee
A. FILMORE HYDE,
J. W. BURDEN,
WHITNEY KERNOCHAN.
F. W. JONES, Jr.,

First running of the New Jersey Hunt Cup won by Arthur Fowler's *Oxygen*, ridden by George Gilder

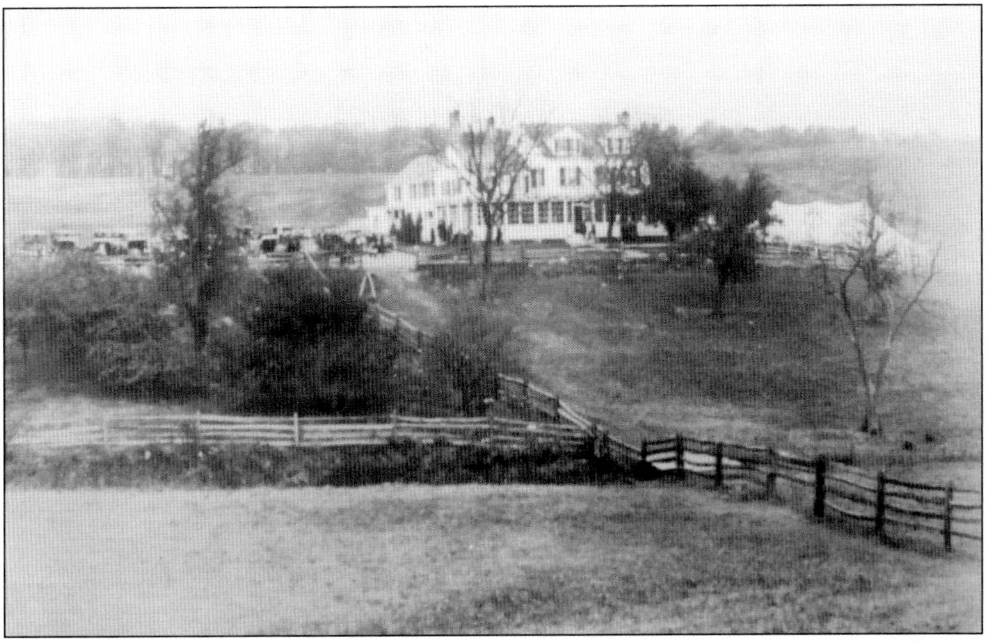

The second annual Farmer's Day Race Meeting was held by the Essex Hunt Club on October 23, 1915. The tent to the right was set up to serve lunch to the farmers. Mr. Pfizer established the Farmer's Day Race Meeting as a way of thanking the farmers for permitting the Essex Hunt to use their land for hunting. At first Farmer's Day was for men only. (James S. Jones.)

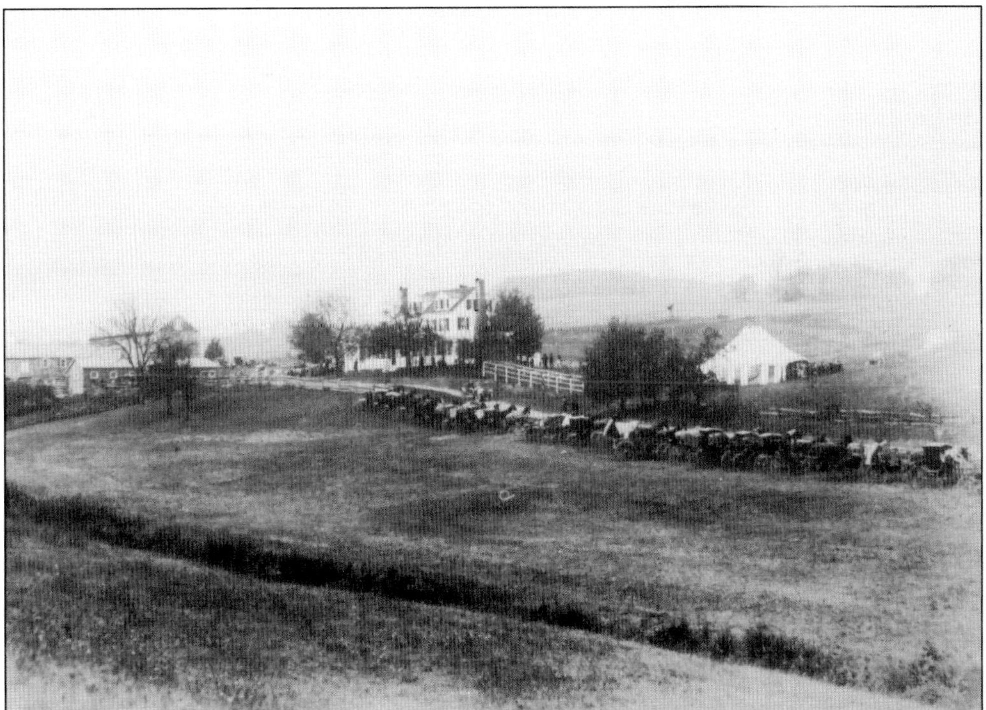

Another view shows the Essex Hunt Club during the second annual Farmer's Day Race Meeting in 1915. Notice all the carriages parked along the driveway. (James S. Jones.)

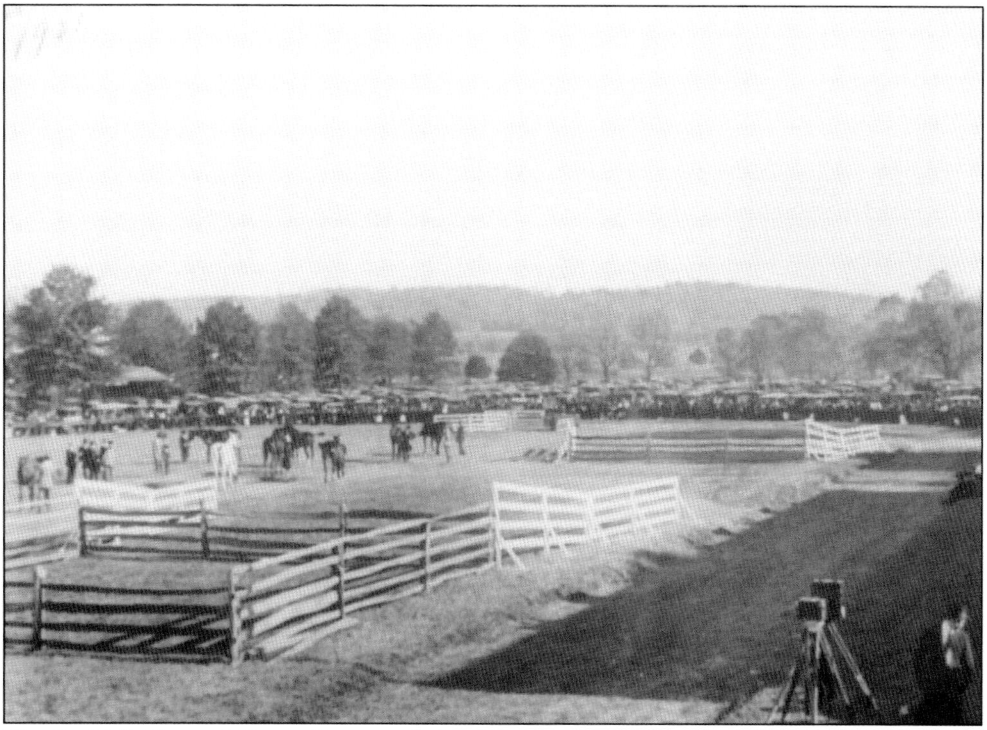

The Far Hills Fair and Horse Show was held at the fairgrounds in 1921. (James S. Jones.)

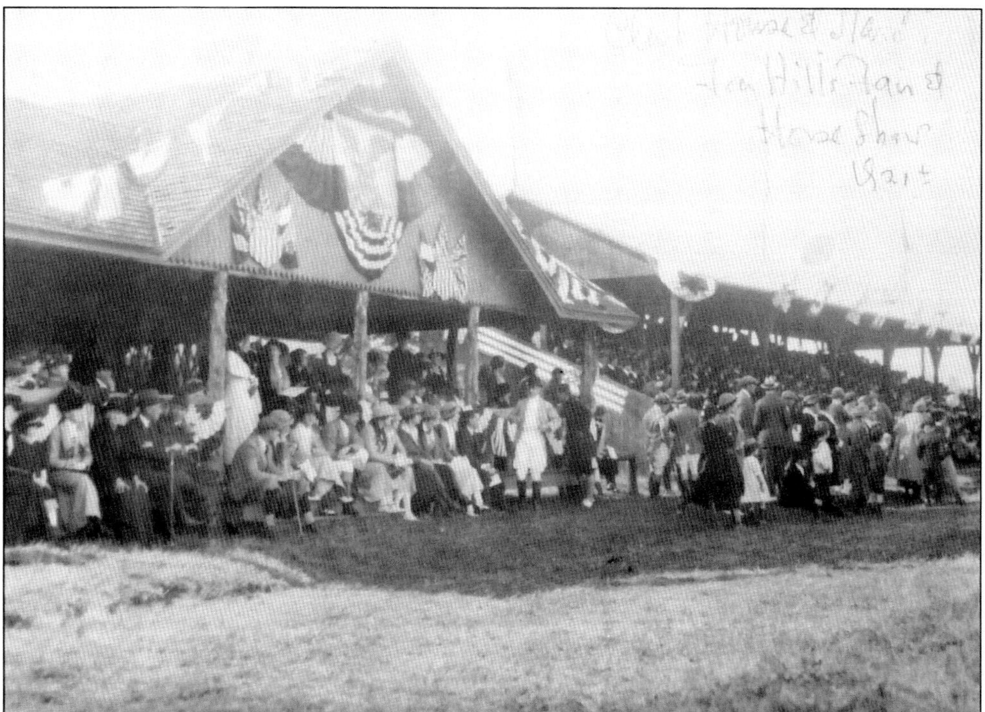

This is the grandstand at the Far Hills Fair and Horse Show in 1921. Today this annual celebration is continued at the Far Hills Race Meeting. (James S. Jones.)

Prior to 1949, the United States Cavalry furnished and subsidized the equestrian teams that represented our country. With the mechanization of the cavalry, we were left with no equestrian representation for the Olympic Games and other international events. To fill this gap, the United States Equestrian Team was founded in 1950. Its headquarters is in Gladstone, in the James Cox Brady stables at Hamilton Farms. Here National Champion Lisa Singer, from Pennsylvania, practices for the World Pairs Championship. She is driving a phaeton drawn by two morgan horses named Farm and Chance. (Collection of the authors.)

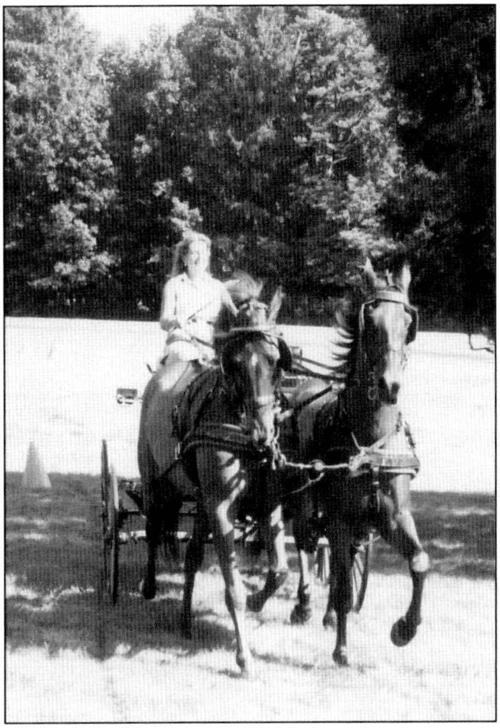

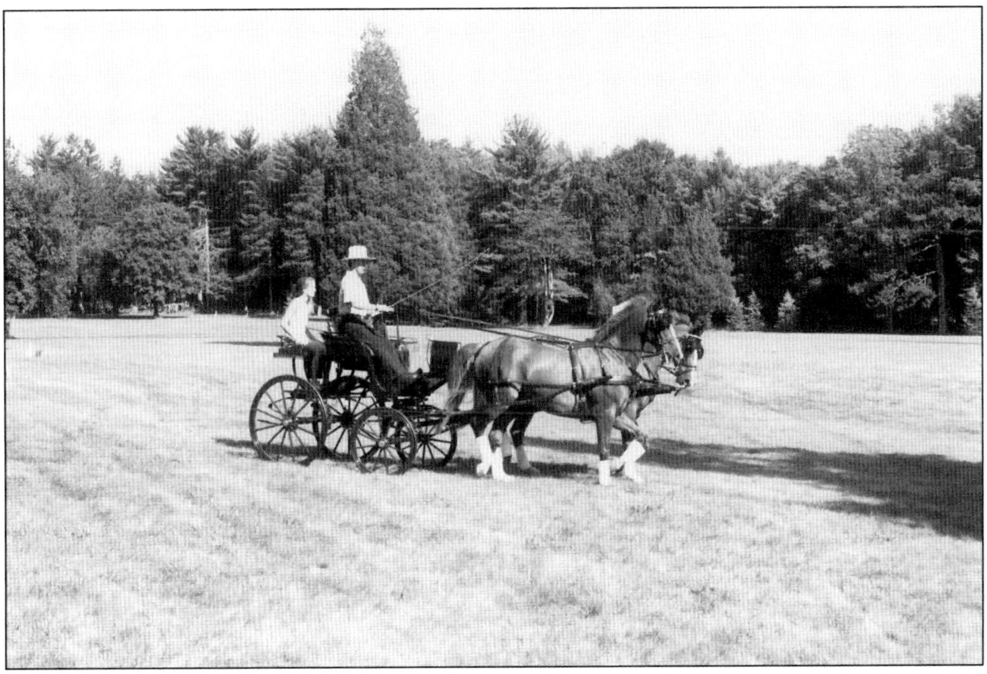

Larry Poulin is a national champion from Maine. He is seen here practicing for the World Pairs Championship with two of his Dutch warmbloods named Brian and Carlos. Many events, which are open to the public, are held here each year. People are welcome to visit the stables and offices and to watch the riders and drivers when they are practicing. (Collection of the authors.)

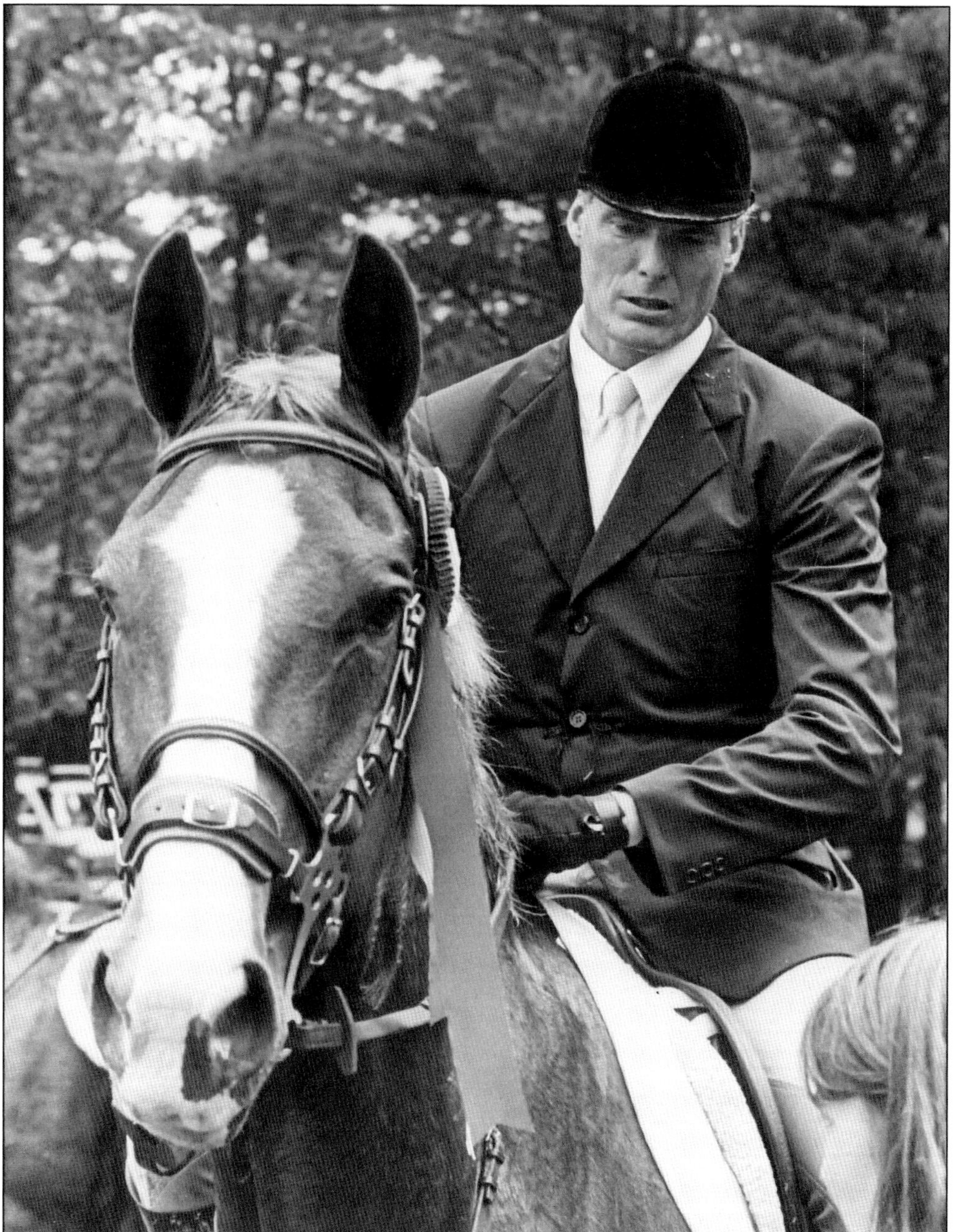

Local events at the United States Equestrian Team include the Essex Horse Trials, the Festival of Champions, and the Gladstone Driving Event. Celebrities often participate in these events. Here Christopher Reeve, on Nicholas, rides in the Festival of Champions in better times. (The *Bernardsville News*.)

Three

Newcomers

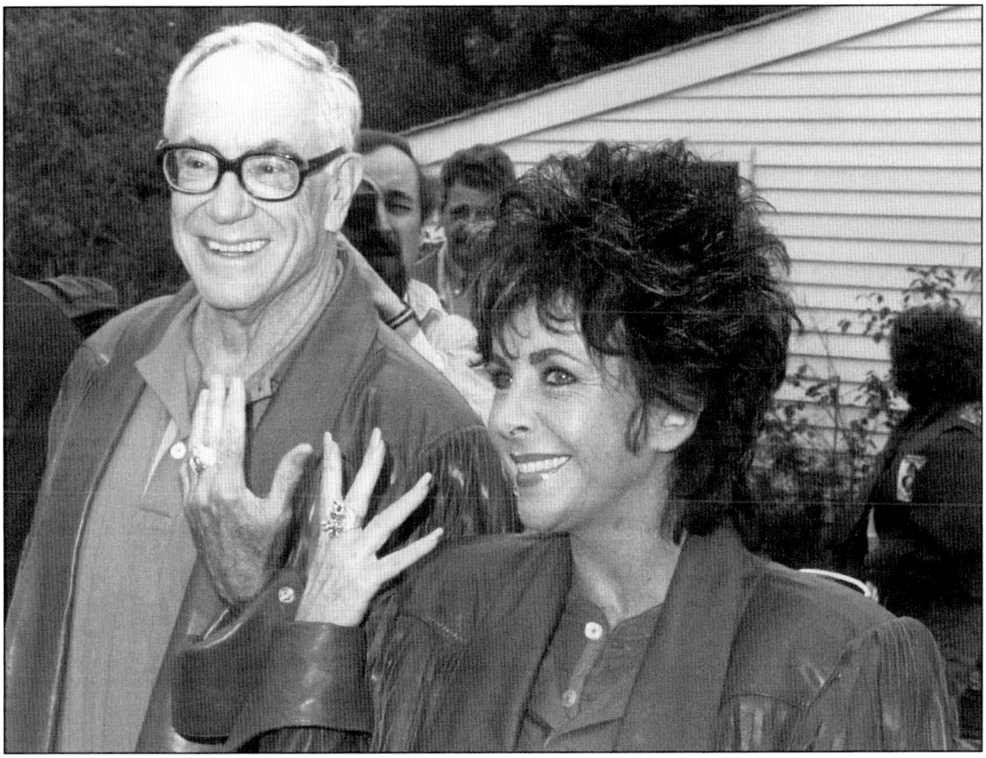

Malcolm Forbes and Liz Taylor, sporting matching rings and matching jackets, prepare for an afternoon ride with his motorcycle club. He made Miss Taylor a gift of a pink Harley Davidson. She was on his arm during his seventieth birthday bash in Tangiers, a party that hosted almost a thousand guests, including the King of Morocco, and continued around the clock for three days. Malcolm knew how to live, and is greatly missed. (The *Bernardsville News*.)

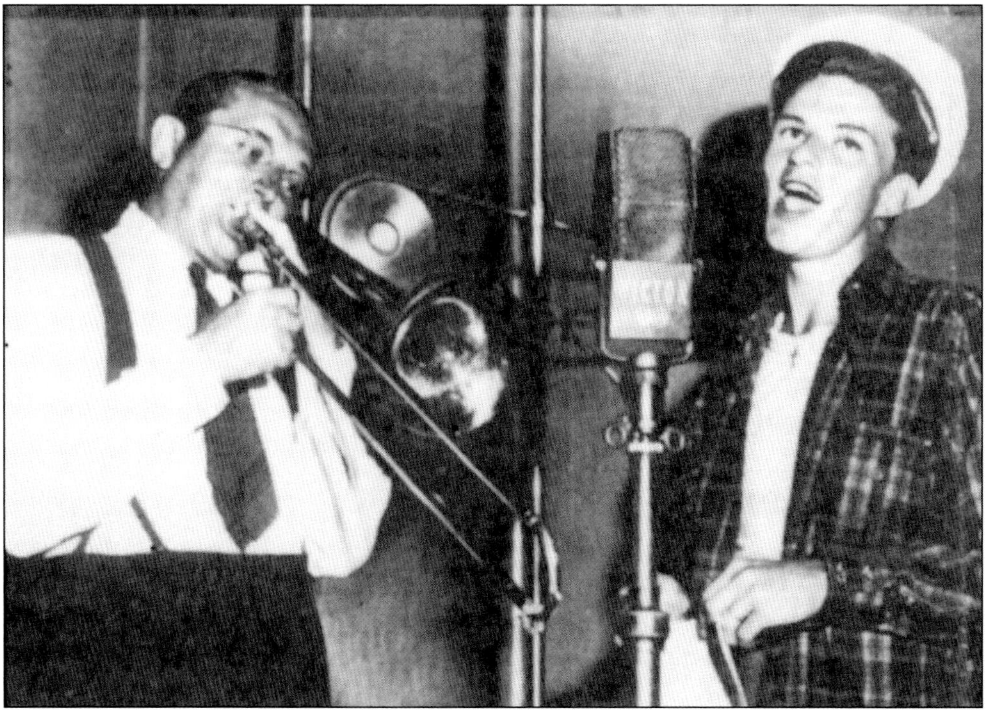

Frank Sinatra was a vocalist in the Tommy Dorsey band. Here he is seen singing with Tommy Dorsey while practicing in Bernardsville. (The *Bernardsville News*.)

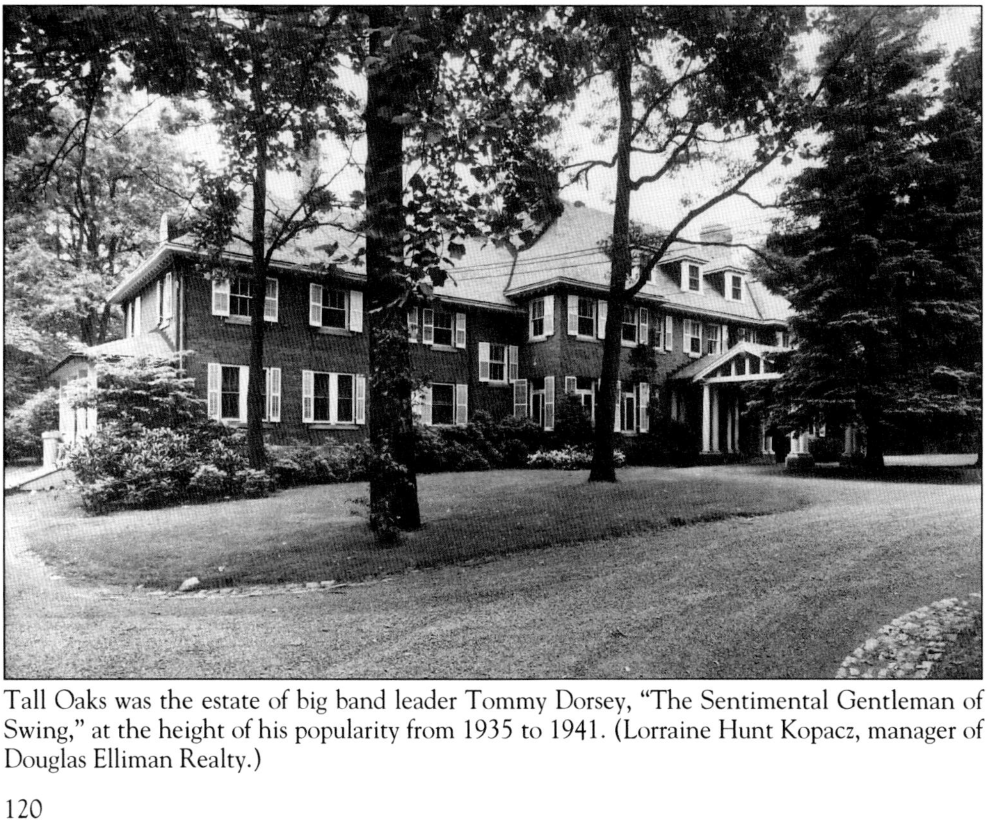

Tall Oaks was the estate of big band leader Tommy Dorsey, "The Sentimental Gentleman of Swing," at the height of his popularity from 1935 to 1941. (Lorraine Hunt Kopacz, manager of Douglas Elliman Realty.)

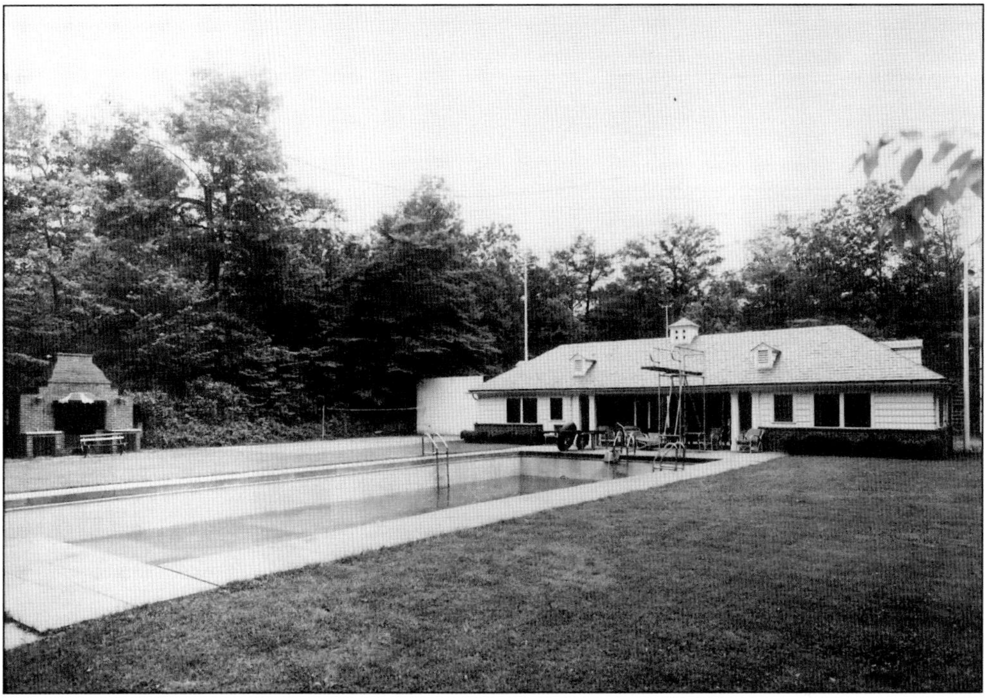

This is the Bing Crosby swimming pool at Tommy Dorsey's Tall Oaks estate. Tommy Dorsey was so enamored of Bing Crosby's swimming pool that he sent his architect to California to copy it exactly. (Lorraine Hunt Kopacz, manager of Douglas Elliman Realty.)

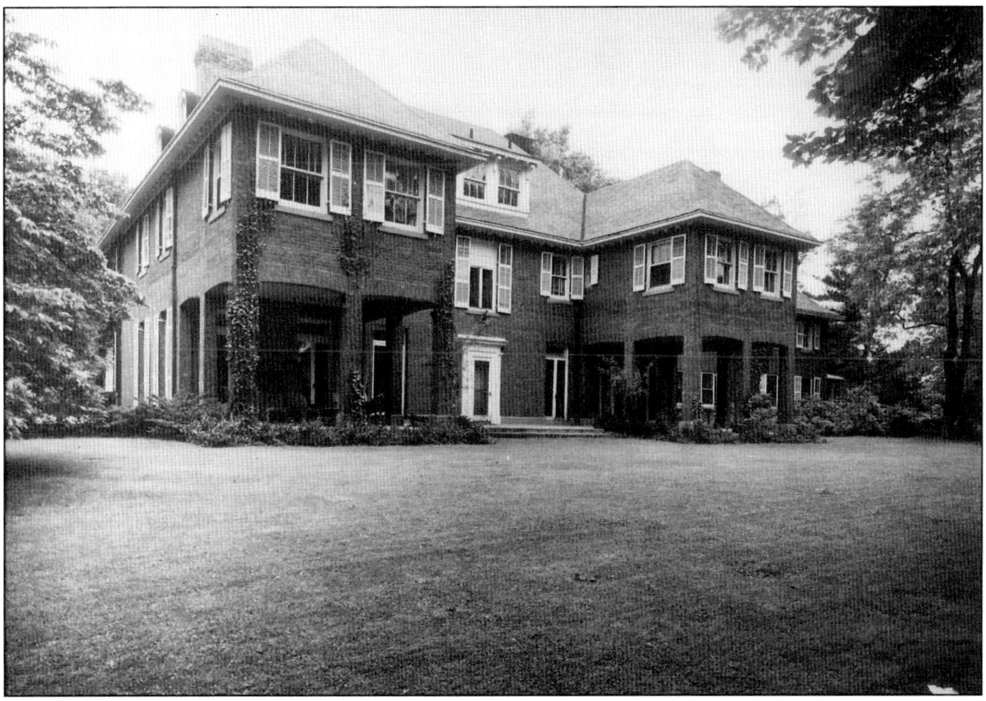

Another view of Tall Oaks shows the estate from the rear. (Lorraine Hunt Kopacz, manager of Douglas Elliman Realty.)

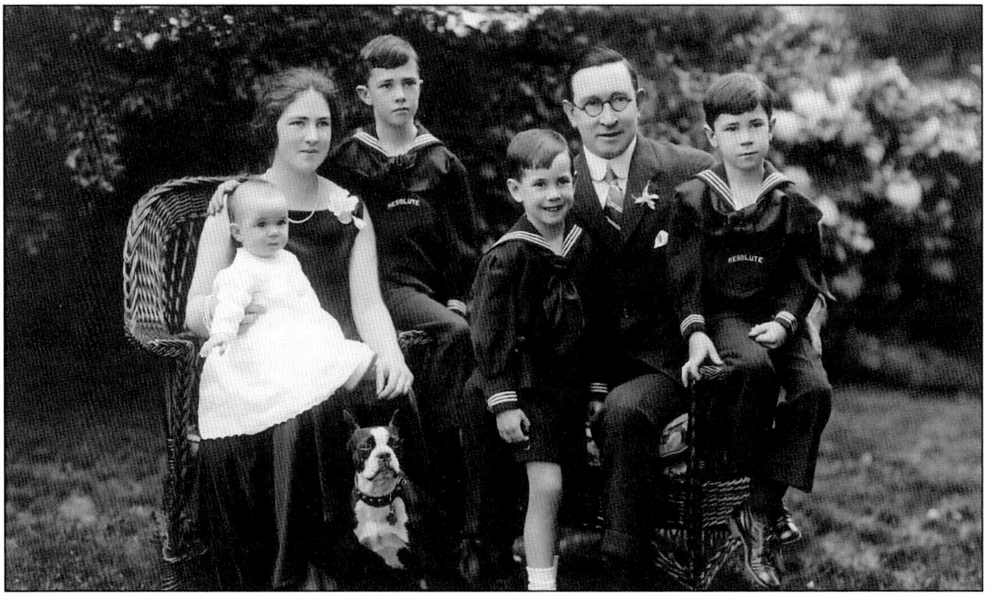

Forbes magazine founder, B.C. Forbes, posed with his family about 1924. They are, from left to right, as follows: Gordon, Mrs. Forbes (Adelaide), Bruce, Malcolm, B.C. Forbes, and Duncan. B.C. (Bertie Charles) was born in Scotland. He came to this country, settled in Englewood, and founded *Forbes* magazine in 1917. It was the first business magazine in the country. To get the business news, B.C. went where the financiers and industrialists socialized: the restaurants and clubs of the financial district. (The Forbes Archives.)

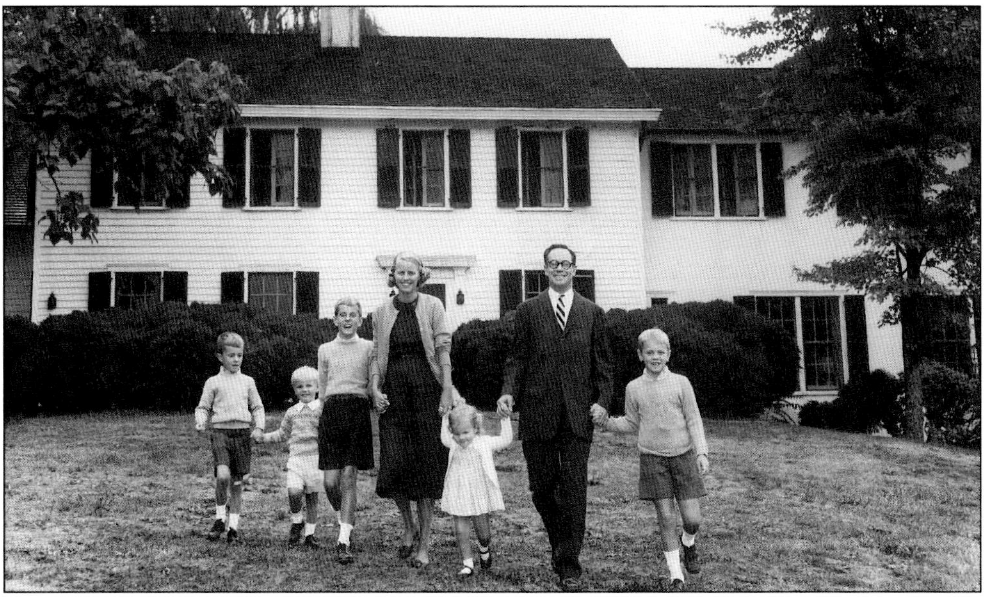

In 1947, Malcolm Forbes and his family moved to Bedminster. He spent six years as a Republican state senator in the 1950s, but was defeated in a bid for governor in 1957. This photograph was used in his gubernatorial campaign. From left to right are the following: Christopher (Kip), Timothy, Malcolm Jr. (Steve), Mrs. Forbes (Bertie), Moira, Malcolm S. Forbes, and Robert. Soon after, Mr. Forbes became editor and publisher of *Forbes* magazine. (The Forbes Archives.)

Steve Forbes and his family posed for this picture at their home in Bedminster. From left to right they are as follows: (front row) Moira and Elizabeth; (back row) Malcolm S. (Steve) Forbes Jr., Sabina and Roberta (twins), Mrs. Forbes (Sabina), and Catherine. (Steve Forbes.)

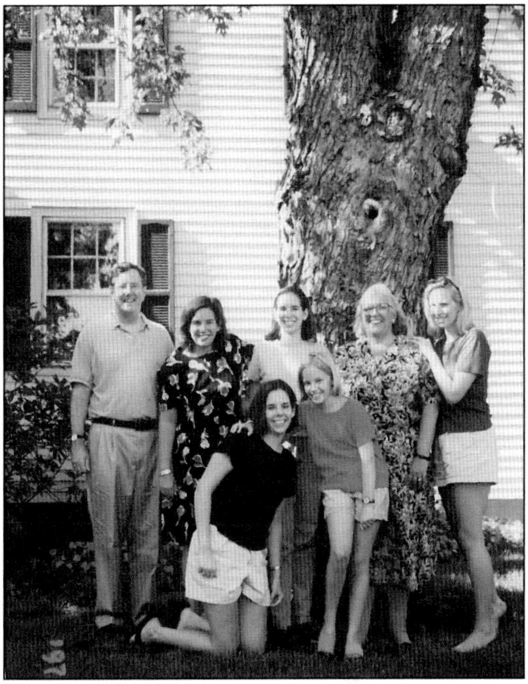

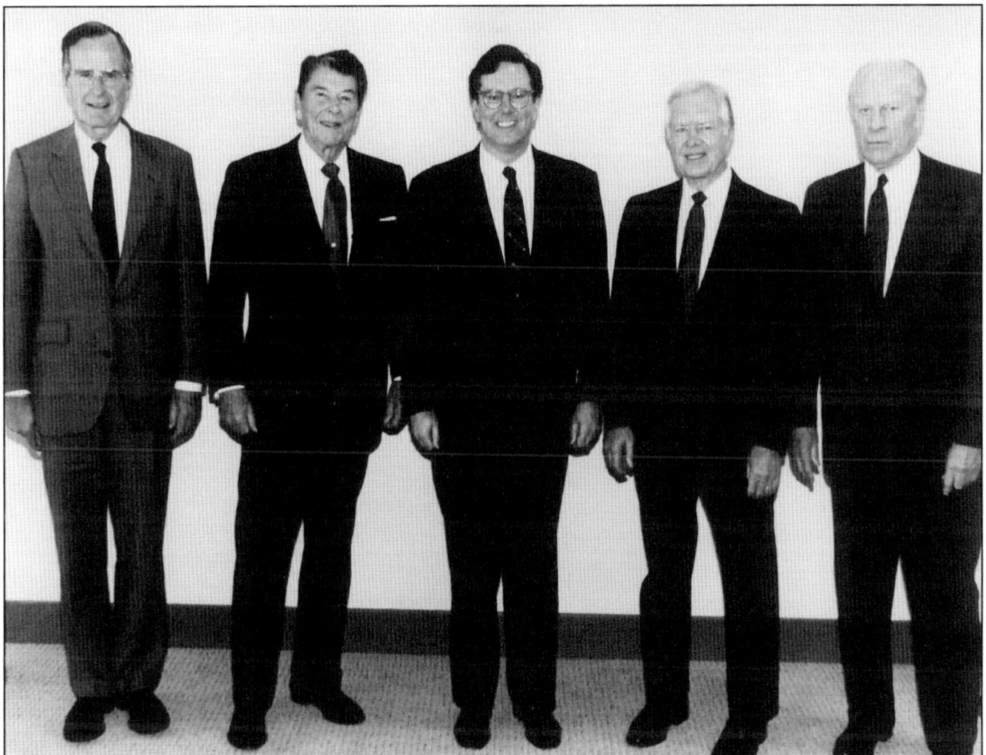

Malcolm S. (Steve) Forbes Jr., is pictured with Presidents Bush, Reagan, Carter, and Ford at the dedication of the Ronald Reagan Presidential Library, Simi Valley, California, November 4, 1991. (Ronald Reagan Presidential Library.)

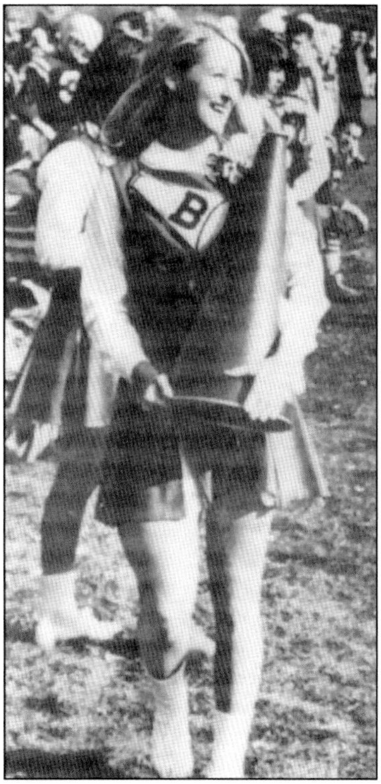

Mary Louise "Meryl" Streep was a cheerleader at Bernardsville High School in 1967. (Bernardsville High School yearbook.)

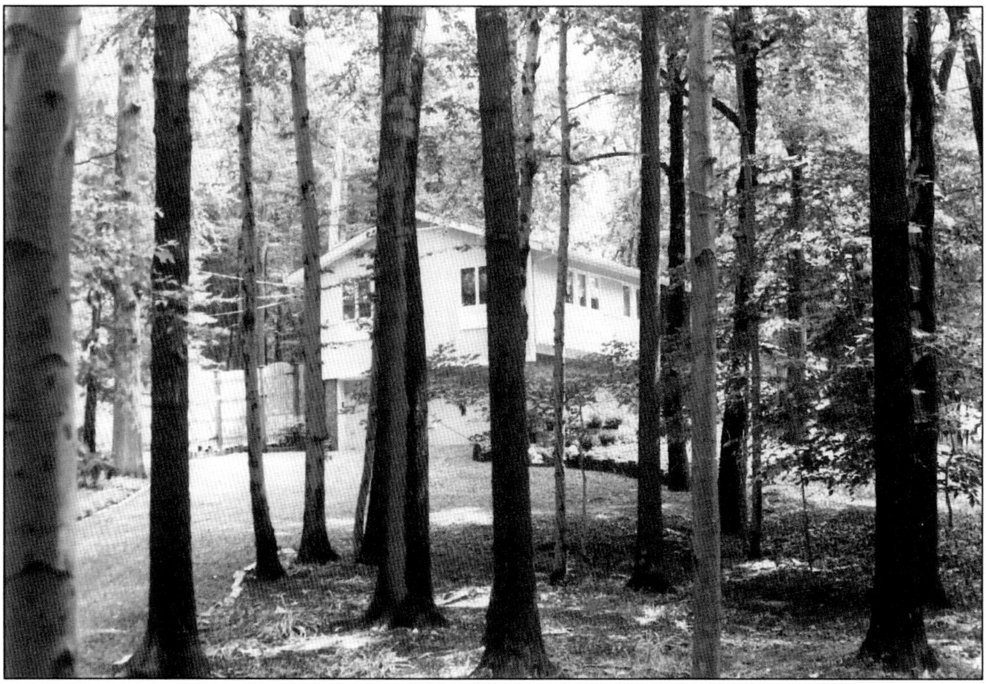

Meryl Streep grew up in this house in Bernardsville. She played Daisy Mae in Bernardsville High School's production of *Li'l Abner*. Meryl went on to attend Vassar and Yale. She has since starred in a number of Hollywood blockbusters and won an Academy Award. (Collection of the authors.)

Jackie Kennedy was a member of the Essex Fox Hounds, and sometimes rode in the Thanksgiving day hunt. Here she is seen at the Far Hills Race Meeting. Caroline and John Jr. were also active in local equestrian events. On the right is Caroline Kennedy participating in the St. Bernards Horse Show. (Bob Collister and A. Carmine, *The Somerset Messenger Gazette*.)

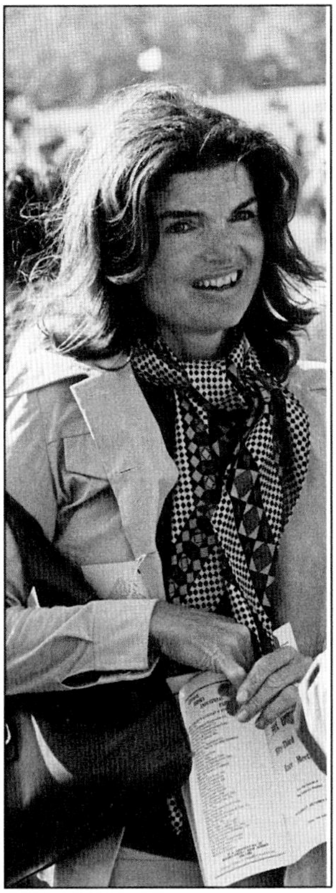

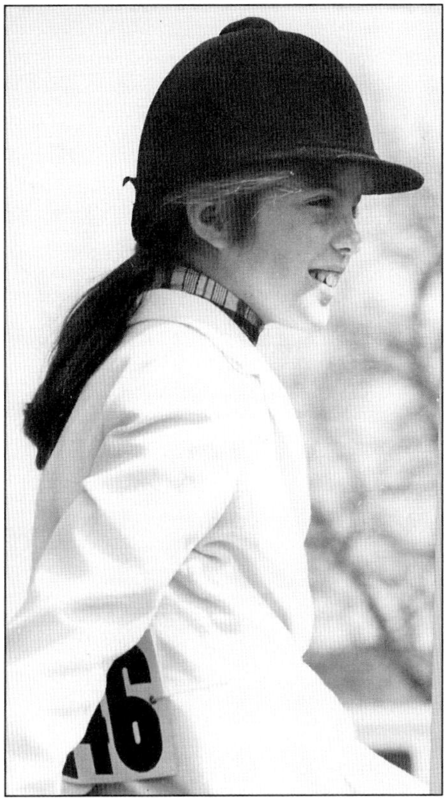

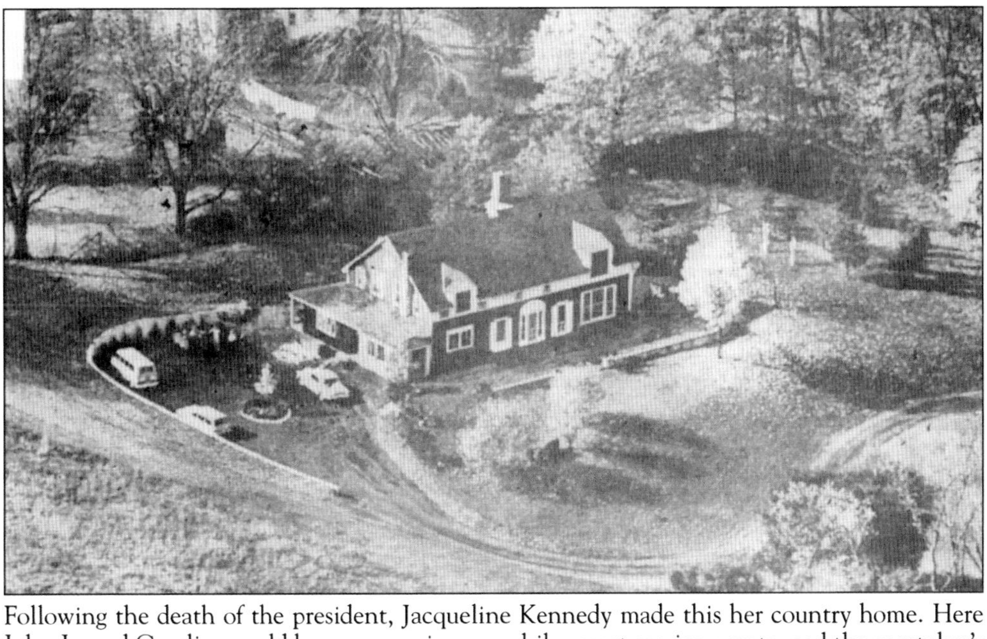

Following the death of the president, Jacqueline Kennedy made this her country home. Here John Jr. and Caroline could be seen growing up, while secret service agents used the caretaker's cottage. Greek shipping magnate Aristotle Onassis also came here prior to his death. (Ted Kell, the *New York Herald Tribune*.)

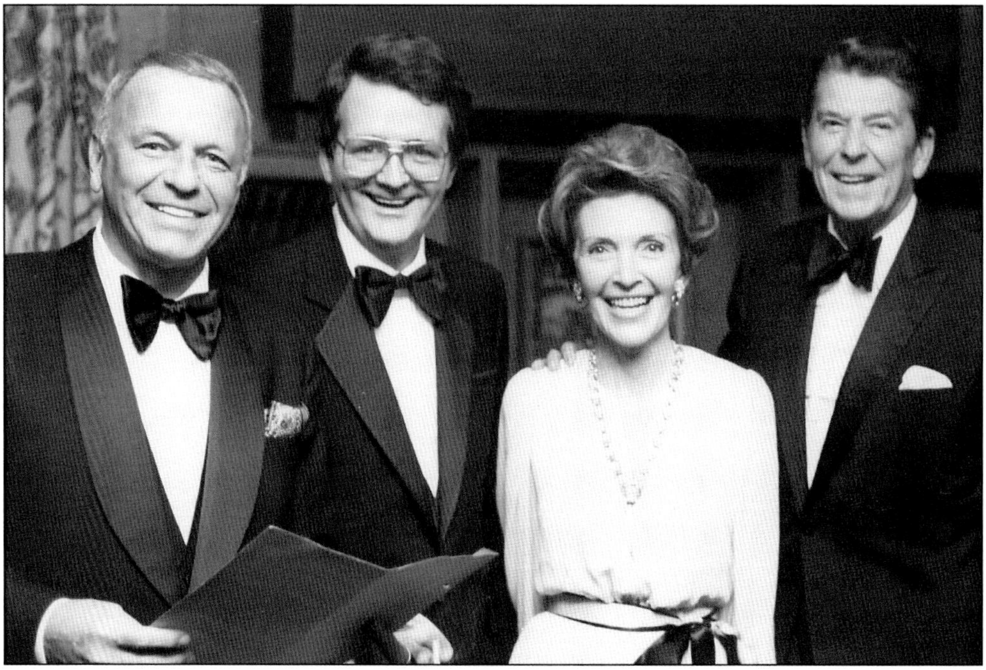

Here is Mr. Raymond Donovan (second from the left) with a few of his friends at the Fiddler's Elbow Country Club in 1979. (The *Bernardsville News*.)

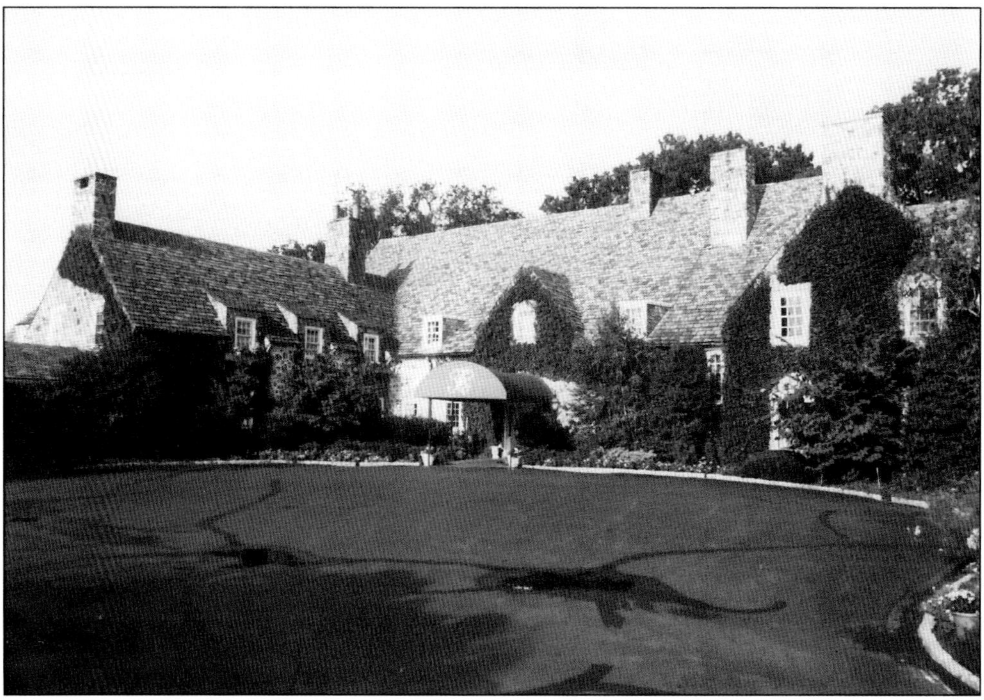

Formerly the estate of New York investment banker Frederick S. Mosley, (Mrs. Mosley was the sister of James Cox Brady) this is now the club house at Fiddler's Elbow Country Club. Mr. Raymond Donovan is a partner in the ownership of the club. Mr. Donovan served as secretary of labor under President Ronald Reagan. (Collection of the authors.)

John Z. De Lorean left his job as vice president of General Motors to found the De Lorean Motor Company in Northern Ireland. Christina Ferrare was Mrs. John De Lorean at the time the couple purchased Lamington House. (*The Somerset Messenger Gazette*.)

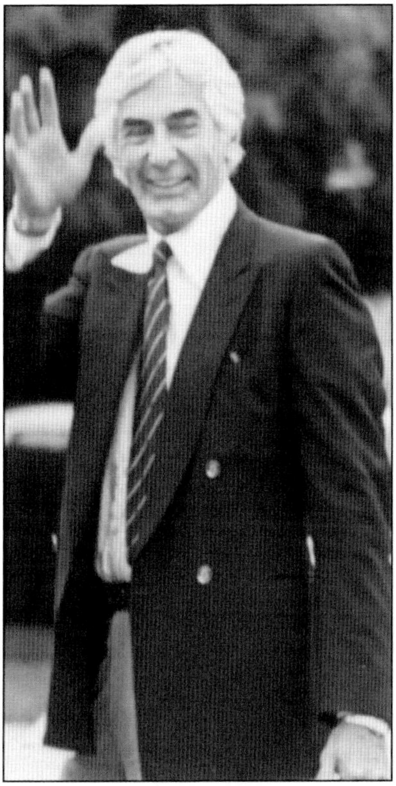

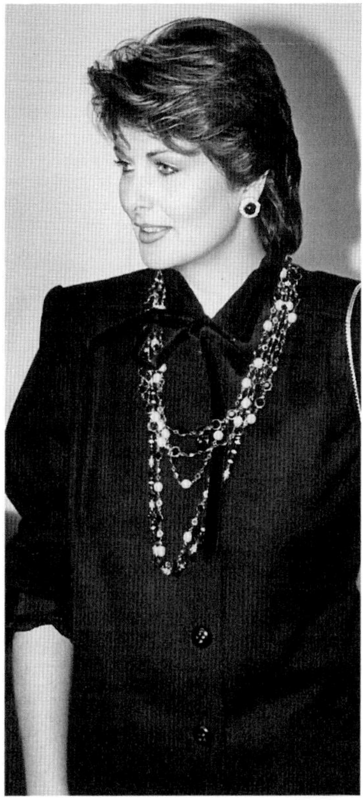

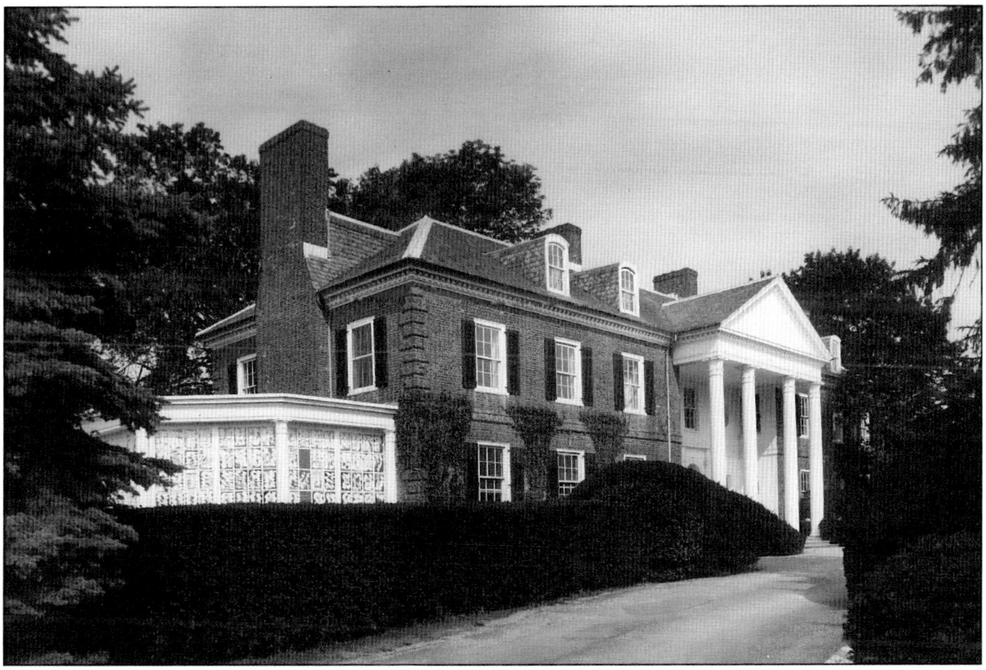

Lamington House was the estate of John De Lorean. When he bought this 433-acre estate in 1981, the $3.5 million price was the highest ever paid for a property in this area. The house was built by John K. Cowperthwaite in 1940. (Turpin Realtors.)

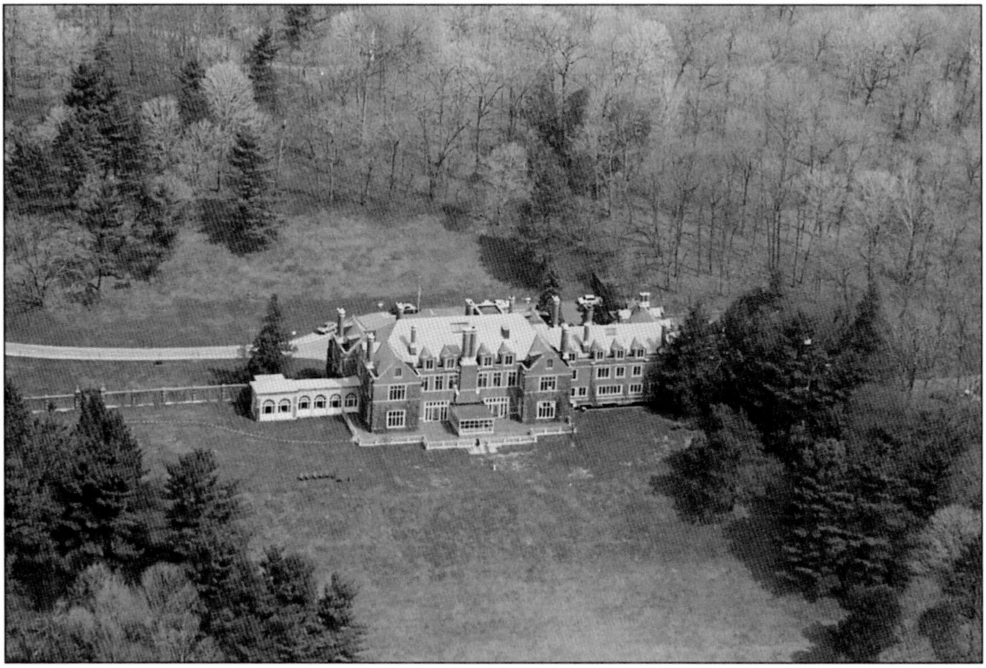

In 1983 King Hassan II of Morocco bought the Kate Macy Ladd House with 328 acres in Peapack and 128 acres in Far Fills for a record-breaking $7.5 million—more than twice the previous record set by John De Lorean in 1981. The King has retained the name Natirar, which was given to the estate by Mr. and Mrs. Ladd. Natirar is Raritan spelled backwards. The north branch of the Raritan River flows through the estate. (Turpin Real Estate.)

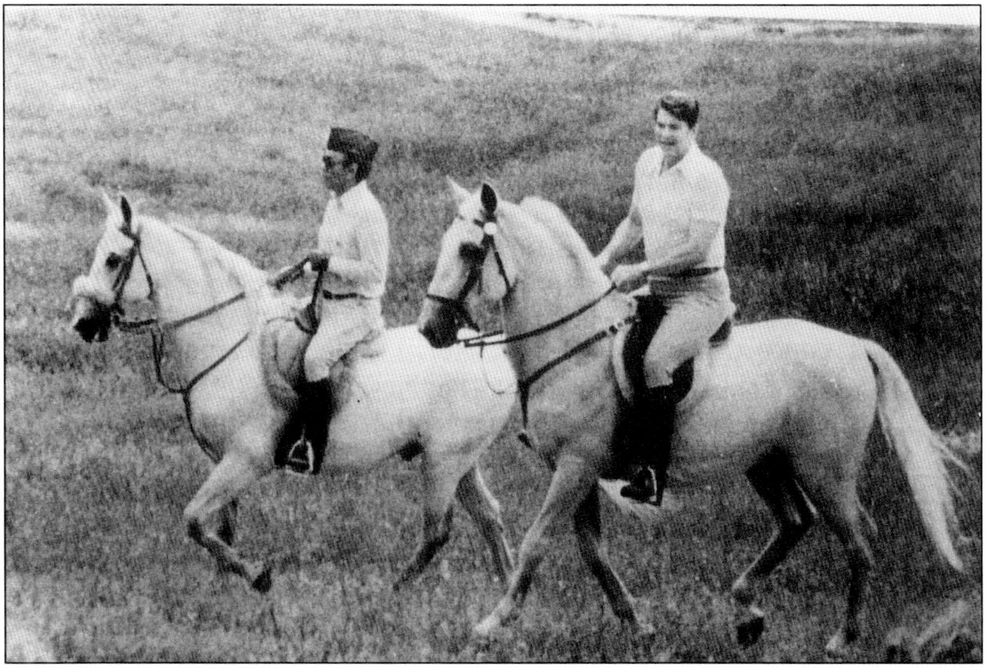

His Royal Highness, King Hassan II of Morocco enjoys a ride on horseback with President Ronald Reagan in 1982. (White House photograph, Michael Evans.)